MW00528455

POLICE BOX
FIRST DOCTOR SOURCEBOOK

CREDITS

LINE DEVELOPER: Gareth Ryder-Hanrahan
WRITING: Darren Pearce and Gareth Ryder-Hanrahan
ADDITIONAL DEVELOPMENT: Nathaniel Torson
EDITING: Dominic McDowall-Thomas
COVER: Paul Bourne
GRAPHIC DESIGN AND LAYOUT: Paul Bourne
CREATIVE DIRECTOR: Dominic McDowall-Thomas
ART DIRECTOR: Jon Hodgson
SPECIAL THANKS: Georgie Britton and the BBC Team for all their help.

"My First Begins With An Unearthly Child"

The First Doctor Sourcebook is published by Cubicle 7 Entertainment Ltd (UK reg. no.6036414).

Find out more about us and our games at www.cubicle7.co.uk

Printed in the USA

CONTENTS

CHAPTER ONE:
INTRODUCTION, PLAYING IN THE FIRST DOCTOR ERA, THE TARDIS

INTRODUCTION

It all began on a November night in 1963. Two schoolteachers followed one of their students, a strange girl called Susan Foreman, back to the junkyard she called home. There, they found a police box that was bigger on the inside, and a cantankerous old vagabond who claimed to be Susan's grandfather.

He was a wanderer, an exile in the fourth dimension, a Lord of Time. He was the Doctor, and from that junkyard, they saw all of time and space. A thousand adventures, seen and unseen, followed on from that cold November night.

Who knows what adventures you'll discover, if you walk down the right street and see a strange blue box waiting there for you?

HOW TO USE THIS BOOK

The First Doctor Sourcebook is primarily a Gamemaster's resource for running adventures either with or in the style of the First Doctor. While players will certainly benefit from the background information on the Doctor and his Companions, all of the rules needed to create or portray the First Doctor's Companions are found in the Player's Guide from the main *Doctor Who: Adventures in Time and Space* boxed set.

This book is designed to be a primer on capturing the feel of the First Doctor's era and incorporating it into your adventures. **Chapter One** describes the Doctor, his remarkable time-travelling machine, and the style of the adventures he had in his first incarnation.

Chapters Two to Ten describe the First Doctor's adventures. Each adventure has the following sections:

- **Synopsis:** Where did the TARDIS materialise? Who did the Doctor meet? And what horrible fates awaited the travellers there? This section summarises the key events of the adventure as experienced by the First Doctor and his companions.

- **Running this Adventure:** Next, we discuss how to run the adventure. We get into the nuts and bolts of plotting and gamemastering, how to adapt the adventure to different Doctors or different groups of player characters, and how to use bits and pieces of the adventure in your own games.

- **Characters, Monsters & Gadgets:** If there are important non-player characters, interesting monsters, or shiny new gadgets in the adventure, you'll find them here. Sometimes, we'll give you full statistics for a character. At other times, when their Attributes and Skills are obvious or irrelevant, we'll just list their key Traits.

- **Further Adventures:** So, what happens after the Doctor leaves? (Or what happened before he arrived?) These further adventure seeds give ideas on spin-offs, sequels and alternate histories that expand on the Doctor's initial adventures.

There are lots of ways to use these adventures. You can use our suggestions for Further Adventures, or build your own adventures using the material provided. In fact, if your players aren't familiar with these classic stories, then you can substitute your player characters for the First Doctor and his companions and 'rerun' the adventures. Maybe your player characters will take other paths and make different decisions – can they stop the *Dalek Invasion of Earth*, or escape the *Reign of Terror?* Can they avoid sneezing humanity into slavery in *The Ark*?

PLAYING IN THE FIRST DOCTOR ERA

"Back when I first started, at the very beginning, I was always trying to be old and grumpy and important, like you do when you're young."

Once upon a time, a daft old man stole a magic box and ran away with his granddaughter.

Of course, calling the First Doctor 'a daft old man' probably wouldn't go down well. He was a scientist, a genius, a citizen of the universe and a gentleman to boot... which translates as a 'grumpy, daft old man' who might, one day, appear randomly on your world and save the day. The First Doctor's directionless wanderings brought him and his companions to many different alien worlds and historical periods, all filled with danger and intrigue. The great spirit of adventure began when those two teachers stepped into that fabled junkyard!

When running or playing games in the style of the First Doctor (either using the Doctor and his companions as player characters, or just mimicking the form), keep the following in mind.

THAT MISERABLE OLD MAN

Later incarnations of Doctor invite interesting people to travel with them on the TARDIS, to see the galaxy through their young eyes and to feel wonder again. The First Doctor appears old, but he's by far the youngest of the Doctors (obviously), so he doesn't need companions for that. More to the point, he doesn't *want* companions for that. He was quite content to wander the universe with Susan, especially as she indulged his curiosity and hardly ever argued with him.

He took Ian and Barbara with him to protect himself – they had stumbled onto the TARDIS, and could not be allowed to reveal what they had seen to the outside world. Initially, he treated them with suspicion, as though they were stray dogs who followed Susan home and had to be kept in the shed instead of being put back on the street.

While this incarnation of the Doctor may like some people – scientists and young people, mainly – he's cantankerous and self-important, and should be played as an intelligent, imperious but somewhat senile old man. He switches between Father Christmas and a grump according to his whim.

In this era, arguments and disagreements between the TARDIS travellers could be much more bitter and long-lasting than in later years. One side or the other often has to be dragged into the adventure. The Doctor has to be forced to intervene in many cases; in others, he deliberately manipulates events to satisfy his own curiosity. It's hard to imagine a later (wiser) incarnation sabotaging his own TARDIS to strand the travellers in a dangerous swamp just so he can investigate an alien city.

This Doctor is also physically frail. While he does occasionally demonstrate superhuman endurance or strength, he is easily winded and has to rest frequently. He often relies on Susan or another companion for support.

When playing the First Doctor, the trick is to balance niceness and grumpiness. Every once in a while, the Doctor should decide something that absolutely infuriates the other player characters (from *'we're not interfering, even though we've arrived in the middle of an absolutely ghastly situation'* to *'we shall help these aliens instead of the humans, for I have no loyalty to your species'* to *'I shall spend my time tinkering with this scientific phenomenon instead of dealing with the more pressing problem'*). The Doctor should never, ever explain himself to the troublesome children he finds himself babysitting across time and space.

NEW TRAIT

FAULTY HEART (MAJOR BAD – TIME LORDS ONLY)

One of the Time Lord's hearts is defective or weak and fails during moments of extreme stress or exertion, causing great pain followed by unconsciousness and, on rare occasions, regeneration.

Effects: During a period of great stress (as determined by the GM, but typically only once per adventure unless the character is particularly active or stressed), the Time Lord's weak heart will suffer an attack and they must make a Strength + Resolve roll at Difficulty 18. On a success, the Time Lord feels a bit weak, adding a +1 Difficulty to all of their rolls until they can rest for D6 minutes, but they are otherwise fine.

On a failure, they are stunned into inaction for D3 rounds due to the pain, after which they add +1 to the Difficulty of their rolls until they can rest for D6x10 minutes.

On a Bad Failure, the heart fails, knocking the Time Lord unconscious for D6x10 minutes or until CPR is applied to the weak heart. If examined during this period of unconsciousness, only one heart will be heard beating.

On a Disastrous Failure, the heart seizes and a chain reaction takes out the second heart as well, causing the Time Lord's body to begin the regeneration process.

TROUBLESOME CHILDREN

The Doctor's companions can be divided into two groups. There are the young replacements for Susan, like Vicki or Dodo, who the Doctor takes with him because he misses his granddaughter. These bright young people are innocent, enthusiastic and kind, and they rarely disagree with the Doctor or force him to intervene.

Then there are the older travellers – Ian and Barbara, Steven and so on – who argue back. They don't accept the Doctor's age and wisdom, they challenge his self-image as the wisest man in the room, and they demand he intervene. They force the Doctor to break his own rules about non-interference. He respects the skills and passions of these companions even as they irritate him to high heaven. These companions often take the lead when dealing with the situations the TARDIS brings them too, and can be more 'heroic' than the Doctor.

In general, none of the First Doctor's companions carry weapons. Ian, Steven and Ben were all surprisingly good at fighting (well, not so surprising for Steven), and could disarm guards and steal weapons, but keep combat as a reaction on the part of the players.

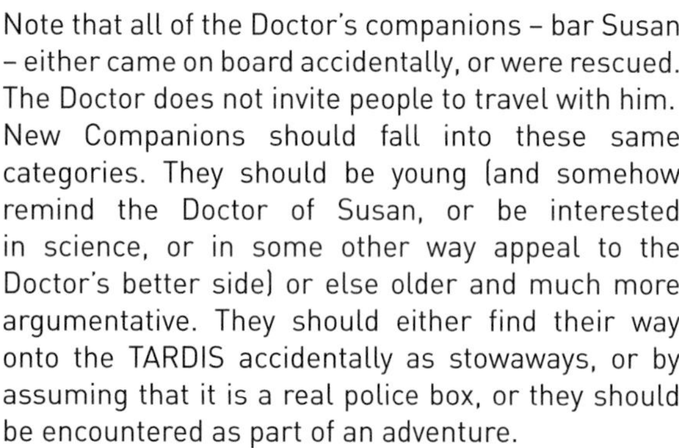

Note that all of the Doctor's companions – bar Susan – either came on board accidentally, or were rescued. The Doctor does not invite people to travel with him. New Companions should fall into these same categories. They should be young (and somehow remind the Doctor of Susan, or be interested in science, or in some other way appeal to the Doctor's better side) or else older and much more argumentative. They should either find their way onto the TARDIS accidentally as stowaways, or by assuming that it is a real police box, or they should be encountered as part of an adventure.

It is the time-honoured duty of the Companion to wander off and get into trouble, or to meet someone in desperate straits who needs saving, or to get captured and learn vital bits of plot. Likewise, it is the Doctor's burden to rescue people from their own foolishness...

EXILES IN THE FOURTH DIMENSION

The TARDIS in this era is... unreliable, to put it mildly. The Doctor tries to drop Ian and Barbara off in 1966, and the closest he gets is the Reign of Terror in France. He has many excuses – I'm sorry, there are many reasons for this inaccuracy. First and foremost, the TARDIS is old and still in need of repair. Once the Doctor borrows a component from the Meddling Monk's TARDIS, he is able to steer the ship right back to Kembel, suggesting that the main problem is the dilapidated control mechanisms. Second, the Doctor may have left his notebook (containing the key codes to the various systems) in 100,000BC, which means he is now guessing which code means what, and his memory is not... not... not faulty at all! Just like the TARDIS!

Third, the Doctor prefers to make calculations and observations before taking off – and he rarely has time for that. Usually, the companions pile back into the TARDIS and flee some ongoing threat instead of taking the time to do painstaking calculations with the astral map.

So, cast aside any thoughts of going on holiday to nice planets or visiting your favourite historical figures, and just go with the flow of the Vortex. The TARDIS may eventually go where the Doctor wants to go, but only after multiple false starts and detours. This also means that the First Doctor is unlikely to be able to do any of the fancy TARDIS tricks he manages later in his career, like materialising the TARDIS around an object or flying it through space. The ship gets the travellers from one place to another, equally perilous place. Anything more than that calls for spending lots of Story Points.

Also, to maintain the tone of a First Doctor adventure, stay away from any mention of the Time Lords or Gallifrey. Leave the Doctor's past and people 'off-screen'. They are wanderers far from home, and do not expect to meet any others of their kind again.

THE FAULTY TARDIS

Not only is the TARDIS unreliable, it's downright dangerous. Components break with alarming frequency – in the Doctor's adventurers, we see the TARDIS lose life support and internal temperature control, shrink to the size of a matchbox (and also shrink its occupants), nearly drive everyone insane with telepathic warnings, and blow its fluid links and other key systems on every third planet. Even on the very first trip with Ian and Barbara, it knocks everyone on board unconscious. It's like a rattling old car with bad breaks, a temperamental engine, the doors are held on with string, and there's an alarming smell of burnt wiring whenever you switch on the radio.

The faulty TARDIS can be used as an all-purpose plot device. The characters arrive in the Swamps of Horrible Death, only to discover that the fluid link just went 'pop' and they need to find some mercury or they'll be stranded forever. They arrive in 19th century New Zealand, right on top of a volcanic eruption that floods the console room with poisonous gas, so they have to flee and watch the ship be engulfed by lava. They're stuck until they dig it out, which means getting involved with colonial-era strife with the Maori tribes. The characters arrive in present-day 1966 and try to keep a low profile, only the Chameleon Circuit glitches and the TARDIS is suddenly in the shape of an Egyptian pyramid.

THE SWINGING 60S

'Now' for the First Doctor is the 1960s. Any 'contemporary' player characters should come from this era. The Beatles are the coolest thing in the universe, supercomputers have lots of magnetic tapes and blinking lights, and England just won the world cup. Stories set on present-day Earth should take place in the 1960s, leaving the 21st century for rocket-powered space exploration and Dalek invasions. Susan picked the middle of the 20th century out of all of time and space to live in (the Doctor, by the way "tolerates this century, but doesn't enjoy it". Obviously, it grows on him.)

WHERE ARE WE? WHAT'S GOING ON?

Future incarnations of the Doctor know pretty much everything there is to know about alien invaders and distant planets. He pokes his head out the door and announces to his companions that they've arrived on Helegropo 6 where the natives are living sound waves. He spots the alien monster and can instantly give a potted biography of the species, complete with their one weakness. He's seen it all before.

Not so, for the First Doctor. While he does sometimes run into familiar planets and races (for example, he recognises the approach of Mondas in *The Tenth Planet*, and he visited Dido and Mira previously on his travels), most of the time he's in unfamiliar territory. That means that the Gamemaster should stay away from convenient info-dumps through Knowledge rolls. The players have to go out and ask where they are and what's going on instead of asking the Doctor or consulting the TARDIS database. This means that First Doctor stories are inevitably going to be slower and involve more talking instead of jumping straight to the action. Manic Time Lords and impatient companions need not apply.

Instead of trying to wrap a whole adventure up in one or two game sessions, give the players plenty of time to investigate. Expect to spend the whole first session of a new adventure just introducing NPCs and factions. Look at adventures like *The Daleks* or *The Massacre* or *The Tenth Planet* as models. In each case, there's a lengthy period of wandering around meeting friendly Thals/Huegenots/Snowcap base personnel before actual danger shows up.

This slower pace also allows for more complicated plots. Have multiple groups and factions involved. *The Web Planet*, for instance, isn't just about the conflict between the Menoptera and the Animus – it

also brings in the Zarbi, and the Optera. Develop rich, complicated settings instead of paring everything down to the bare bones. Add in characters that don't have an immediate function in the plot, and throw in elements that don't seem immediately relevant. Give the story room to grow as you play through it.

THE GRAND SCOPE

One hallmark of the First Doctor era is the sheer scale of his adventures. Obviously, epics like *The Dalek's Master Plan* encompass many worlds and have a huge cast of supporting characters, but this Doctor also tends to spend more time at each place he visits. The Romans, for example, takes place over several weeks. So too does Marco Polo.

Think big. No, bigger than that. Let the characters stay in one place for months of game time, or bounce them between half a dozen different places linked by a big overarching plot. When the First Doctor visits an alien planet (*The Daleks, The Sensorites, The Keys of Marinus, The Web Planet, The Space Museum*), his actions and those of his companions literally change the world.

That big cast of characters can also add to the scope. Look at *The Dalek's Master Plan*. How many villains are in there? The Daleks, obviously, but you've also got Mavic Chen, the various sinister Masters of the Galaxies, the Meddling Monk, Karlton and the Space Security Service, and that's not including the one-shot monsters like the Visians or the outlaws of Desperus. The actions of the player characters could provoke any of those factions or villains to do something unexpected. What if the player characters offer to sell the Taranium core to each of the Seven Masters? What if Karlton gets killed, and Sara Kingdom becomes head of the SSS?

ALIEN CULTURES, NOT ALIEN MONSTERS

That big scope and slow development means that the First Doctor's adventures often delved into the depths of an alien culture, instead of just facing alien monsters. Every creature encountered should have a backstory and a place in the world; even the villains have compelling reasons to do what they do. The First Doctor's encounter with the Cybermen, for example, has him facing enemies who are oddly noble from one perspective. We get to spend a lot time in the company of aliens on the Web Planet or the Sense-Sphere.

Even the Daleks are initially presented as part of a complex web of historical conflicts and environmental degradation.

So, instead of just coming up with a monster to threaten your players, give them a culture to interact with. The First Doctor approach draws from classic science fiction and historical travelogues, so take the time to explore each world you land on. (That doesn't mean you can't have, say, random eight-foot-tall invisible apes – it's just that random invisible apes should not be the focus of the adventure.)

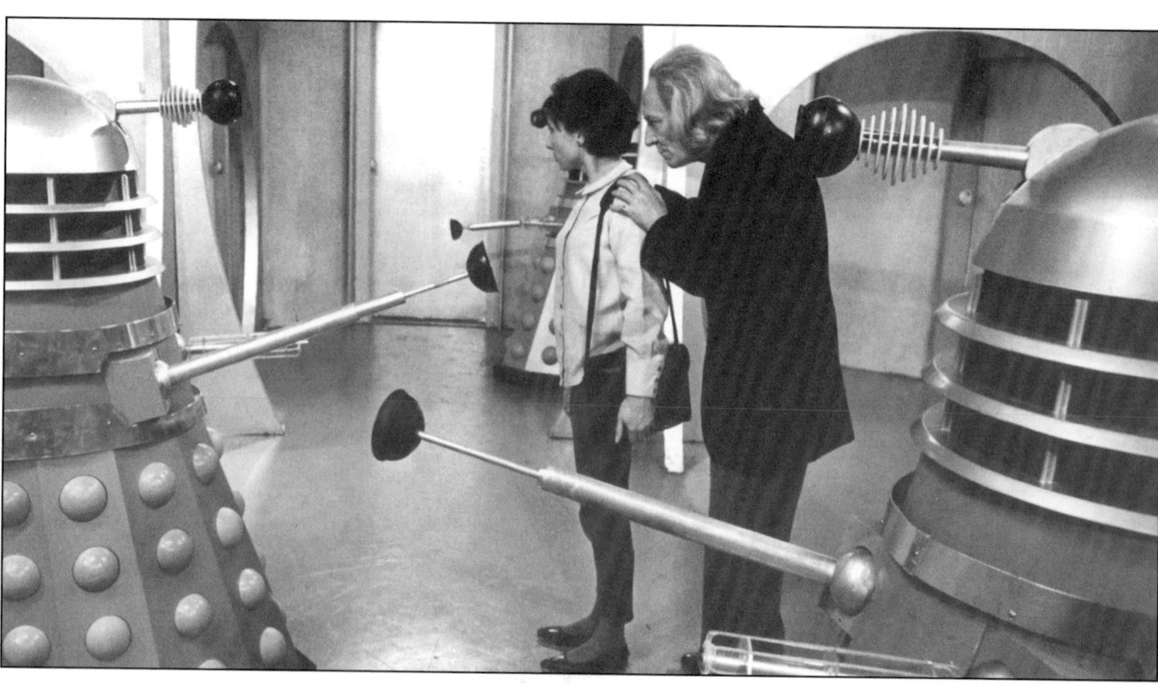

ADVENTURE SEEDS

THE END OF THE CURTAIN

The TARDIS materialises in Edo, Japan in 1853, soon after Commodore Perry's fleet bombarded the Japanese capital to force the Emperor to open negotiations. The travellers are mistaken for Christian missionaries – or Western spies – and have to navigate the dangers of a closed culture that has suddenly been forced to open up.

Notable Characters:

- Commodore Perry, the commander of the American squadron, here to force Japan to open up to American goods and trade
- Abe Masahiro, the chief senior counsellor and the representative of the government.
- Hotta Masayoshi, another counsellor, strongly opposed to the Americans.
- Yoshida Shoin, a Japanese scholar who tried to sneak aboard Perry's ship to learn Western technology.

Things to Do: Helping Shoin get onto Perry's ship, rescuing Shoin from prison, dealing with Masayoshi's scheme to force Shoin to build a cannon capable of blasting Perry's ships.

Action Scenes: Running away from vengeful samurai; sneaking onto Perry's ships, fighting Masayoshi's assassins.

Problems: One of Perry's lieutenants has fallen in love with a Japanese girl, and tries to take her with him. Unfortunately, she's Masahiro's niece.

THE STAR KINDLERS

It is the immensely far future. Most of the stars went out long ago, leaving the sky dark and the universe cold and dark. The distant descendants of mankind survive by kindling artificial stars that burn for only a few hours before burning out. The Star Kindlers who operate these titanic machines are an elite priesthood, cut off from the huddled masses who rely on those mayfly stars to survive. There are three inhabited planets in this artificial solar system, all of which are increasingly at each other's throats as resources dwindle.

The TARDIS arrives and the Doctor befriends the Master Kindler. Soon afterward, an assassin poisons the Kindler. Who will take his place – and is this a plan to seize control of the Kindling machine and use it as a weapon to destroy one of the three worlds?

Notable Characters:

- The Master Kindler
- His two apprentices
- The squabbling Masters of the Three Worlds

Things to Do: Investigate the murder, indulge in Jack Vance-style wordplay and whimsy at the end of time.

Action Scenes: Chasing the murderer; dodging the Dwellers in the Darkness who attack when the sun fails; stopping the sun from engulfing the three worlds.

Problems: The characters are framed for the murder.

DEAD YESTERDAY

The Agency is a top-secret branch of the British secret service that deals with new dangers and threats born of this age of science. It's all catsuits and spy chic – and they've been watching the Doctor ever since the events of *The War Machines*. Now, they need his help to stop a madman from releasing a deadly plague that will wipe out all life on Earth, but there's a catch. He did it yesterday.

Notable Characters:

- Adam Black and Toni Ryder, agents of the Agency!
- Dr. Horgus, the insane plague-maker
- The Syndicate, a sinister criminal network and their mutant assassin, Bullfrog

Things to Do: Travel back in time to save the day; sixties swinging spy action! Wander off course several times before finally hitting yesterday! Race to stop Horgus from releasing the plague, and stop the Syndicate from stealing the TARDIS.

Action Scenes: Bullfrog kidnaps one of the Doctor's companions; fights on Horgus' airship laboratory.

THE TARDIS

THE FIRST DOCTOR'S TARDIS

Probably the most iconic thing about the Doctor's TARDIS is that it resembles the Police 'Public Call' Boxes found in London in the 1960s. These dark blue boxes contained a telephone with a direct link to the local Police station, so that Police Officers on patrol could report back without having to physically return to the station, and could be communicated with if an emergency arose (the station controllers could remotely activate the electric light on top of the box to signal that they needed to talk). Members of the public were also permitted to use the telephone in an emergency – the telephone was behind a hinged panel so that you could access it even if the box was locked.

The boxes were often made of concrete with wooden doors and, aside from the telephone, contained an incident book, a first aid kit, a stool, a table, brushes and dusters, a fire extinguisher, and a small electric heater. The exterior of the Doctor's TARDIS was a near-perfect replica, and often confused members of the local constabulary as to why a new Police Box had suddenly appeared, and why they couldn't get into it. And who knows who you'd end up talking to on the emergency telephone....

WHY A POLICE BOX?

TARDISes have a particular component called a Chameleon Circuit, which allows them to blend-in at any location it visits. The Doctor's TARDIS decided that a Police Box was the perfect camouflage for London in 1963, and so adopted that form. Then something went wrong with the circuit and, despite the odd glitch, his TARDIS has retained that form ever since. The Doctor and Susan were quite surprised to discover the problem, as they stepped outside and looked back at the blue box sticking out like a sore thumb in the Paleolithic era!

THE TARDIS INTERIOR (CONSOLE ROOM)

Beyond the dark blue outer shell of the time machine is a dimensional gateway, a form of 'dimensional interface' that links both TARDIS exterior and interior together. It is protected by a pair of double doors set with the very distinctive TARDIS circular roundel panels that was predominant upon Type 40 TT capsules.

The whole console room is a bright pristine white and very utilitarian in design, with a few comforts such as a hat stand, clock, chairs and a few tables. The walls are covered with roundels, behind which lurk some of the TARDIS' more important circuits and systems.

The hexagonal console dominates the middle of the room. Set back from that is the TARDIS scanner, with a screen that allows the Doctor to view feeds from outside of his ship and determine if the outside environment is safe. Behind this is the Fault Locator, a computer device that can pinpoint a problem with the TARDIS systems.

The control console itself hosts a myriad of gadgets, switches, dials and flashing lights with the time rotor safely encased in a clear tube, lit from within. When the TARDIS is in motion the tube rises and falls as the time rotor spins.

Beneath the console is the energy source of the machine, powerful enough to destroy the TARDIS and its occupants if it were to get out of control. The Doctor almost experienced this when his faulty Fast Return switch stuck and propelled the TARDIS to the events of the Big Bang.

For more information on TARDIS systems and time travel, take a look at *The Time Traveller's Companion.*

NEW GADGET

THE DOCTOR'S RING (SPECIAL GADGET)

The Doctor wears a large blue crystal ring throughout his first incarnation. This ring demonstrates several unusual properties – it focuses the rays of the sun to unlock the TARDIS on one world, and he uses it to free Dodo from WOTAN's hypnosis.

The ring is a link to the TARDIS' reserve of Artron Energy. It can manifest any reasonable Gadget trait for a single action by tapping the TARDIS' Story Points.

Buying a Minor Trait costs 2 Story Points; buying a Major Trait costs 4. The Doctor must concentrate to activate the Ring. Only a Time Lord can use the ring.

THE FIRST DOCTOR'S TARDIS

AWARENESS	3	PRESENCE	3
COORDINATION	3	RESOLVE	4
INGENUITY	4	STRENGTH	3

THE TARDIS: Time and Relative Dimension in Space, the Doctor's stalwart companion over the years and a constant friend to him when all others have left his side. The TARDIS is a sentient time machine, but during the time of the First Doctor it was still developing its powers and personality. Yet, even at this early stage of their relationship, it reflects the Doctor's own cantankerous nature and is prone to breaking down at the drop of a hat, plunging the old man and his companions into mortal peril before bringing them home safely.

SKILLS

Knowledge 8, Medicine 2, Science [Temporal Physics +3] 6, Technology 4, Transport 3

TRAITS

Face in the Crowd, Argumentative, Clairvoyance, Impulsive, Feel the Turn of the Universe, Psychic, Telepathy, Vortex, Scan [x3], Transmit, Restriction [Tricky Controls, 6 Pilots], Forcefield (Minor), Resourceful Pockets

ARMOUR: 30

HIT CAPACITY: THOUSANDS

SPEED: 12 (MATERIALISED)

STORY POINTS: 15

CHAPTER TWO:
AN UNEARTHLY CHILD, THE DALEKS, THE EDGE OF DESTRUCTION

AN UNEARTHLY CHILD

"Fear makes companions of us all, Miss Wright."

SYNOPSIS

England, 1963.

Two schoolteachers, Ian Chesterton and Barbara Wright, were fascinated by one of their students, Susan Foreman. At times, Susan was brilliant – she knew more about physics and chemistry than Chesterton did, although she occasionally blurted out answers that seem either nonsensical, or beyond comprehension, when she talked about higher dimensions and future discoveries. In Barbara's history class, Susan was equally unpredictable. She knew the oddest details about history, but was also ignorant of basic facts about modern-day culture. The girl tried to fit in, and seemed otherwise normal, but there was something uncanny about her.

The two teachers followed Susan to her home address, which turned out to be a junkyard at Totter's Lane. Searching the yard, they found a strangely out-of-place police box which seemed to hum. Their investigation was interrupted by a strange old man, Susan's Grandfather: the Doctor. He attempted to convince them to leave, and told them they were mistaken when they thought they heard Susan's voice, but Ian suspected the old man had kidnapped the girl and barged into the police box.

Ian and Barbara were amazed to discover that the inside of the box was far larger than its exterior could possibly allow. They had discovered the Doctor's ship, which Susan refers to as the TARDIS – Time And Relative Dimension In Space.

Susan pleaded with her Grandfather to let the two teachers go, to trust them to keep what they've seen secret, but he refused. She even threatened to leave with the teachers, and in response the Doctor activated the ship. The TARDIS flew a hundred thousand years back in time, and materialised in the Paleolithic era.

There, they met a tribe of primitive humans, to whom fire was a mysterious wonder. Three factions divided the tribe. The son of the previous leader, Za, should have been the leader, but his father died without teaching him the secret of making fire. His rival for the position was Kal, who was adopted from another tribe. The third power in the tribe was the Old Woman, a priestess of their tribal deity, Orb. She feared fire, and plotted to stop the tribe from rediscovering the secret.

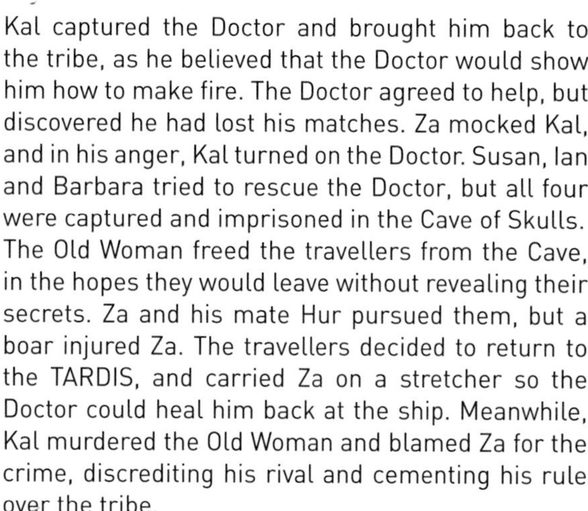

Kal captured the Doctor and brought him back to the tribe, as he believed that the Doctor would show him how to make fire. The Doctor agreed to help, but discovered he had lost his matches. Za mocked Kal, and in his anger, Kal turned on the Doctor. Susan, Ian and Barbara tried to rescue the Doctor, but all four were captured and imprisoned in the Cave of Skulls. The Old Woman freed the travellers from the Cave, in the hopes they would leave without revealing their secrets. Za and his mate Hur pursued them, but a boar injured Za. The travellers decided to return to the TARDIS, and carried Za on a stretcher so the Doctor could heal him back at the ship. Meanwhile, Kal murdered the Old Woman and blamed Za for the crime, discrediting his rival and cementing his rule over the tribe.

The travellers arrived at the TARDIS, but were ambushed and recaptured by Kal and his followers. The Doctor tricked Kal into revealing his bloody knife, proving that he and not Za killed the Old Woman. Za became the leader of the tribe, but instead of letting the travellers go, he imprisoned them once again in the Cave. They would join his tribe, he declared, and become firemakers.

Finally, the travellers devised an escape plan. They put skulls atop flaming torches, and the tribe mistook these apparitions for terrifying spirits. The four escaped the cave and fled back to the TARDIS, dematerialising in the nick of time to escape the pursuing tribesmen.

CONTINUITY

The Doctor returns to the junkyard at 76 Totter's Lane several times, most notably in his Seventh incarnation, when the Daleks try to find the Hand of Omega, hidden by the Doctor in 1963...

RUNNING THIS ADVENTURE

There are really two adventures here – the initial discovery of the TARDIS at Totter's Lane and the Palaeolithic drama.

The first adventure is a perfect example of how to set up a *Doctor Who: Adventures in Time and Space* campaign. You've got tension between the characters (Ian and Barbara don't trust the Doctor,

but want to protect Susan, and Susan is the Doctor's granddaughter), you've got an intriguing mystery (what is the strange box in the junkyard), and you drop the players right into the action (the travellers are ambushed by cavemen as soon as they arrive in the Stone Age). Using a similar setup for your first adventure is a great way to kick off a campaign. Note that the Doctor is far less sympathetic here – he mistrusts humans and is mainly interested in his and Susan's safety. Setting the Doctor up as an antagonist so the human player characters can win him over makes the early adventures much more perilous, as the players cannot rely on the Doctor to save them.

The encounter with the cavemen is much more of a conventional adventure. The travellers show up, start exploring, and are drawn into an ongoing conflict.

THE OBJECT OF DESIRE

In the prehistoric adventure, the tribesmen force the travellers to get involved. The Doctor does not want to interfere, but he is physically seized and dragged into the plot. The tribe *want* something from him – in this case, the secret of fire. You could substitute almost anything else for that object of desire. If the TARDIS had materialised in, say, the Middle Ages, then maybe the object of desire would have been the secret of the printing press. The object of desire doesn't have to be scientific knowledge – imagine a race of aliens who are allergic to even mild radiation. A ship crashes on their planet, and it's crammed with all sorts of technological wonders... but they can't go near it, because the ship's reactor is damaged. The level of radiation is harmless to a human, so the player characters can just walk in and retrieve the technology on board.

Make the Object of Desire simple for the player characters to produce, but impossible for the locals to do the same without help. Make it something that the characters can give freely – a piece of knowledge, a show of support, a trivial mundane item – and make sure that giving it is a free choice for the players. Don't make it something that the locals need, like the cure for a disease.

Now, here's the interesting bit. Divide the locals into several factions. The Tribe of Gum had three factions, all after the secret of fire. All the factions want something from the player characters. It's up to the players to choose who to support. The GM could present the three tribal factions as embodying three different ideas – faith (the Old Woman), tradition (Za, the son of the former leader) and innovation (Kal, the stranger). This choice can be presented without complications, as a sort of personality test for the player characters, or shaded with ambiguities. Kal may be the best choice for leader, but he's sneaky and untrustworthy.

Za may be the most sympathetic, but he lets his ambition get the better of him. The Old Woman may be the safest option for the player characters, but what happens when she dies?

Draw the players in to the setting by forcing them to choose who to help.

For example, if the characters go undercover at a hotel, then don't slow the game down by roleplaying your character's confusion about the concepts of 'money' or 'carpets' or 'glass windows', but have fun describing how you build a lean-to shelter out of your bed, or flood the bathroom because you can't stop the magic stream of water.

LOW-TECHNOLOGY COMPANIONS

Most of the Doctor's companions come from the present day (Tech Level 4 or 5) with a few from other time periods, usually the future. However, it is possible to play a primitive tribesperson like Leela of the Sevateem. Maybe Za and Hur could have joined the Doctor instead of returning to the tribe.

A Tech Level 1 companion presents an interesting challenge to both the player and the Gamemaster. On one hand, it's certainly a distinctive character trait! The character has no understanding of any technology more complex than a knife or a bow and arrow – even the most primitive vehicle is a thing of wonder, so a phone booth is just as magical as a TARDIS (*"yes, it is small on the inside, but this mouth speaks with many voices!"*).

On the other hand, this can get very annoying if overplayed. It's no fun if the character holds up play all the time because they get stuck on the most trivial examples of technology. (*"She pushed, and the wall opened! What magic is this thing you call 'door'?"*)

The best approach is to emulate Leela – she may not have understood everything she saw, but she was quick to translate it into terms she could work with. Play the character's unfamiliarity with technology as a source of humour or commentary on society, instead of making it a handicap.

STONE AGE TRIBESMAN

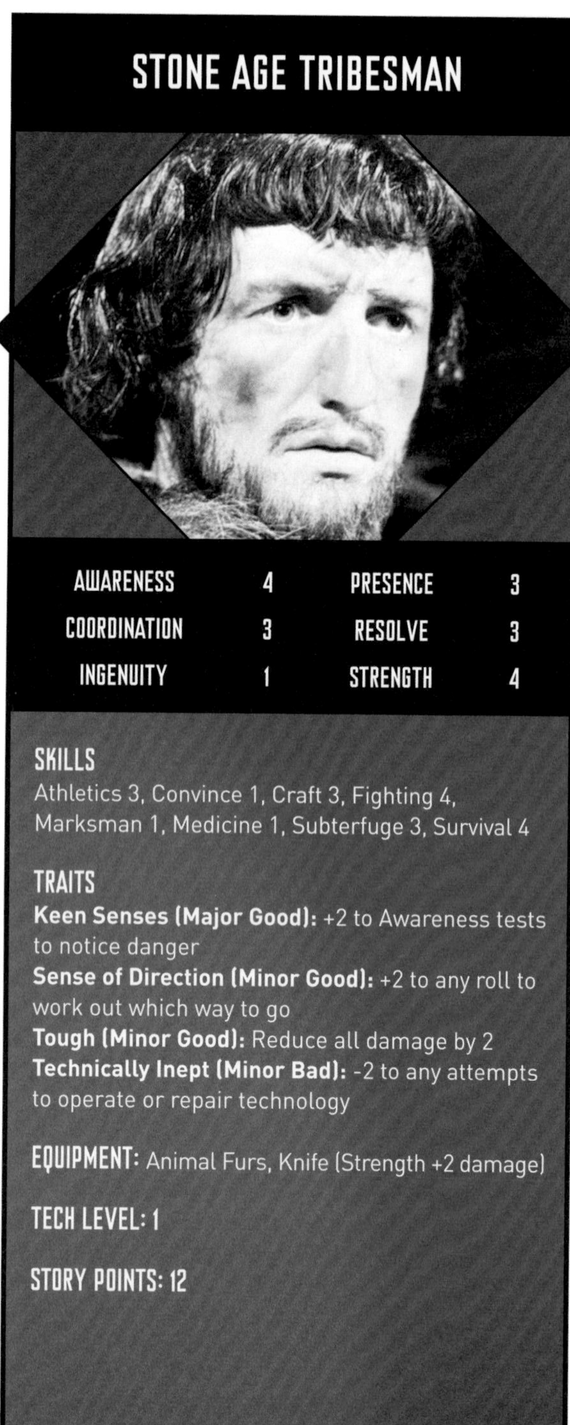

AWARENESS	4	PRESENCE	3
COORDINATION	3	RESOLVE	3
INGENUITY	1	STRENGTH	4

SKILLS

Athletics 3, Convince 1, Craft 3, Fighting 4, Marksman 1, Medicine 1, Subterfuge 3, Survival 4

TRAITS

Keen Senses (Major Good): +2 to Awareness tests to notice danger
Sense of Direction (Minor Good): +2 to any roll to work out which way to go
Tough (Minor Good): Reduce all damage by 2
Technically Inept (Minor Bad): -2 to any attempts to operate or repair technology

EQUIPMENT: Animal Furs, Knife (Strength +2 damage)

TECH LEVEL: 1

STORY POINTS: 12

Remember, a character can spend a Story Point to use *"Is that how it works, Doctor?"* (see page 67 of the *Gamemaster's Guide*), to use a skill possessed by another player character without unskilled penalties – and without the penalties incurred from having a low technology level. Za can press the shiny stones in the right order (and make a Technology roll) if the Doctor tells him what to do first.

THE CAVE OF SKULLS

This shrine was where the tribe kept their prisoners – and their dead. All the skulls in the cave were split open, suggesting either violent deaths or ritual sacrifice. There were two entrances into the cave. A huge stone blocked the main entrance. The tribesmen rolled the stone away when throwing prisoners into the cave (Strength + Resolve, Difficulty 18 to roll aside). A short passage led from this entrance to the tribe's main sleeping cavern, where the whole tribe huddled together for warmth.

There was also a secret back way into the cave from the forest above. Finding this narrow passageway requires an Awareness + Ingenuity roll, Difficulty 18. Only the Old Woman knew about this hidden entrance, which was blocked by bones and other debris.

FURTHER ADVENTURES

- **The Doctor's Post Box:** The Doctor appeared to use 76 Totter's Lane as his address on Earth (certainly, it's on his library card!). Why would a wanderer in time and space need a postal address? Who's writing letters to him? The Doctor could have abandoned all sorts of intriguing plots when he was forced to leave in a hurry. You could start a campaign with one of the characters finding an undelivered letter addressed to the Doctor at 76 Totter's Lane.

- **Mysteries at Coal Hill School:** Two teachers and a student just vanished mysteriously from Coal Hill School. Of course someone is going to investigate. Your player could play other staff from the school, or Susan's classmates (and what did she accidentally let slip during her time in the school?). Even if they never find out what became of Mr. Chesterton and Ms. Wright, there are all sorts of other mysteries to be investigated in this era.

- **Tribe of the Atom:** The Doctor left his Geiger counter behind in the distant past. What could a tribe of Stone Age humans do with a Geiger counter? Well, for one thing, they could locate deposits of magic 'hot rocks'. Fast forward a few thousand years, and imagine a society dominated by atomic priests, who dwell in temples where the walls glow with radium lights, and whose flesh is scarred with the holy marks of the sacred stones!

- **Mysteries of Orb:** The Tribe worshipped a solar deity called Orb. What if there was more to Orb than the Doctor suspected? What caused the strange cold environment around the tribe – an unusually long winter, or something more? Why did they say that Orb no longer shone as brightly? Could there have been a sinister, alien purpose behind the Cave of Skulls?

THE DALEKS

"That's sheer murder."
"NO. EXTERMINATION."

SYNOPSIS

The TARDIS materialised on the alien world of Skaro. Long ago, two races fought a catastrophic neutronic war on this world. One faction, the Thals, was nearly annihilated by the war. The few Thal survivors developed a powerful anti-radiation drug that allowed them to survive on the blasted surface.

Their foes, the Kaled race, retreated to a vast underground city, where they became the hideous Daleks. Their travel machine casings turned them into virtually invincible war machines, but they were restricted to the city as they depended on radiation and static electricity drawn from the floor to power themselves. The two races remained deadlocked for generations.

The travellers, of course, knew nothing of this. Exploring, they found themselves in a petrified forest near a strange city. The Doctor wished to explore the city, and sabotaged the TARDIS' Fluid Link to ensure they could not leave until they had visited the city to repair the link and, completely coincidentally of course, satisfy his curiosity. The Thals tried to warn them of the dangerous levels of radiation on the planet by leaving a box of anti-radiation drugs outside the TARDIS, but the travellers pressed on heedlessly. By the time the Daleks captured the four travellers, they were already suffering from radiation sickness.

After questioning their prisoners (whom they suspected of being Thals), the Daleks permitted Susan to leave the city to retrieve the anti-radiation drugs. In the forest, she met the surviving Thals. Starvation forced them to migrate to this region, and they hoped to bargain with the Daleks for food. Susan agreed to act as their go-between.

The Daleks attempted to lure the Thals into an ambush by offering them food. However, the travellers were able to disable one of the Daleks and found a way out of the underground corridors just in time to raise the alarm. The surviving Thals fled back into the forest with the travellers, leaving the Daleks trapped in the city.

However, the Doctor discovered that the Daleks had taken the Fluid Link he'd removed from the TARDIS when they questioned him. The travellers were stuck on Skaro – unless they could recover the Fluid Link from the city. They convinced the pacifistic Thals to fight back against the Daleks and devised a plan to attack the city. The Thals and their new-found allies divided into two groups – a distraction aimed at the front gate of the city, while a smaller war party sneak across the Lake of Mutations and attack the city through a rear entrance.

Meanwhile, the Daleks hatched their own schemes. Their experiments with a sample of the Thal anti-radiation drug proved that the Daleks were immune to radiation – in fact, they needed it to thrive. To expand their control beyond the city, they had to increase the planet's radiation level. Building another bomb would take too long, but they could overload the city's reactors and throw neutronic fallout into the planet's atmosphere.

The Doctor led the distraction team, and managed to temporarily disable Dalek communications before being captured. In the confusion, Ian and the Thals managed to storm the Dalek control room and disabled the power source that fed static electricity to the city's power grid. Deprived of energy, the Daleks were immobilised and began to die. They begged the Doctor to repair the machine, but he refused. With the Fluid Link recovered and the TARDIS repaired, the travellers bade farewell to their Thal allies and departed.

EARLY DALEKS

These 'version 1' Daleks were more limited than their future descendants. Notably, they are limited by their need for static electricity – they cannot fly or move outside the city's corridors.

The Dalek mutant inside the casing has the attributes in brackets; it has a Speed of 1 and cannot survive for long outside of the shell. It also takes damage as normal once removed from its armoured casing.

AWARENESS	3 [2]	PRESENCE	3 [2]
COORDINATION	2 [3]	RESOLVE	4 [4]
INGENUITY	4 [4]	STRENGTH	5 [3]

SKILLS

Convince 2, Fighting 2, Marksman 2, Medicine 1, Science 2, Survival 4, Technology 3

TRAITS

Armour [Minor]: This is a weaker version of the Dalek's famous Dalekanium armour shell and can only deduct 5 points of damage.

Cyborg

Fear Factor [3]: This hasn't changed much; Daleks are still terrifying once you can get over how strange/silly they look. They gain a bonus of +6 when trying to actively scare someone.

Natural Weapon – Exterminator: The Daleks encountered upon the Dead Planet use a deadly form of this weapon that can emit a beam which either kills or paralyses their victims. (L[2/L/L])

Scan: The Dalek v.1 can interface with computers and complex machines.

Technically Adept: The Daleks are brilliant with computers and other technology; they can use and adapt a variety of technologies.

Restriction: The Daleks from the Dead Planet were unable to leave their city of metal; they required static electricity for power that was distributed through the metal flooring from a central hub generator. A Dalek cut off from the floor (either lifted off the ground, or blocked by a non-conductive object like a cloak) loses 1-6 points of Strength and Resolve each round. When reduced to 0 Strength and Resolve, it shuts down.

Weakness: The Dalek mutant is extremely vulnerable to the effects of the Thal anti-radiation drug. If the mutant is injected with the drug, it falls ill and is reduced to 0 Co-ordination within minutes. Depending on the dose, this could prove fatal.

STORY POINTS: 2-3

RUNNING THIS ADVENTURE

The *Daleks* was one of the Doctor's most important adventures, as it was (subjectively) the first contact between two of the most powerful civilisations in the universe – the Time Lords of Gallifrey and the Dalek Empire. You could say the Time War began in this moment, although neither side realised what was at stake. This was the Doctor's first encounter with the Daleks. These Daleks gave a slightly different account of their history compared to later encounters, claiming to be survivors of the war who started using the travel machine casings to survive instead of admitting they were mutants engineered by Davros. Perhaps they lied, or had forgotten their own history – the war was hundreds of years ago, after all. The Doctor left these Daleks to die, but that did not put an end to the evil race.

The Thals went on to rebuild their civilisation, and battled the Daleks many more times in the future before they were exterminated.

BEHIND THE SCENES: FIRST IMPRESSIONS

The Daleks were never intended to be anything more than a one-shot villain. They were created just for this adventure, and came back because they proved so memorable and popular. Similarly, a villain or monster you create for your games may turn out to be more memorable than you expected. Watch your players – if they really like (or better, really really hate) a villain, then bring them back in a future adventure!

THE DALEK CITY

The city looked relatively small from the surface, but that was because most of it lay underground. It lay in a mist-shrouded valley in the shadow of looming mountains. To the north of the city was a toxic lake, presumably where the Daleks dumped poisonous waste products from the city's underground factories. The towering buildings that made up the city were almost all scientific laboratories, sensor arrays and weapons systems. Notably, instruments there monitor radiation levels in the surrounding area.

At this point in the city's history, the surface sections are sparsely occupied, suggesting there are few Daleks living there.

The city had few external defences – at least, none that were active – other than its protective wall that ran around the west, south and east perimeter. The travellers and the Thals were able to walk straight into the city, although it is possible that the Daleks had concealed weapons that they chose not to use.

KEY LOCATIONS

- **Audience Chamber:** This large chamber was where the Daleks ambushed the Thals. It may have been a meeting room or public space, as it was in the heart of the surface city.
- **Laboratories:** There were numerous research laboratories throughout the city.
- **Prison Cells:** The Daleks held their prisoners in cells under the city. Security cameras monitored these cells constantly, and any suspicious action risked attracting the attention of Dalek guards.
- **Monitoring Towers:** These towers contained the city's laserscopes and communications relays. The laserscopes functioned like long-range telescopes, allowing the Daleks to spy on the Thals. However, a bright light source could interfere with the laserscopes and disrupt the functioning of the towers.
- **Farms:** The Daleks produced food using artificial sunlight in huge hydroponic farms under the city. Presumably, the mutants still needed to consume organic matter to survive. Later Daleks could synthesise their own nourishment.
- **Control Room:** From this chamber, the Dalek commanders could direct the operations of their subordinates. Notably, they could monitor events outside the city using their laserscopes. The control room also contained the static electricity distribution hub, a key component of the Dalek infrastructure.
- **Reactors:** These reactors powered the entire city. They vented hot air through shafts in the north of the city, near the Lake of Mutations.

NAVIGATING THE CITY

The city was designed for Daleks. All the doors and corridors are Dalek-sized, so they seem low and cramped to humans. There is no furniture or other amenities in the city – no chairs, no beds, nothing except cold metal and machinery. Elevators connect different levels of the city. These elevators travel up and down open shafts, suggesting that different vehicles used these shafts as well as the elevator cars encountered by the travellers.

All the doors in the city are controlled by light beam switches; interrupting the light beam triggersthe opening mechanism. The doors could be locked and overridden from the control centre. Physically forcing open a door is Difficulty 15.

Security cameras and vibrascopes feed information on the movements of intruders to the Daleks in the control centre. The security cameras are articulated, so they can twist and move to watch their targets. The vibrascopes pick up on the noises made by footsteps, which were obviously quite unlike the sounds made by Daleks. Sneaking through the city is therefore quite tricky (Difficulty 15 for Co-ordination + Subterfuge tests).

All the floors in the city are charged with static electricity. This energy field is harmless to humans, but can be accessed by the Daleks or by a suitable device. It is possible that the Daleks can turn this field into a weapon, making the whole floor deliver a stunning or lethal shock to anyone touching it without suitable protection.

THE THALS

Before the great war, the ancestors of the Thals were belligerent and militaristic, while the Kaleds were more peaceful and focussed on science. The war transformed both cultures. The Kaleds became the xenophobic, monstrous Daleks, but the Thals abandoned their warlike ways and became pacifists.

The few surviving Thals retreated to an isolated plateau in the mountains that was less affected by the radiation than the rest of the planet. There, they eked out an existence as best they could. The Thals still possessed some knowledge of technology (around TL5), but had no weapons. They concentrated their efforts on biochemistry and medicine; they developed their anti-radiation drugs and found ways to grow crops in the blighted soil of Skaro.

DALS OR KALEDS?

According to the Thals, the Daleks evolved from a rival race called the Dals, not the Kaleds. As the Doctor later visited Skaro at the height of the wars, when the mad genius Davros created the Daleks, he discovered the mutants were called Kaleds. Perhaps 'Dal' was the Thal nickname for their enemies, or maybe the TARDIS translation matrix had a glitch that day.

THAL CHARACTERS

The Thals are virtually identical to humans. Only the fittest of them survive in the harsh conditions, so they tend to be strong and tough, with high Strength and Resolve scores. Most have the Distinctive trait of white-blonde hair, and the Code of Conduct of Pacifism. All Thals have the Survival skill at 2 or higher.

- **Temmosus:** The original leader of the Thals, who led them down from the Plateau. Temmosus believed that the Thals and Daleks could work together to rebuild their world and overcome the mistakes of the past. He died when the Daleks lured him and his followers into an ambush. Traits: Voice of Authority, Obsession (saving the Thal people).

- **Alydon:** Young Alydon was Temmosus' chosen successor, and became leader of the Thals when his mentor died. Like Temmosus, Alydon believed in the path of peace, and was hesitant to fight back against the Daleks. However, Ian convinced him that there could be no compromise with the monsters, and that the only way to survive was to strike back. Traits: Obligation (the Thals), By The Book

- **Ganatus:** Unlike the rest of the Thals, the hunter Ganatus mistrusted the Daleks. He survived the ambush and was among the first to support fighting back. He was much less passive than the other Thals. Traits: Brave, Argumentative, Lucky

- **Dyoni:** Dyoni was Alydon's lover. She was fascinated by the technology of the travellers, especially the TARDIS. After Temmosus's death, she became the custodian of the Thal archives. Traits: Insatiable Curiosity.

ANTI-RADIATION DRUG

Gadget Traits: Environmental, Restricted

One dose of this drug gives immunity to nuclear radiation for several days. It can also reverse the effects of radiation sickness, restoring Ability points lost to radiation damage. The drug is not addictive and has no side effects – at least, not on humans. The drug makes Daleks (and possibly other mutants) sick and disorientated.

Cost: 1 Story Point

SCARRED SKARO

The war between Daleks and Thals was fought with nuclear weapons – specifically, a form of neutron bomb designed to kill organic beings while leaving structures intact. Other weapons were also used, including poisonous distronic explosives that blighted the environment of Skaro.

The background radiation makes Skaro extremely hazardous to visitors. Anyone exposed to the radiation without suitable protection (like a radiation suit or the Thal drug) loses 1 point of Strength per hour; when the character's Strength is reduced to 0, the radiation saps Coordination and Resolve.

The toxic Lake of Mutations and the swamps surrounding it behind the Dalek city is home to many especially horrible mutants. Crossing the swamp requires the Survival skill (Difficulty 12-18, depending on how deep into the wetlands you go). Creatures like magnedons and swamp horrors may be encountered here.

MAGNEDON

These creatures are bizarre 'magnetic lizards'. They may be native to Skaro, but given their unlikely biology, they are more likely to be artificially created lifeforms, perhaps left-overs from one of Davros' experiments. Magnedons look like reptiles, but are made of living metal animated by an internal magnetic field. They prey on other, similar magnetic creatures, and may also be able to feed off natural magnetic or static electrical fields.

AWARENESS	3	PRESENCE	2
COORDINATION	3	RESOLVE	2
INGENUITY	1	STRENGTH	2

SKILLS

Athletics 2, Fighting 1, Subterfuge 3, Survival 3

TRAITS

Alien
Alien Appearance (Major Bad): It's a metal lizard.
Alien Senses (Minor Good): Magnedons can 'smell' electromagnetic fields.
Armour (Minor Good): 5 point of Armour.
Climbing (Minor Good): Magnedons clamber around trees and caves, and have a +4 bonus to Coordination + Athletics rolls when climbing:
Magnetic Control (Special Good): Magnedons can control magnetic fields. They usually use this ability to attract prey, but could also use it to disrupt sensors or energy weapons. The Thals hunt the magnedons and drain their natural electromagnetic fields into batteries, leaving the creature's inanimate carcass behind.

SWAMP BEAST

The nightmarish swamp beast spotted by Ian as he skirted around the Lake of Mutations may be a relative of the slyther (see page 69). This monster looked like a sort of cancerous octopus, with two sinister glowing eyes. It appeared cowardly and fled when challenged, but later returned to kill one of the Thals.

AWARENESS	3	PRESENCE	2
COORDINATION	3	RESOLVE	2
INGENUITY	1	STRENGTH	4

SKILLS

Athletics 3, Fighting 2, Survival 3

TRAITS

Alien
Alien Appearance (Major Bad): Cancerous octopus!
Fear Factor 1 (Minor Good): The swamp beast gets a +2 bonus when trying to scare people.
Tentacles (Special Good): The swamp beast can grab foes with its long tentacles. The beast rolls Coordination + Fighting to attack, and can drag victims into the water if it wins. The tentacles do Strength damage (2/4/6) on a hit. However, damage to the tentacles does not injure the main body of the beast. Each tentacle can survive 5 points of damage.
Whirlpool Vortex (Special Good): The swamp beast can churn up the waters around itself, making it almost impossible to swim. A character dragged into the water by the swamp beast must make Strength + Athletics rolls at Difficulty 20 to stay afloat, or at Difficulty 24 to escape the whirlpool.

FURTHER ADVENTURES

- **Exploring the City of the Daleks:** What did the Daleks leave behind in their city? There could be all sorts of gadgets and monsters lurking in the steel corridors of the bunker.

- **The Art Collector**: At one point, Ian and Barbara throw a sculpture down a lift shaft to block an approaching elevator full of Daleks. Hang on, a sculpture? In a Dalek city? Who made it? Was it a relic from the days when the Kaleds were philosophers and teachers? Or did the Daleks themselves make it? Could it have been a rare example of Dalek art, and if so, what does it say about the psychology of their race? An art collector might pay any price to have that piece recovered.

- **Skirmishes in the Time War:** The Time Lords and the Daleks both returned to this city again and again, their timelines crossing and criss-crossing until the whole tangled mess was locked away by the Doctor. Still, there might be echoes of the Last Great Time war here, fugitive glimpses of the vanished Dalek Empire and temporal strike teams from Gallifrey. This city is a haunted place, a twisted nexus point. You might meet anywhen in those endless corridors...

THE EDGE OF DESTRUCTION

"You see? The machine's been warning us all along!"

SYNOPSIS

The Doctor attempted to return Barbara and Ian to Earth by activating the Fast Return switch on the TARDIS console, but something went wrong. The ship dropped out of the Time Vortex in mid-flight and refused to move or open the doors. The scanner displayed seemingly random images of previous landing sites instead of showing them what lay outside. Clocks and watches on board began to behave strangely.

The passengers, too, were affected by some odd force. All four of them suffered from bouts of amnesia and paranoia. Susan, in particular, became almost murderous and threated to stab Barbara and Ian.

Touching the console triggered an immediate blast of pain, so the travellers were unable to tell the TARDIS to take off again. The Doctor tried to examine the ship's Fault Locator to determine the source of the problem, but could not focus on the readouts and was left baffled. As frustration fuelled the travellers' mounting sense of fear and paranoia, the Doctor offered them all a nightcap to help them relax. Secretly, he had drugged these drinks, and the other three fell asleep.

The Doctor tried to use the console controls, but was interrupted by a semi-conscious and belligerent Ian, who attacked him. The Doctor's own self-control cracked – he accused Ian and Barbara of sabotaging his ship, and decided to throw them off the ship no matter where the ship had landed. Susan pleaded for his clemency, and as she did so, an alarm sounded from the depths of the TARDIS. The ship – and its passengers – were in mortal peril.

Fighting against the disruptive influence, the Doctor convinced the others to work together to find the source of their problems. They had only minutes to locate what was wrong, as the TARDIS was on the brink of tearing itself apart. The Fault Locator still could not identify the underlying problem.

Barbara realised that the TARDIS itself was trying to help them. Whenever the scanner screen displayed a safe place, they could touch the console and open the doors without suffering psychic feedback. Whenever it displayed a dangerous location, the doors were sealed. Outside the doors, though, was nothing but the empty void.

The Doctor explained that he had used the fast return switch, so they examined that control and discovered that the spring beneath it was broken. The control was stuck in the 'on' position – the TARDIS had returned to Earth, but then kept going. Unlocking the switch freed the TARDIS from its self-destructive loop, returning the ship to normal flight.

CONTINUITY

The events of *Edge of Destruction* draw the TARDIS crew together. Afterwards, they are much more friendly and less suspicious of each other.

The alert klaxon may be an earlier form of the Cloister Bell.

RUNNING THIS ADVENTURE

Edge of Destruction is an example of a short adventure that can be inserted between two bigger scenarios. It's a great idea to have a few ideas like this ready to play, so you can use them if there's an unforeseen gap between adventures (*"I never thought you'd solve that one so quickly, and I don't have anything ready for next week... I mean, everything's proceeding exactly as I planned, for I am a wise and all-knowing Gamemaster!"*), or if some of the players are missing and you want to run a short and ultimately inconsequential adventure for the remaining characters.

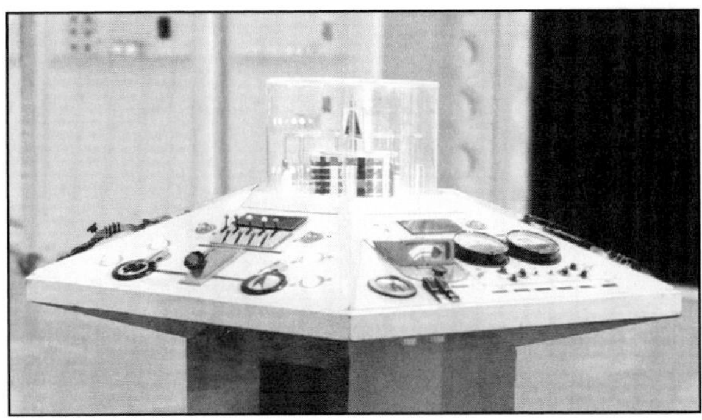

In the case of *Edge of Destruction*, the 'villain' is ultimately nothing more than a broken spring. (That's the sort of problem you run into when you steal an old Type 40 TARDIS and fly it around the universe!) That one small failure causes a cascade of problems for the characters. The broken spring means the TARDIS keeps rewinding, and that will eventually hurl it into the elemental chaos of the Big Bang. However, as the fast control subsystem is still working, the Fault Locator cannot help, forcing the TARDIS to try to warn its crew in indirect ways like the telepathic circuits – and scrambling the telepathic circuits like that has harmful effects on the passengers' mental states.

Don't slavishly follow the plot of *Edge of Destruction* – if you do, then the first thing the players will do every time they get on board their time machine is check the springs for faults! Instead, follow this formula:

- Some insignificant subsystem (let's call it A) goes wrong
- That failure causes a bigger problem, B
- A side effect of B, which we'll call C, stops the characters from immediately fixing the first problem

In *Edge of Destruction*, A is the Fast Return Switch, B is the ship's headlong plunge towards destruction, and C is the telepathic communication that drives the crew into paranoia and madness. Substitute your own A, B and C for your own adventures. For example:

The Drowning TARDIS:

A: The swimming pool springs a leak.

B: The water short-circuits the defence systems, leaving the TARDIS vulnerable to attack from other travellers in the Time Vortex.

C: The corridors between the characters and the console room are flooded – they'll have to find a way to breathe underwater or otherwise divert the tidal flood of water.

The TARDIS of Babel:

A: The translation circuit malfunctions. The characters cannot understand each other's speech, nor can they read any text at all. They can only communicate through gestures.

B: That means they can't read the little message on the console that says "Danger! Incoming Dalek fleet".

C: One of the characters has had their language remapped to the magical tongue of the Carrionites. Every time she speaks, she summons minor imps – pesky, hungry little beasts that want to eat the characters.

The Throwback Filter:

A: The temporal shields have partially failed. The characters are de-evolving into animalistic, ancestral forms as their DNA gets shifted back in the timestream.

B: If the temporal shield isn't repaired, causality on board will collapse and the ship will be destroyed!

C: Firstly, the characters have to overcome their new animal instincts to act rationally. Secondly, evolution is working much faster in other parts of the ship. The companions tracked mud onto the ship on the last planet, and the slime mold in that mud just evolved into sentience and has taken over the console room.

CHAPTER THREE:

MARCO POLO, THE KEYS OF MARINUS, THE AZTECS

MARCO POLO

"When great Kublai Khan appears, you will make your obeisance to him, so that he may look kindly upon you, and spare your worthless lives."

SYNOPSIS

The TARDIS, still damaged from the previous adventure, arrived on Earth in 1289. Outside was a harsh, snowy, mountainous landscape. However, the companions were forced outside to explore, as the Doctor told them that the ship's heating, light and water systems were damaged and need repair. Unless they found shelter, they would perish.

Exploring, the travellers encountered a Mongol warrior named Tegana who had a small army of warriors with him. Tegana denounced the strangers as evil spirits and commanded that they be put to death. As things looked dire for the time travellers a man of European descent interceded on their behalf. This man was none other than the legendary Marco Polo.

Marco Polo explained that he commanded the caravan, and intended to travel from the Pamir Plateau, also called the Roof of the World, to the court of the Kublai Khan himself. Tegana was the lieutenant of a rival of the khan, the warlord Nogai, and was accompanying him as his guest. Tegana's mission was to negotiate peace with the great Khan. Also in the caravan was a young girl named Ping-Cho, who was intended as a bride for one of the Khan's advisers.

The companions were forced to join the caravan when Marco Polo seized possession of the TARDIS. He loaded it onto the back of a cart with the intent of presenting it to Kublai Khan as a gift. Meanwhile, Tegana had his own schemes. He plotted to steal the TARDIS for his master Nogai, but also intended to murder Kublai Khan.

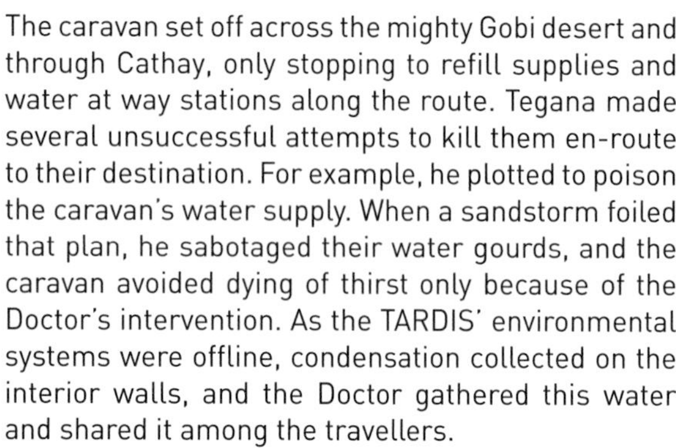

The caravan set off across the mighty Gobi desert and through Cathay, only stopping to refill supplies and water at way stations along the route. Tegana made several unsuccessful attempts to kill them en-route to their destination. For example, he plotted to poison the caravan's water supply. When a sandstorm foiled that plan, he sabotaged their water gourds, and the caravan avoided dying of thirst only because of the Doctor's intervention. As the TARDIS' environmental systems were offline, condensation collected on the interior walls, and the Doctor gathered this water and shared it among the travellers.

Tegana also plotted with bandits to ambush the caravan. Later, after a messenger from the Khan ordered Polo to hasten his journey, Tegana had his thieves steal the TARDIS when it was left behind with a slower cart. The ship was recovered only by chance – Ping-Cho fled the caravan and Ian was sent to find her, and he interrupted the thieves.

With each misadventure, Marco Polo became more suspicious of the travellers even as they became more suspicious of Tegana. After many hardships, the caravan arrived in the Khan's domain. There, the Doctor entertained the Khan by playing a masterful series of backgammon games. He won a huge pile of treasure, wagered it all for possession of the TARDIS – and lost. The 'magic box' now belonged to the Khan. The Khan questioned Marco Polo about the origins of the box, and was angered when he learned that Marco Polo stole the box from the Doctor. The Khan was displeased with his servant's behaviour, but as he had won the TARDIS fairly in his own game, he retained possession of the ship.

With the TARDIS firmly in the grasp of the Great Khan, it seemed like there was not a single silver lining, other than the unlikely death of Ping-Cho's betrothed husband. The elderly man died after drinking an aphrodisiac potion. Ping-Cho now pursued her romance with the Khan's dispatch rider, Ling-Tau.

The Khan had the companions imprisoned while he considered their allegations about Tegana. Convinced that someone has to stop the villain, the travellers broke out of their prison and warned Marco Polo, who rushed to the throne room. He arrived in the nick of time to save the Khan from an assassin's blade. Tegana's plan was to kill Kublai Khan, throwing the Mongol Empire into chaos and opening Nogai's path to victory.

Tegana and Polo fought a bitter sword duel that ended with Tegana's defeat and suicide. As a reward for his heroism, the Khan freed Marco Polo and gave him permission to return home to Venice. To repay his own debts, Polo returned the TARDIS' keys to the Doctor and helped him and his companions escape. The Khan's court watched in amazement as the box vanished into thin air.

RUNNING THIS ADVENTURE

Marco Polo is another example of an historical adventure – an adventure involving no alien or supernatural elements, just real-world history. While Marco Polo's relationship with Kublai Khan was probably exaggerated, everything in this adventure is based or at least inspired by history. Kublai Khan did have a fractious relationship with his warlords (although it was with his nephew Kaidu Khan, not Nogai Khan).

When plotting a historical adventure, start with history. Grab a biography or a history book on some period that attracts you, and then start thinking about what could happen when the player characters get involved. Look for interesting events, mysteries, or places where the action of individuals can make a huge difference. The player characters can't stop World War II, but look at World War I where the assassination of a single person – Archduke Ferdinand – triggers the whole conflict. Don't worry too much about historical accuracy when coming up with your plots. Feel free to stick characters together, ignore dates and places, and condense complex events into simpler ones. After all, sometimes the accepted interpretation of events can be wrong, especially the further back you go!

Once you've got your inspiration, creating a historical adventure works just like any other adventure. You may not have the convenient plot devices of alien technology and monsters, but people work just as well, especially if lubricated with Story Points. Having the plot turn on convincing Kublai Khan of Tegara's treachery is just like having the plot turn on an alien supercomputer – instead of finding the control codes so they can turn on the ancient planetary force shield, they've got to find proof of Tegara's malice so the Khan orders his arrest.

One word of warning – be careful of the impact of technology, especially firearms. If your characters routinely carry guns, unlike the Doctor and his companions, then they may be able to get out of problems through brute force and intimidation when facing very low-tech opposition.

MARCO POLO

AWARENESS	3	PRESENCE	4
COORDINATION	3	RESOLVE	4
INGENUITY	3	STRENGTH	4

Born in Venice, he travelled east with his father Niccolo and his uncle Maffeo. The older Polos were already great explorers who had completed a previous expedition to China and returned alive. This second expedition lasted 24 years, as the Khan became very fond of the European explorers and would not give them permission to return home despite their many requests. When finally given leave to depart, Marco Polo returned to his beloved Venice, where – after the brief inconvenience of being taken prisoner by the army of Genoa and locked in a cell for several months, during which time he dictated his famous book – he became a wealthy and prosperous merchant.

SKILLS

Athletics 3, Convince 3, Fighting 3, Marksman 1, Knowledge 4, Science 1, Subterfuge 2, Survival 3 (Travel 5), Transport 4

TRAITS

Lucky (Minor Good Trait): Reroll double 1s
Sense of Direction (Minor Good): +2 to any attempts to determine the best route to travel
Obligation (Major Bad): Servant of the Great Khan

TECH LEVEL: 2

STORY POINTS: 5

THE PERILS OF LONG JOURNEYS

The Doctor doesn't usually do long journeys. When you've got a TARDIS, it's as easy to travel to the far side of the universe as it is to pop down the shops for a pint of milk. (On the far side of the universe, you can get anti-milk, which becomes a powerful explosive when added to hot tea.) Sometimes, though, the only way to get from A to B is the long, boring, slow way that involves crossing through all the points in between.

For long journeys, such as the journey from the Roof of the World to the Khan's summer palace, use the Survival skill. Call for Resolve + Survival rolls from all the player characters every few days of travel, with the DC determined by the nature of the terrain.

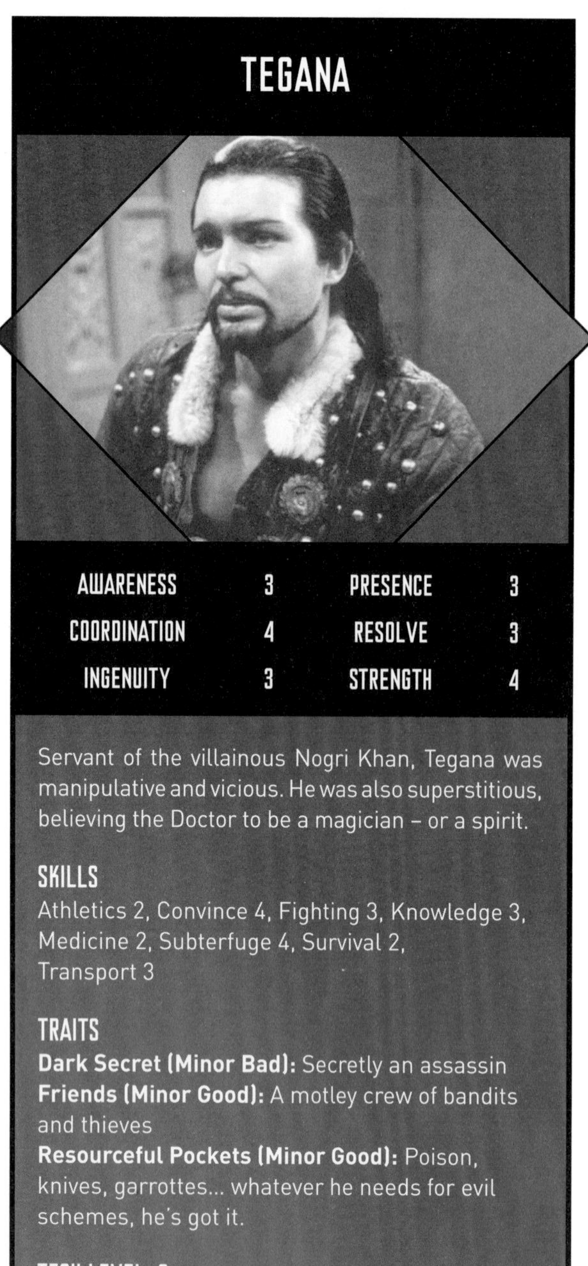

TEGANA

AWARENESS	3	PRESENCE	3
COORDINATION	4	RESOLVE	3
INGENUITY	3	STRENGTH	4

Servant of the villainous Nogri Khan, Tegana was manipulative and vicious. He was also superstitious, believing the Doctor to be a magician – or a spirit.

SKILLS

Athletics 2, Convince 4, Fighting 3, Knowledge 3, Medicine 2, Subterfuge 4, Survival 2, Transport 3

TRAITS

Dark Secret (Minor Bad): Secretly an assassin
Friends (Minor Good): A motley crew of bandits and thieves
Resourceful Pockets (Minor Good): Poison, knives, garrottes... whatever he needs for evil schemes, he's got it.

TECH LEVEL: 2

STORY POINTS: 3

KUBLAI KHAN

AWARENESS	4	PRESENCE	6
COORDINATION	3	RESOLVE	5
INGENUITY	5	STRENGTH	4

The great Kublai Khan was quite unlike his barbaric grandfather Genghis. He considered himself to be of "the clan of the statistician and the administrator", and was quite polite and civilised, even meek. Despite this, he was a man of iron will and the ruler of a vast empire.

SKILLS

Athletics 3, Convince 4, Fighting 2, Knowledge 4, Science 3, Subterfuge 2, Survival 2, Transport 3

TRAITS

Owed Favour (Major Good): By the entire Mongol empire. It's good to be the Khan.
Indomitable (Major Good): +4 to any attempts to resist hypnosis.
Voice of Authority: +2 to any attempts to use Presence or Convince. He's the Khan.
Code of Conduct (Major Bad): Even the Khan is bound by tradition and law.

TECH LEVEL: 2

STORY POINTS: 6

A gentle plain might be TN9, while a jungle or mountainous region might be TN15 or higher. Those who succeed in their rolls avoid any problems. Those who fail take 0/1/2 damage from exposure to hostile conditions or exhaustion. Next, look at the lowest result. If it's something interesting (like a Disastrous Failure or a marginal *no, but* Failure), then come up with an encounter for the whole group. Examples might be:

- **Bad weather:** A storm hits the group. They've got find shelter immediately or take more damage.
- **Bridge washed away by heavy rains:** How do they cross the raging torrent?
- **Attack by bandits:** Desperate thieves plot to ambush the characters as they travel. They attack at night, or when the characters travel past a good spot for a surprise attack.
- **Lost in the wilderness:** The characters take a wrong turn and end up very, very lost. They're not going to make any progress until someone succeeds at an Awareness + Ingenuity roll, at a Difficulty based on the surrounding terrain. In a trackless desert, you're going to end up going around and around in circles; in a mountain range made of living rock, the trick is spotting the sleeping mountains that don't move and using them as landmarks.
- **Panicked animals:** If the characters travel with riding animals or beasts of burden, then something spooks their mounts. Presence + Transport rolls (modified by Animal Friendship) are needed to calm them down. Oh, this hazard can also be applied to vehicles, which might break down or get stuck. Obviously, you wouldn't use Presence + Transport then, it'd be Ingenuity + Technology. Well, I suppose you could use Presence if it was an intelligent robot vehicle. Although then what would spook an intelligent robot vehicle? Look, I guess you can use Presence + Transport in a situation where your intelligent robot car gets spooked by some unknown force, but to be honest, anything that scares a *metal car* is probably worth running away from...
- **Intrigue by night:** One of the characters' fellow travellers plots against them – maybe he sabotages their equipment, or hires bandits to attack them, or changes their map so they get lost. Why is he plotting against them? That's for the characters to uncover!
- **Damaged supplies:** Some vital supplies get damaged or spoiled, and must be replaced promptly. For the Doctor and his companions in Mongolia, it was their water supply, but it could be food, fuel, batteries, oxygen tanks or something more exotic.
- **Bad choice of route:** The guide makes a bad decision and takes the company into unusually difficult terrain. The characters have a choice – turn back and retrace their steps, which takes a long time, or press on and try to push through the more difficult terrain ahead.
- **Changing mode of transport:** Circumstances dictate that the characters have to change how they're travelling. (Road to boat, boat to train, train to zeppelin, zeppelin to giant riding centipede, giant riding centipede to sewer surfing and so on).

ACCESS TO THE TARDIS

A TARDIS is a wonderful thing. It's an impenetrable fortress jam-packed with all sorts of exotic gadgets, vitally needed supplies, spare parts and other wonders. Oh, and it travels in time and space. It's the best way to travel in the whole universe.

In fact, if the characters have access to a TARDIS, then it solves lots of their problems, no matter where or when they are. If the TARDIS landed close to the scene of the action, then you can expect the characters to run back to the ship regularly. If it landed far away, then the further the characters get from the TARDIS, the more danger they're in.

If you deny the characters access to the TARDIS – say, by dropping it down a deep hole, or surrounding it with armed guards, or having Marco Polo steal the keys – then expect the players to concentrate on getting it back. They may even ignore your plot in favour of focussing on ways to recover their ship. The best thing to do is to make sure that getting the TARDIS back is accomplished by following your main plot. For example, if you want the characters to meet Kublai Khan, then arrange events so that talking to the Khan is the best way to get the TARDIS back.

FURTHER ADVENTURES

- **Kublai Khan, Time Conqueror:** *I told you about the Buddhist monks. They will discover its secret. A caravan that flies. Do you imagine what this will mean to the Khan? It will make him the most powerful ruler the world has ever known. Stronger than Hannibal. Mightier than Alexander the Great.*

What if Kublai Khan kept the characters' TARDIS? It is a wonderful magic box, after all, able to hold any amount of things or people within it. Soon, the Khan discovers the box can be used as a weapon – he places a whole horde of his Mongol warriors inside, then has a sailor bring the box to Japan. Getting a whole army across the sea in boats is exceedingly difficult, but a single box is no problem! Japan soon falls to the horde.

One of his new subjects is a Confucian sage, who discovers the box can be controlled using the strange hexagonal plinth in the central chamber. In fact, the box can travel into the heavens, and even swim back and forth in the river of time like a particularly ungainly yet wonderful fish. With all of time and space to conquer, the Khan and his Mongol horde sets forth on the greatest invasion of history in history.

Then the Celestial Invention Agency show up, give the characters a replacement TARDIS, and order them to go clean up their mistakes.

- **The Secret Diary of Marco Polo:** In the 21st century, a Venetian historian claims to have discovered something amazing – a lost diary written by Marco Polo himself! The media and other authorities are sceptical, as the diary mentions meeting a strange 'traveller in time and space' who possessed a magic cabinet. Even stranger, the diary has Polo confessing that he stole a 'machine' from the cabinet, and that it brought him nothing but bad luck and weirdness on his journey home.

What did Polo take from the TARDIS, and what happened on the way back? The characters have to get a copy of the diary, then travel back to 1289 and follow Polo on his journey home to Venice.

- **A Visit to Kan'po Rimpoche:** The Doctor visits Tibet several times on his travels. He picks up a Buddhist relic at Det-Sen monastery in the 1600s, and brings it back in 1930 (*The Abominable Snowmen*). His old friend and fellow Time Lord Kan'po Rimpoche lives in retirement at another monastery somewhere in the mountains, too (*Planet of the Spiders*). The Doctor's use of the Fast Return Switch to get here suggests he visited Tibet relatively recently, perhaps before he brought Susan to school at Coal Hill.

Why was the Doctor there? Did he leave something in Tibet, just like he left the Hand of Omega hidden in Coal Hill in 1963?

THE KEYS OF MARINUS

"For seven centuries we prospered, and then a man named Yartek found a means of overcoming the power of the machine. He and his followers, the Voords, were able to rob, exploit, kill, cheat. Our people could not resist because violence is alien to them."

SYNOPSIS

Marinus was a peaceful world – but that peace was forced upon it by a machine called the Conscience of Marinus. The Conscience broadcast a telepathic signal that eliminated evil impulses in the population. It was located on a small island in the midst of an acidic sea, far from any danger. An official named Arbitan, together with a small staff, maintained the Conscience.

One of the races (or factions) kept in check by the Conscience was a hostile force of assassins named the Voord. Under the guidance of their leader Yartek, they had become immune to the pacifying effects of the Conscience. Arbitan discovered a way to modify the machine's signal so that it would also affect the Voord, but to do so, he would have to reactivate the Conscience, and do to that he needed the five control keys. He possessed only one of the keys. As a security measure, the other four keys had been scattered long ago across the face of the planet.

Arbitan dispatched his staff to find the keys, but they never returned. As the Voord closed in on his island fortress, Arbitan looked for other agents to send in search of the keys... and then, hope arrived in the form of the TARDIS and its travellers.

He asked the Doctor and his companions to travel across Marinus to recover the four missing keys, and when the Doctor refused, Arbitan placed a force field around the TARDIS. He would open the field only when he had all five keys in his hands. He gave the travellers teleportation devices called Travel Discs so they could cross the acid ocean.

Their first stop was the city of Morphoton. This city appeared to be a beautiful paradise, full of luxuries and wonders. Everything the travellers desired was there – but Barbara suddenly began to perceive the city differently. She saw it as a degraded ruin instead of a paradise. They discovered that the citizens of Morphoton were under the telepathic influence of giant brains in jars. Using telepathic relays attached to the foreheads of all citizens, they projected images of wealth and pleasure while in reality the citizens were slaves of the brains. One such slave was Sabetha, the daughter of Arbitan. She had found the second Key, but then fallen under the thrall of the brains. Unable to resist directly, she managed to sabotage Barbara's control relay.

Barbara managed to free Sabetha, and the two destroyed the brain cases, freeing the city's population along with the other three travellers. They also freed Sabetha's companion Altos, another of Arbitan's agents.

The group then split up. The Doctor went in search of one key in the City of Millenius, while the others braved the jungles and the ice caves in search of the other two.

The plants of the Screaming Jungle were both hostile and telepathic, but the five travellers fought their way through the defences and found their way into a ruined temple. The third key lay on a plinth, but a close examination revealed that this key was a fake, and taking it triggered a trap. The real key lay in a laboratory under the temple.

The fourth key was hidden in a cave in an icy wasteland, guarded by mechanical ice soldiers. On their way there, the travellers were tricked and imprisoned by a trapper named Vasor who tried to steal their travel discs, but he was killed by a rampaging Ice Soldier.

Finally, they travelled to the City of Millenius. Soon after arriving, Ian was arrested by the guards on suspicion of murdering Eprin. This victim was another of the seekers sent out by Arbitan. The Doctor appeared and acted as Ian's defender, and managed to solve the mystery of Eprin's death – he was murdered by Kala, the wife of one of the guards in a plot with Eyesen, the Court Prosecutor. The final Key was found among Eyesen's possessions.

With all of the keys in their possession the travellers now returned to Arbitan's island and tower. However, Yartek of the Voords had already infiltrated the tower and murdered Arbitan. Disguised as the old Keeper, he took the first four keys from Altos and Sabetha. When the Doctor arrived, he saw through Yartek's ruse and tricked him by giving him the false key from the Screaming Jungle instead of the fifth key. When Yartek tried to use the keys to seize control of the Conscience, the machine's security systems activated a self-destruct mode, and the resulting feedback killed Yartek and the Voords.

Arbitan's followers were shocked to see their machine destroyed, but the Doctor told them that they must find their own answers on Marinus now, instead of being ruled by machines.

RUNNING THIS ADVENTURE

The Keys of Marinus is a classic 'find the plot tokens' adventure – the characters go from one mini-adventure to another, picking up the items they need to complete their main quest. Arbitan's approach is a little heavy-handed, and a more generous, interfering Doctor than the crotchety first incarnation might have willingly gone looking for the missing keys.

THE CONSCIENCE OF MARINUS

The Conscience is a highly advanced telepathic computer system built more than two thousand years ago to enforce justice and harmony across Marinus. Originally, it was designed as a judge, but then upgraded to telepathically control the population. For seven hundred years, it functioned perfectly, but then became unreliable.

When functioning correctly, the Conscience is a 4-point Special Gadget with the traits Scan x2, Transmit, Telepathy x2 and a Restriction that it only affects the minds of the natives of Marinus. If active, the Conscience gives the Major Bad Trait Code of Conduct to all those affected by its telepathic field, guiding them to behave 'properly' and preventing them from committing crimes.

To protect the Conscience from tampering, it was placed in a tower on an island in the middle of an acidic sea. The controls for the Conscience could only be activated by someone in possession of all five key microcircuits. When the Voord learned to resist the Conscience's effects, the machine was deactivated and the control keys scattered. This precaution prevented the Voord from using the Conscience as a weapon, but unfortunately meant the end of the golden age on Marinus. Without the Conscience to eradicate injustice, other corrupt governments (such as the Morpho Brains) flourished.

ARBITAN'S TOWER

This pyramidal structure was built to house the Conscience. There was no obvious entrance – instead, the only way in was via secret doors. Inside, the Pyramid contained living quarters and life support on the lower levels, laboratories on the middle levels, and the great chamber of the Conscience at the summit.

TRAVEL DISCS (MINOR GADGET)

These wrist-watch-like devices can teleport the wearer to any of several pre-set destinations. The discs are not especially precise, and will deposit the traveller somewhere near the destination instead of on the exact spot. The discs are easy to use, and can be triggered just by pressing a button.

Trait: Teleport, Restriction (Limited Destinations).

ARBITAN

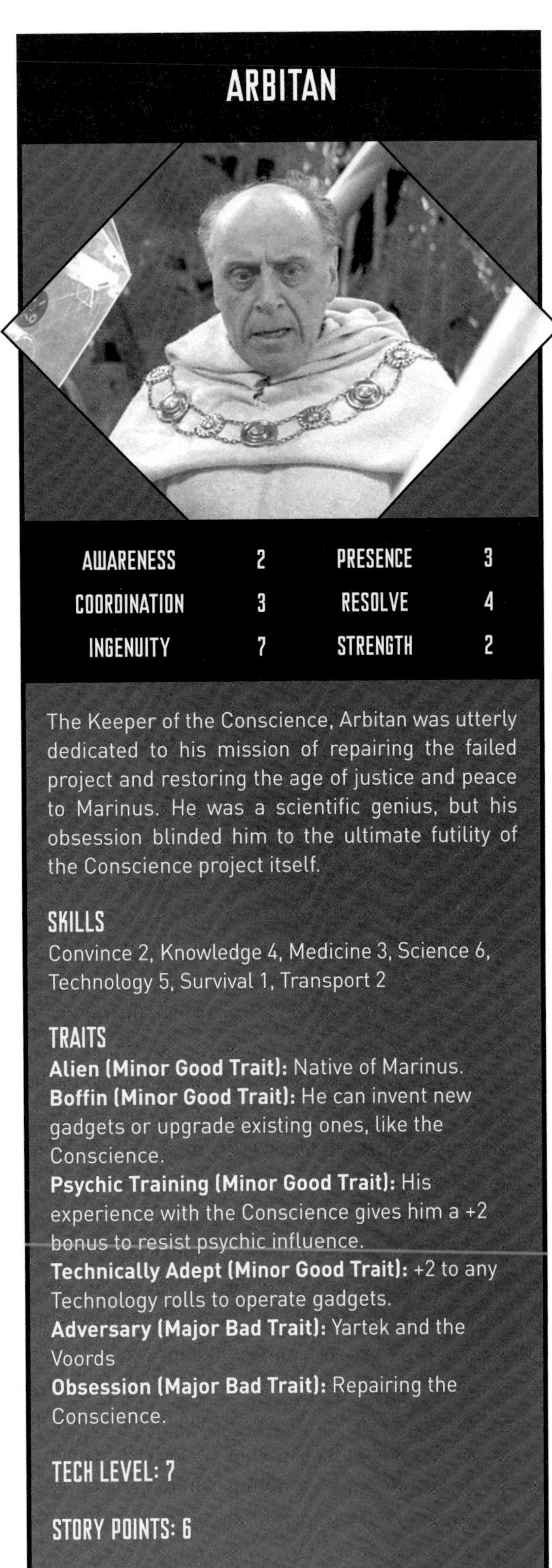

AWARENESS	2	PRESENCE	3
COORDINATION	3	RESOLVE	4
INGENUITY	7	STRENGTH	2

The Keeper of the Conscience, Arbitan was utterly dedicated to his mission of repairing the failed project and restoring the age of justice and peace to Marinus. He was a scientific genius, but his obsession blinded him to the ultimate futility of the Conscience project itself.

SKILLS

Convince 2, Knowledge 4, Medicine 3, Science 6, Technology 5, Survival 1, Transport 2

TRAITS

Alien (Minor Good Trait): Native of Marinus.
Boffin (Minor Good Trait): He can invent new gadgets or upgrade existing ones, like the Conscience.
Psychic Training (Minor Good Trait): His experience with the Conscience gives him a +2 bonus to resist psychic influence.
Technically Adept (Minor Good Trait): +2 to any Technology rolls to operate gadgets.
Adversary (Major Bad Trait): Yartek and the Voords
Obsession (Major Bad Trait): Repairing the Conscience.

TECH LEVEL: 7

STORY POINTS: 6

THE VOORD

The monstrous Voord are a mysterious army of conquerors. They may be native to Marinus, or they may be invaders from beyond. They may be a faction from the same humanoid species as Arbitan and the other inhabitants of Millenius and Morphoton, or they could be another faction entirely.

The Voord wear black armour and elaborate helmets with swept-back 'wings' and antennae. These helmets may be connected to their telepathic powers – not only could they resist the Conscience's impulses, but they can also communicate with one another to plot their attacks. They carry razor-sharp knives as their primary weapons, but clearly have the technology for more advanced and destructive weaponry.

The explosion of the Conscience killed Vartex and disrupted most of the Voord as psychic backlash exploded through their telepathic network, but it is possible that some Voord survived and now plot their revenge on Marinus.

AWARENESS	3	PRESENCE	2
COORDINATION	4	RESOLVE	3
INGENUITY	3	STRENGTH	4

SKILLS
Athletics 3, Fighting 3, Subterfuge 4, Survival 4

TRAITS
Alien

Alien Appearance (Major Bad): The Voord wore distinctive helmets (or maybe they have distinctive heads. Either way, they're pretty distinctive).

Alien Senses (Minor Good): Voord can sense the mental activity of other creatures and use it to hunt.

Enviromental: Acid

Networked (Minor Good): All Voord can communicate with one another.

Telepathic (Special Good): Voord can read minds.

WEAPONS: Voord knife (3/**6**/9 damage)

TECH LEVEL: 7

VOORD MINI-SUBMARINES

Arbitan's tower is protected by a sea of corrosive acid that eats away the hulls of any ship that tries to cross it. A few miles offshore, a howling ring of winds prevents flying machines from crossing to the island. The only way to reach the tower is via teleportation, and Marinus' teleportation technology is limited.

The island was believed to be impenetrable, until the Voord developed glass-hulled mini-submarines. These one-Voord submersibles were capable of resisting the acidic liquid and travelling from the mainland to Arbitan's island.

While the Voord are unlikely to use the same vehicles in other situations – a glass submarine is something of a specialist item – it does show that they are creative and willing to take risks to accomplish their goals.

YARTEK

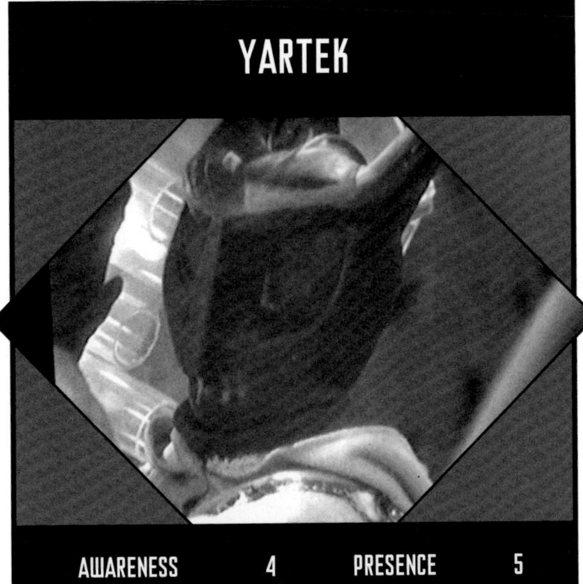

AWARENESS	4	PRESENCE	5
COORDINATION	3	RESOLVE	5
INGENUITY	4	STRENGTH	4

The villainous leader of the Voord, Yartek planned to seize control of the Conscience and use it to telepathically dominate all of Marinus. Indeed, if he had succeeded, he might also have put the Doctor and the other travellers under his spell and gained access to the TARDIS, spreading his evil to many other worlds.

SKILLS

Athletics 1, Convince 3, Fighting 4, Knowledge 5, Science 4, Technology 4, Survival 4

TRAITS

Alien
Alien Appearance (Major Bad): Yartek did not have the distinctive antennae of his followers.
Alien Senses (Minor Good): Voord can sense the mental activity of other creatures and use it to hunt.
Armour (Minor Good): 5 points of Armour against most attacks. Cutting attacks (knives, claws, swords) ignore Voord armour.
Networked (Minor Good): All Voord can communicate with one another.
Telepathic (Special Good): Voord can read minds.
Shapeshift (Minor Good): Yartek can use his telepathy to affect the perceptions of others. He used this power to disguise himself as Arbitan and steal the keys.

TECH LEVEL: 7

STORY POINTS: 5

THE CITY OF MORPHOTON

Morphoton is two cities in one. Its inhabitants believe they live in a beautiful palace, where their every wish is attended to and every desire is fulfilled. The luxurious chambers of Morphoton contain anything you can imagine. The Doctor asked for a laboratory, and behold, the next morning he found one equipped with every scientific device and instrument imaginable. Should another dream of a hoard of gold, or a theatre of marvels, or a garden of golden flowers, then Morpoton will provide.

That is because Morphoton is a lie. In reality, the city is a drab ruin. The ruling brains of Morphoton – the Morphos – broadcast a telepathic signal called the mesmerant. This signal convinces the population that they are living in luxury, enslaving their minds while the Morphos use their bodies as slaves. A citizen of Morphoton dreams that she lives the life of a queen, lounging on cushioned couches eating the finest foods fed to her by servants, while in reality her body toils in endless service to the brains.

SOMNAR DISCS (MINOR GADGET)

These coin-sized discs were used by the brains to solidify their control. Anyone wearing such a disc suffers a -4 penalty to all rolls to resist mesmerant waves. The brains can also use the discs to put victims to sleep.

MORPHO BRAINS

The secret rulers of Morphoton are the Morpho Brains. These creatures resemble overgrown human brains in glass jars. Without bodies, they are incapable of physical action, so they used the citizens of their city as slaves. The origin of the brains was never revealed, but they may have been created by the citizens as a replacement for the Conscience. Perhaps the people feared the disorder and chaos that erupted when the Conscience was deactivated, and created these hideous mutants to control their own base impulses.

AWARENESS	2	PRESENCE	4
COORDINATION	0	RESOLVE	5
INGENUITY	4	STRENGTH	0

SKILLS

Convince 2, Knowledge 5

TRAITS

Alien
Alien Appearance (Major Bad): It's a brain in a jar.
Dependency (Major Bad): Human slaves.
Psychic
Telepathic (Special Good): Powerfully telepathic.
Mesmerant Wave (Special): The brains can produce a special psychic wave called the Mesmerant to delude their victims. This wave affects everyone in the city. Victims of the wave have their perceptions altered by the brains.

The brains can produce one such wave every four hours. Generating extra waves is a strain (costing one Story Point per extra wave). Those struck by a wave must roll Presence + Resolve against the brain's Presence + Resolve; if the brain wins, it dictates the victim's perceptions for the next four hours. A character already under the brain's control suffers a -4 penalty to any rolls to resist mesmerant waves.

TECH LEVEL: 7

STORY POINTS: 2

THE SCREAMING JUNGLE

This region of Marinus is extremely dangerous. The plants of the jungle grow with terrifying speed. Their vines and branches snake out astonishingly quickly to enwrap and engulf unwary travellers. Those who travel in the jungle must make Strength + Survival rolls against Difficulty 15 and consult the table below.

RESULT	EFFECT
Fantastic Success (25+)	The character makes excellent time through the jungle and isn't slowed down at all. Furthermore, if the character is telepathic, he gains a +4 bonus to his next roll to resist the screams.
Great Success (19-24)	The character makes it through the jungle, but only slowly.
Normal Success (15-18)	Thorns and branches claw at the character, inflicting 3 points of damage, but he manages to make some progress through the forest.
Failure (12-14)	The character makes no progress in the jungle, but takes no damage from the thorns.
Bad Failure (7-11	The character gets lost in the jungle and takes 3 points of damage.
Disastrous Failure (6 or less)	The character gets lost in the jungle, takes 3 points of damage, and gets trapped by fast-growing vines. Unless someone rescues him, he'll get eaten by the plants.

The plants are also telepathic. This low-level telepathy is imperceptible to most people, but any vulnerable character (those with the Psychic trait) can hear the constant anguished screaming of the trees. This vegetable cacophony of thought distracts the character, giving them a -2 penalty to any rolls made within the Screaming Jungle.

VASOR THE TRAPPER

AWARENESS	4	PRESENCE	2
COORDINATION	3	RESOLVE	3
INGENUITY	2	STRENGTH	4

The frozen ice caps of Marinus are home to many fearsome creatures, like huge snow-wolves and ice soldiers, but treachery can be more dangerous than claws or spears. Vasor the Trapper lived alone in a small cabin, hunting wolves and other furry animals. In the autumn, he would trek south to a trading town to sell his furs and buy supplies. Robbing the dead and waylaying travellers were bright spots in this otherwise hardscrabble existence.

Vasor's usual tactic was to pretend to 'rescue' parties of stranded travellers, then split them up. Tough-looking individuals would be sent to fetch firewood or on some other errand that put them in the path of the wolves; weaker victims were brought back to his cabin.

SKILLS
Athletics 3, Convince 2, Fighting 3, Marksman 2, Knowledge 1, Medicine 1, Subterfuge 2, Survival 4, Transport 2

TRAITS
Tough (Minor Good Trait): Reduces damage by 2.
Dark Secret (Major Bad Trait): Murderer.
Outcast (Minor Bad Trait): Lives along on an icecap.

TECH LEVEL: 5

STORY POINTS: 3

ICE SOLDIERS

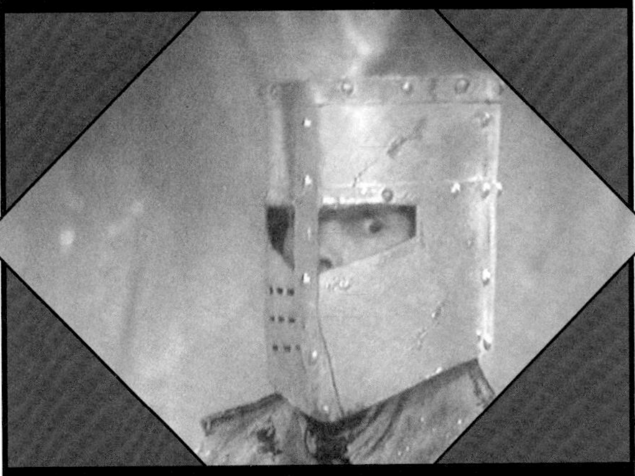

AWARENESS	2	PRESENCE	1
COORDINATION	2	RESOLVE	5
INGENUITY	1	STRENGTH	7

These strange creatures resemble medieval knights in armour, coated in a rime of frost. Four of them guard the fourth Key. If they are not mechanical robots beneath their mail, then they must be some sort of genetically engineered artificial creatures, as they slept beneath the ice for years until disturbed by the travellers.

Ice Soldiers are fairly slow and cumbersome, but relentless. They tracked the travellers across the frozen wastes to Vasor's cabin to recover the key, and killed the trapper in the ensuing struggle.

SKILLS
Athletics 2, Fighting 3, Survival 2

TRAITS
Alien
Armour (Minor Good): 5 points of Armour against attacks.
Clumsy (Minor Bad): They're not very agile at all.

WEAPONS: Big Sword (6/**11**/17 damage)

THE CITY OF MILLENIUS

Millenius is the largest city on Marinus, and is notable for its harsh justice system where the accused are considered guilty until proved innocent. (Perhaps this policy was created in response to the loss of the Conscience, as the authorities tried to contain a population suddenly freed from the enforced ethics of the machine.) Unfortunately, many of the judges and prosecutors are corrupt and venal. Eyesen, for example, tried to steal one of the Keys.

Assuming one does not break the law (or, in Ian Chesterton's case, get framed for a crime), then Millenius is one of the more pleasant places to live on Marinus. Sabethan and Altos returned after the destruction of the Conscience with the aim of settling there and reforming its government.

FURTHER ADVENTURES

- **Return of the Voord:** Yartek and the Voord were defeated by the destruction of the Conscience, but there could be more Voord out there. Yartek planned to reprogram the Conscience to mind-control the whole planet, so future Voord schemes would probably involve clandestine schemes and commando raids instead of all-out attacks. For example, a Voord attack on present-day Earth could have Voord warriors sneaking in to take out UNIT space-radar installations, followed by an attempt to broadcast subliminal mind-control waves through the internet. The Voord might also use some of the other dangerous entities from Marinus as pawns. For example, they could deploy Ice Soldiers as shock troops, or keep Morpho Brains in jars as living weapons.

- **Fall of the Conscience:** The period just after the first Voord attacks on Arbitan's island is a very interesting one. Imagine if the companions visited the peaceful, egalitarian planet of Marinus around then. They arrive on a world where crime and injustice are literally unthinkable... and then, overnight, all the evil and nastiness suddenly floods out when the Conscience fails.

- **Wild Travel:** Travel discs are a handy alternative to TARDIS travel... for the Gamesmaster, that is! Give a character a travel disc pre-programmed with a dozen perilous locations, and you can whisk them from erupting volcano to murder mystery to alien fungus pit to monster lair at the touch of a button.

THE AZTECS

"If I could start the destruction of everything that's evil here, then everything that is good would survive when Cortes lands."

SYNOPSIS

The TARDIS landed inside an Aztec tomb. Barbara took an arm bracelet from the corpse buried there, which meant she was mistaken for a goddess when they left the tomb. She played along, claiming to be the incarnation of the goddess Yetaxa. The other three travellers were deemed to be her servants. Ian was assigned to the temple guard, Susan was her handmaiden, and the Doctor was seen as one of her priests. Barbara's divinity was confirmed by the two high priests of Yetaxa. One, Autloc, was the High Priest of Knowledge and appeared to be a gentle soul. The other, Tlotoxl, was High Priest of Sacrifice and embodied everything that the travellers found ghastly about the Aztec civilisation. Barbara argued that the Aztecs had many admirable qualities beyond human sacrifice, and lamented the fact that Cortes's invasion would wipe away the good along with the bad and erase an ancient civilisation from history.

The Doctor had more pressing concerns – the door in the tomb only opened out. Unless the companions could find another way into the tomb, they could not return to the TARDIS. He visited the Garden of Peace where the wise elders of the Aztecs dwelled, and there he met a charming woman named Cameca. From her, he learned that the designer of the temple had passed away, but his son was now a guard in the retinue of the temple. Meanwhile, Ian was introduced to the warrior Ixta, another guard. Ixta was a mighty warrior, proud of his martial skills and his exalted rank within the temple – a rank he was unhappy to share with this stranger. Chief among his duties was escorting the prisoners to the sacrificial altar.

Ian was appalled at the prospect of abetting murder, and appealed to the Doctor. The Doctor warned him that their position was precarious as long as they were cut off from the TARDIS, and advised Ian to go along with the horrible deed. Barbara, however, was unwilling to tolerate murder in her name. She decided, over the Doctor's objections, to try to change history. If she could stop the Aztec practice of human sacrifice, she would remove Cortes's justification for destroying their civilisation and thus preserve Aztec culture into the future. At the sacrificial altar, Barbara commanded Tlotoxl not to sacrifice the anointed victim. The victim protested, and at Tlotoxl's suggestion, threw himself over the parapet. At the same time, Susan cried out, breaking the taboo about speaking on sacred ground. Tlotoxl demanded that she be punished, but Barbara managed to convince Autloc to take Susan to the priest's seminary instead.

Barbara's ban on sacrifice set Tlotoxl against her, and the High Priest of Sacrifice now doubted her divinity. He began to question and undermine her, forcing her to rely on Autloc's uncertain support. He pitted Ixta against Ian; Ian was able to use his martial arts training to defeat Ixta in their first bout, but Ixta demanded a rematch, and promised that next time he would be ready for Ian's tricks.

Meanwhile, in the seminary, Susan astounded Autloc and his aide Tonila with her understanding of the scriptures.

Cameca introduced the Doctor to the son of the temple builder – who turned out to be Ixta. The Doctor bargained for Ixta's knowledge of the temple. In exchange for the Doctor showing Ixta a poisonous thorn that would paralyse his foe, Ixta promised to give the Doctor his father's secret drawings of the temple. The Doctor had no idea that Ixta intended to use the thorn on Ian, or that Ixta was lying – there were no such drawings. The secrets of the temple died with its builder.

At the duel, the Doctor tried to warn Ian, but it was in vain – Ixta scratched Ian with the thorn, paralysing him. Tlotoxl told Ixta to kill Ian, and when Barbara objected, Tlotoxl told her to use her divine powers to save her servant – if she truly had such powers, doing so would be easy for her. Instead, she darted across to the High Priest's side and held a knife to his throat. If Ian died, so would Tlotoxl.

Thwarted, Tlotoxl recruited Tonila to his cause, and planned another test for Barbara. This time, he would poison her. A goddess would be unaffected by the poisoned drink, but a treacherous mortal would die. Ian warned Barbara of this scheme, but Tlotoxl's suspicions were confirmed, and he was now sure that Barbara was not the divinity Yetaxa that she claimed to be. Other intrigues engulfed the travellers. Susan was chosen as bride by the Perfect Victim, a madman destined to be willingly sacrificed at the upcoming eclipse. In the days before his death, his requests could not be refused, no matter how outrageous they were, and he chose to marry Yetaxa's handmaiden.

The Doctor continued to speak with the wise elder Cameca. He learned that her former lover was the builder of the temple, and that he brought her an amulet from the tomb before disappearing, suggesting that there was another way into the tomb. The Doctor also accidentally became engaged to Cameca – a not entirely unpleasant state of affairs, but a somewhat larger consequence to drinking a cup of cocoa than he expected.

The intrigues came to a head at the eclipse. The Doctor and Ian uncovered a secret passage that led to the tomb of Yetaxa and the TARDIS. When they returned to fetch Barbara and Susan, Tlotoxl had Ixta attack Autloc and frame Ian for the deed. Ian was arrested. Barbara asked Autloc to intercede, but his faith in her was broken, and he resolved to leave the city.

With both Susan and Ian in custody, and Barbara's influence crumbling thanks to Tlotoxl's machinations, all seemed lost. Fortunately, Cameca was able to distract the guards and free Ian and Susan, and they were able to disrupt the ceremony in time for the Doctor to open the door to the tomb. The four fled into the TARDIS, while outside Tlotoxl plunged his sacrificial dagger into the Perfect Victim, ending the eclipse and confirming the power of the gods.

RUNNING THIS ADVENTURE

The Aztecs is a fascinating adventure. It's structurally beautiful, with a cast of intriguing characters and strong conflicts, and it does it all without needing science-fiction plot devices. It's a wonderful model for a historical adventure.

BALANCE OF POWER

Like *The Tribe of Gum, The Aztecs* puts the power and the decision-making authority on the player characters. Barbara is accidentally thrust into the position of goddess by sheer chance – she happened to pick up the bracelet before wandering out of the tomb. Once she has that power, though, she starts using it. Unlike the *Tribe of Gum*, where the travellers just wanted to escape, here Barbara has a goal in mind. She wants to stop human sacrifice, despite the Doctor's objection that time cannot be rewritten here.

Now look at the supporting cast. There are the two High Priests, one venerating Knowledge and the other embodying Sacrifice. This gives Barbara a clear way to accomplish her goal – all she needs to do is make sure that Autloc ends up in control and not Tloxotl. By making her abstract goal of 'stop human sacrifice' into something concrete, the Gamemaster ensures that all the players have something to focus on.

Next, when the characters split up, each player character is given a chance to use their particular talents to shine, and is paired with a complementary non-player character or two. Barbara gets to use her diplomacy skills and her knowledge of history as she contends with the High Priests. Ian gets to be a two-fisted man of action, and is matched with Ixta. The Doctor continues to be manipulative, high-handed and a little bit sinister, with his insistence that human sacrifice cannot be stopped. He's paired with Cameca, a woman who matches his wisdom but has the gentleness to humanise him a little. Even Susan, despite being a little side-lined, gets to reprise her *Unearthly Child* role as the supernaturally intelligent student, picking up on Aztec lore through telepathy. The travellers split up and uncover bits of the plot, then meet up again and share information in a safe place.

The adventure is also wonderfully economic with its use of non-player characters. Ixta, for example, is not just the temple guard – he's *also* the son of the builder and therefore may be in possession of the secret of the hidden door. Tonila is introduced as a throw-away minor character, Susan's tutor in the temple, but becomes more important when Txototl recruits him. Keeping the number of NPCs small makes the plot richer – if the Gamemaster had divided the roles of temple guard and son of the builder between two characters, then the dramatic sequence where the Doctor ends up sabotaging Ian's duel would never happen.

CHANGING HISTORY

If you've got *Feel The Turn Of The Universe*, you can tell if a particular section of time is fluid or fixed. Mere humans, though, sometimes struggle against the inevitability of fate. In another place, another time, then maybe Barbara's heroic attempt to reform Aztec civilisation might have worked. Here, it can lead only to tragedy.

Pure historical adventures work best with unchanging history. (Well, if you bring aliens in, then it's probably an alternate and therefore fluid history by default, unless it's a very subtle alien invasion). The Doctor exaggerated slightly when he said that *"you can't rewrite history! Not one line!"* – the presence of the travellers did change history, just not very much. If Barbara had never been there, then Autloc would still be a faithful High Priest, instead of a disillusioned wanderer.

In games where history cannot be changed, make sure the players have a second challenge that can be overcome. Barbara cannot change history, but the question of whether or not the travellers will escape back to the TARDIS is more uncertain. If the characters could just walk away, then the whole adventure would be hollow – the struggle to enter the tomb gives the characters something they can achieve, beyond Barbara's quixotic scheme.

THE TEMPLE & ENVIRONS

The Temple of Yetaxa is a huge step pyramid in the heart of the vast Aztec city. The tomb of Yetaxa lay deep within the pyramid, and was accessible only via a one-way stone door. The door could easily be opened from inside, but opening it from the outside was almost impossible (Strength + Resolve, Difficulty 40 – the Doctor and Ian set up a pulley, which brought the Difficulty down to a mere 18). The Aztecs believed in the possibility that Yetaxa would reincarnate, so they left an exit within the tomb for the reborn god.

The upper levels of the temple contain the chambers of Yetaxa, ceremonial chambers for the priests, and a balcony overlooking the whole city. Here is found the sacrificial stone, stained red with the blood of thousands of victims. The High Priest of Sacrifices cuts out the victim's heart, which is said to contain a fragment of the sun.

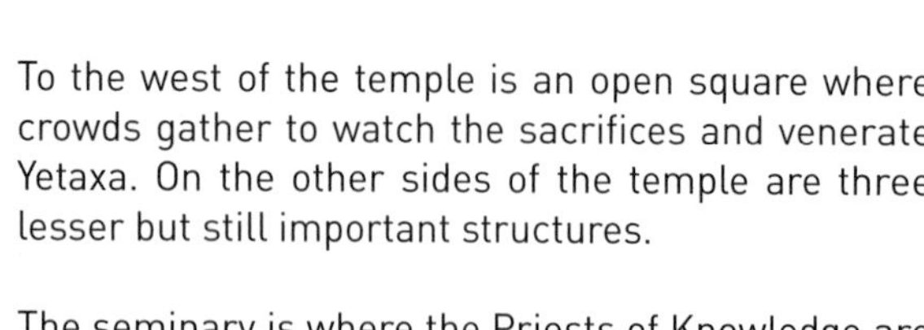

To the west of the temple is an open square where crowds gather to watch the sacrifices and venerate Yetaxa. On the other sides of the temple are three lesser but still important structures.

The seminary is where the Priests of Knowledge are taught and trained. This building also contains the city's records and scrolls. The Priests of Knowledge know a great deal about certain topics, notably herbalism, astrology and the prediction of weather patterns.

On the opposite side to the seminary is the barracks. Here is where the temple guards live and train. These guards serve as bodyguards for the priests, and also assist with the rituals. Prisoners are kept in the dungeons beneath this structure.

Note that the sacrificial victims are not always prisoners – to the Aztecs, being sacrificed can be an honour and a great blessing, so some people volunteer to give their lives to the gods. This is especially true for the sacrifices at eclipses and at the end of each 52-year cycle.

The Aztecs believe that the universe risks collapse every 52 years, and that if the gods lack the strength to reignite the sun, all will be plunged into eternal darkness.

Finally, the Garden of Peace adjoins the temple. This tranquil area is for those who have reached the venerable age of 52. They rest and walk in these gardens, and pass on their wisdom to the young. In the centre of the gardens is a stone that, when moved aside, leads to a dark, water-logged tunnel that runs under the temple. This passageway provides access to the sealed tomb of Yetaxa.

AUTLOC

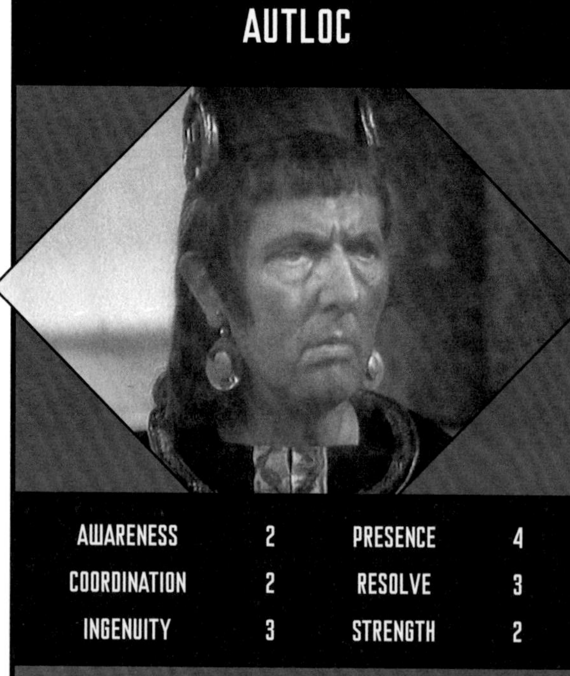

AWARENESS	2	PRESENCE	4
COORDINATION	2	RESOLVE	3
INGENUITY	3	STRENGTH	2

The High Priest of Knowledge was sympathetic to Barbara's plan to end human sacrifice – if the gods commanded that the old ways be abandoned, then as far as he was concerned there must be a good reason for it. In time, though, he came to see that the gods were as blind and foolish as mortals. He lost his faith in Yetaxa, and abandoned his post to leave the city in search of wisdom in the wilderness.

As High Priest, Autloc was a man of wealth and status; he entrusted his wealth to Cameca to bribe the guards holding Ian.

SKILLS

Convince 2, Knowledge 4, Medicine 2, Science 1, Survival 2

TRAITS

Voice of Authority (Minor Good): He's the High Priest of Knowledge.
Code of Conduct (Minor Bad): Loyal servant of Yetaxa.

TECH LEVEL: 1

STORY POINTS: 1

TLOTOXL

AWARENESS	3	PRESENCE	5
COORDINATION	3	RESOLVE	4
INGENUITY	3	STRENGTH	3

Tlotoxl was the High Priest of Sacrifice. Though ugly and lame, he has an undeniable charisma, a magnetic force of personality.

SKILLS

Convince 4, Fighting 2, Knowledge 3, Medicine 3, Survival 1, Transport 1

TRAITS

Hypnosis (Minor Good): +2 bonus to Convince rolls when commanding people.
Argumentative (Minor Bad): He believes he's always right.
Distinctive (Minor Bad): There's no mistaking Tlotoxl.

TECH LEVEL: 1

STORY POINTS: 3

CAMECA

AWARENESS	3	PRESENCE	3
COORDINATION	2	RESOLVE	4
INGENUITY	4	STRENGTH	1

Wise Cameca was one of the most respected elders in the Garden of Peace, and even managed to charm the Doctor. In another universe, she might have joined him on the TARDIS as a special companion.

SKILLS

Convince 2, Knowledge 4, Medicine 1

TRAITS

Charming (Minor Good): +2 to Convince rolls to win someone's trust
Slow Reflexes (Minor Bad): Always goes last in a phase.

TECH LEVEL: 1

STORY POINTS: 3

IAN CHESTERTON, MARTIAL ARTIST

In his first fight with Ixta, Ian demonstrates a surprising mastery of martial arts. In game mechanics, martial arts attacks can be easily modelled using the detailed resolution rules and called shots. Instead of trying to inflict damage, Ian might try to knock over, incapacitate or distract a foe. A Yes, But result might be "Ian flips Ixta, but his foe does not drop his weapon", a Yes, And result might knock Ixta over and deal damage equal to Ian's Strength.

Joint locks and pressure point attacks can be called shots. By taking a -2 penalty to his attack, Ian does damage to Ixta's Coordination or Resolve instead of splitting the damage between Ixta's other Attributes.

IXTA

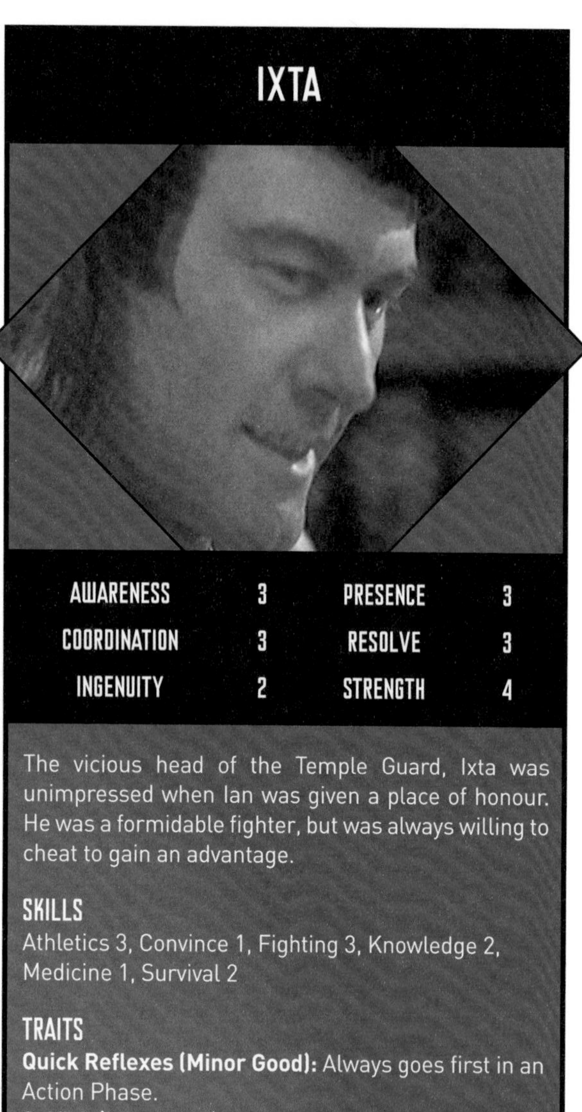

AWARENESS	3	PRESENCE	3
COORDINATION	3	RESOLVE	3
INGENUITY	2	STRENGTH	4

The vicious head of the Temple Guard, Ixta was unimpressed when Ian was given a place of honour. He was a formidable fighter, but was always willing to cheat to gain an advantage.

SKILLS

Athletics 3, Convince 1, Fighting 3, Knowledge 2, Medicine 1, Survival 2

TRAITS

Quick Reflexes (Minor Good): Always goes first in an Action Phase.
Selfish (Minor Bad): Looks out for himself.
Obligation (Minor Bad): Servant of the Temple.

TECH LEVEL: 1

STORY POINTS: 3

AZTEC WEAPONS

The Aztecs did not know iron-working, so most of their weapons were made from wood, stone or copper. Ixta, for example, carried a heavy stone club (Strength +2 damage), while Tlotoxl had a sharpened stone knife to cut out his enemy's heart (again, Strength +2 damage).

The thorn given to Ixta by the Doctor secreted a paralytic poison. A character struck by such a thorn loses 1 point of Coordination per Action Round until the wounded is treated with Medicine or the character hits 0 Coordination and cannot move. The poison wears off after half an hour or so.

FURTHER ADVENTURES

- **The Doctor Lies:** That's rule #1, even back in his first incarnation. What if he lied to Barbara? What if time could be changed, and the only reason he lied was to hasten the travellers' departure? Maybe Barbara could have changed history, and preserved the Aztec empire! The characters arrive in a parallel 21st Century Earth where all of Central and North America is ruled by the Aztec Empire. Human sacrifice stopped five hundred years ago – but now a cult of serial killers plot to bring it back!

- **The Failing Gods:** According to Aztec belief, the universe risked collapse every 52 years. That sounds like a cyclic temporal pocket being propped up by channelled bio-psychic energy to me. The Aztec sacrifices power some alien device that keeps reality intact. Who built it... and who's sabotaging it? Maybe the elders in the Garden of Peace – survivors of the previous cycle – know more than they're saying...

- **Clash of Cultures:** Barbara guessed that they arrived in the 15th century, but she could have been wrong. Maybe it was closer to 1520 – and the Spanish are coming. The characters could return to the temple just in time to get entwined in the clash of civilisations!

CHAPTER FOUR:
THE SENSORITES, THE REIGN OF TERROR, PLANET OF GIANTS

THE SENSORITES

"It's suspicion that's making them enemies. You don't understand the Sensorites."

"Do you think I don't understand? Trust is a two-sided affair."

SYNOPSIS

The TARDIS arrived on the bridge of an Earth starship that was trapped in orbit around a mysterious planet called the Sense-sphere. The crew – a pair of astronauts named Richmond and Maitland – appeared dead, but were soon discovered to be in artificial comas. They explained that the alien inhabitants of the world below, the Sensorites, kept them from leaving. The Sensorites possessed powerful telepathic powers, and could induce comas, drive their victims insane or even control their actions. The ship's mineralogist, John, had already fallen victim to their psychic influence.

The Doctor stabilised the ship's orbit, and Susan was able to block the alien's influence over John. They discovered that the planet below was rich in minerals, especially molybdenum, a vital component in Earth engineering.

Sensorites on board the Earth ship disabled the TARDIS by cutting away the external lock, while a Sensorite ship launched from the planet surface to collect the human prisoners. The Sensorites had decided to move the explorers, as well as the Doctor and his companions, to a reservation on the planet to live out the rest of their lives.

From his observations of the Sensorites, the Doctor determined that their eyes were adapted to bright conditions, and that they were therefore vulnerable to darkness. When the aliens arrived to take the crew into custody, he switched off the lights, disorientating them. He parleyed his advantage into a meeting with the Sensorite leaders.

Sensorite society was divided into several castes. The Elders ruled and governed, the Warriors fought, and the common folk, the Sensorites, played and worked. At the head of the Elder caste were the First and Second Elder, although the City Administrator was nearly as important. It was this City Administrator who objected to the presence of humans in the city, and even plotted to use the Sensorite's ultimate weapon, the Disintegrator on them. However, the Elders confiscated the firing key before he could incinerate their guests.

The Elders explained that the Sensorites suffered from a mysterious plague that started several years ago when humans first visited their world. Those initial visitors died when their ship exploded, but the Elders sensed that the explorers in the orbiting ship had learned of the planet's mineral wealth, and would bring more intruders and more disease with them.

During the meeting, Ian fell ill, and the Doctor realised that the 'plague' was actually poison in the water supply. He convinced the Sensorites that he could find a cure, and was given a laboratory. He quickly developed a treatment that could temporarily cure the symptoms, but he knew that the only way to permanently solve the problem was to find the source of the poison. He visited the tunnel entrance, but was attacked by something in the darkness and barely escaped with his life.

Meanwhile, the City Administrator attempted to seize power. All Sensorites looked extremely alike, so he was able to masquerade as the Second Elder by attacking him and stealing his sash. He tried to frame the Doctor for the attack and steal a disintegrator key, but that plan failed. He did convince the First Elder to promote him to Second Elder.

The Doctor and Ian set off into the tunnels, armed with Sensorite weapons and map. However, both had been sabotaged by agents of the City Administrator, and were useless. In the tunnels, they wandered lost until they discovered a group of humans. These explorers had landed on the Sense-sphere several years previously. Exposure to the Sensorite's telepathic signals had driven them insane, and they now believed they were at war with the native inhabitants.

Fortunately, Susan and Barbara had discovered the City Administrator's treachery, and led an expedition of Sensorite warriors into the tunnels. Using her telepathic powers, Susan was able to find the Doctor and ambush the insane humans. The madmen were returned to the spaceship in orbit, and Maitland and Richmond were permitted to return home. The villainous City Administrator was exiled, and the First Elder returned the missing TARDIS lock to the Doctor.

RUNNING THIS ADVENTURE

The Sensorites shows how to present an intriguing alien race in different ways. At the start of the adventure, the Sensorites seem sinister and invincible. Their motives are unclear – why keep the humans trapped, instead of destroying them – but their power is undeniable. Not only do they demonstrate their mind-control ability, they also violate the TARDIS, trapping the travellers. They are depicted as all-powerful masterminds.

Then the Doctor undercuts their superiority by showing that they are scared of the dark, and Susan shows that their mind control can be beaten. Suddenly, the Sensorites turn from a threat into equals that can be negotiated with. Their society is presented as a harmonious commune where everyone has their place and everyone is happy, and that they were dangerous only because they were threatened.

The introduction of the City Administrator shows this to be a lie. The Sensorites might claim to be united and harmonious, but some of them are so xenophobic that they are willing to betray their leaders and plot bloody murder.

Finally, there is the concept of the Sensorites as victims. Human greed and madness is the root of the evil on the Sense-sphere. The Sensorites did not start this war, and tried desperately to spare the humans instead of killing them.

TELEPATHY

Both Susan and the Sensorites make extensive use of telepathy in this adventure, and we get to see some of the more interesting – and dangerous – things telepathy can do. It's not just reading thoughts and winning at poker!

Telepathic Conditions: Some worlds have "an extraordinary number of ultra-high frequencies" that make telepathy easier. On such planets, characters who are Psychic find their powers are temporarily enhanced. If you've got Psychic Training, you're now Psychic. If you're already Psychic, you're now Telepathic. If you're already Telepathic, then you get another trait like Clairvoyance or Telekinesis. If you've already got all those traits, then...well, you really don't need any more powers, but it's still a nice place to be.

Furthermore, any skill tests to use psychic powers get a +2 bonus.

Resisting Telepathy and Telepathic Blocks: So, you don't want someone poking around in your private thoughts? You can try resisting. Roll your Ingenuity + Resolve (plus Psychic Training if you have it). Anyone trying to use Telepathy has to beat the total of your roll.

Those with the Telepathy trait themselves can do more, and can set up Telepathic Blocks by spending an extra Story Point when they roll. Telepathic Blocks protect anyone nearby – telepathy works on line of sight to some degree, so if someone erects a Telepathic Block between the telepath and their target, it will protect the target. Blocks last for several minutes or even longer, depending on the relative strengths of the telepaths and local conditions.

Assisting Telepathy: It's possible to assist with a telepathy roll even if you're not Psychic. This uses the *You Can Do It* option for Story Points – hold hands, close your eyes, concentrate really hard on helping your Psychic pal – and give them one of your Story Points.

Telepathic Attacks: Characters with Telepathy only need to roll the dice if someone's trying to block or disrupt their telepathy, or in stressful situations, or if they're trying to inflict telepathic damage. Telepaths can use their target's Bad Traits against them – if they know what they are! If the target has a Bad Trait like a Phobia, or is already terrified, or is Obsessed with something, then the telepath can 'ride' on that trait. If you're scared of, say, Jammy Dodgers, and the telepath attacks your brain with a psychic image of a Jammy Dodger, then it's easier to get inside your brain. The telepath gets a +2 bonus (for a Minor Bad Trait) or a +4 bonus (for a Major Bad Trait).

Telepathic Damage: Telepaths can do more than just read minds – they can plant bad thoughts and beliefs, or just zap your mind. To inflict telepathic damage, the telepath must beat the Difficulty by at least 4. If he succeeds at this, he may either inflict damage equal to half his Resolve (this damage ignores Armour, but not the Tough trait), or give the victim a temporary Minor Bad Trait (something like Phobia, Obsession, Amnesia or Eccentric fits the bill). If the attack beats the difficulty by 8 or more, then that's full-Resolve damage or a temporary Major Bad Trait.

Side Effects of Telepathy: Even if you're not telepathic, exposure to too much telepathy can be dangerous. Imagine living in an apartment with really thin walls, where you can hear everything your neighbours say and do. Now, imagine that all those neighbours are actually dentists, and they never stop practising with their drills. All drilling, all the time – no wonder the human explorers went insane...

THE EXPLORERS

The human explorers came from 28th century Earth, and briefly described conditions back home. London was now called 'Central City' and occupied half the country. They did not have time travel technology themselves, but were comfortable with the concept of time travel and recognised the Doctor's companions as coming from the distant past.

Both ships were prospectors. The Sense-sphere was rich in molybdenum, a mineral used in the making of steel, which was vitally needed for the hungry Earth economy.

HEART RESUSCITATOR (MINOR GADGET)

All Earth astronauts carried these useful gadgets. The Heart Resuscitator uses ultrasonics to massage and stimulate cardiac tissue, repairing damage and improving blood flow. In game terms, it can be used to restore lost Strength with a successful Ingenuity + Medicine roll. The Difficulty for this roll is usually a 9, and using the machine results in the recovery of 1/2/3 points of Strength.

Traits: Heal, Restriction (Limited Use)
Cost: 1 Story Point

THE SENSORITES

The Sensorites are a race of thin-limbed humanoids with large eyes and whitish upturned whiskers. They are physically almost identical to one another, with no discernable difference between genders (or maybe they don't have gender – no-one's looked beneath those jumpsuits). They live on a planet called the Sense-sphere, which is in the same solar system as the Ood-sphere. In fact, the Sensorites are very similar to the Ood; both races look alike (maybe there are tentacles beneath those Sensorite beards), have psychic gifts, use handheld devices to communicate, and have a strict social structure. They're probably cousins.

Sensorite society is divided into castes. Being a member of a higher caste is not necessarily an honour – castes are assigned based on thought patterns and emotional suitability. You get assigned to the Elder caste of leaders because you like ordering people around and dealing with problems, so you'll be happy and well suited for that role.

At the top, there are the Elders, led by the First Elder and Second Elder. The Elder caste also includes local leaders, like the City Administrator. As all Sensorites look alike, rank is denoted by badges and sashes.

Next are the Scientists, who develop the Sensorites' technology, and the Warriors, who protect the city from wild beasts and other dangers. The bottom caste are referred to as the Sensorites; they have no special responsibilities in their society.

All Sensorites are mildly telepathic. They carry devices called mind transmitters to improve their ability to communicate over long distances.

AWARENESS	2	PRESENCE	2
COORDINATION	2	RESOLVE	3
INGENUITY	4	STRENGTH	2

SKILLS

Sensorite skills depend on their caste.

Sensorite: Convince 1, Craft 2, Knowledge 1, Transport 1
Scientist: Convince 1, Craft 1, Knowledge 2, Science 3, Technology 3, Transport 1
Warrior: Fighting 1, Marksman 2, Subterfuge 2, Technology 2, Transport 2
Elder: Convince 3, Knowledge 4, Subterfuge 4

TRAITS

Alien, Alien Appearance
Face in the Crowd (Minor Good): All Sensorites look alike.
Impaired Senses (Minor, Vision)
Psychic (Special Good): Sensorites can detect psychic emissions...
Telepathic (Special Good): ... and read minds.
Weakness (Major Bad): Sensorites are incapacitated by loud noises or darkness.

TECH LEVEL: 6

SENSORITE TECHNOLOGY

Mind Transmitter (Minor Gadget)
Traits: Transmit
Cost: 1 Story Point

All Sensorites carry mind transmitters. When pressed to the forehead, it increases the range of their telepathic powers, increasing the user's Resolve by 3 for the purposes of calculating telepathic range.

Paralyser Beam (Minor Gadget)
Traits: Paralyse
Cost: 1 Story Point

The standard weapon carried by Sensorite warriors, this weapon shoots a beam that freezes those it hits. The weapon is fired using the Marksman skill, and inflicts damage to Coordination at a rate of 1/2/ Paralysed. The paralysis wears off after only a few minutes.

Cutting Beam (Major Gadget)
Traits: Weld, Blast
Cost: 2 Story Points

This gadget was designed as a cutting torch, but can also be used to fry enemies. Sensorite cutting beams are powerful enough to damage the exterior hull of the TARDIS. If used as a weapon, it uses Marksman and inflicts 4/L/L damage.

Disintegrator (Special Gadget)
Traits: Delete, Scan
Cost: 3 Story Points

The disintegrator is the ultimate weapon of the Sensorites. Like the cutting beam, it was probably originally created for peaceful purposes like excavating the aqueducts under the city. It requires time to calibrate, as the user must give the machine a precise set of co-ordinates. When the disintegrator activates, it deletes any matter at those co-ordinates.

It's very exact – the City Administrator plotted to disintegrate the hearts of the intruders to the city – but of limited use as a weapon as you have to know exactly where your foes will be (you know, it's a lot easier to do that if you invite your foes to dinner with assigned seating, or if you can mind-control them into being where you want them to be.) If you line everything up properly, though, then poof! They're dust. As a safety precaution, the Disintegrator can only be used when a firing key is installed. Firing keys are kept by the Elders and the Senior Warrior.

CITY OF THE SENSORITES

The Sensorite city is a pleasant if sterile environment of curved metal walls and brightly lit corridors. Yellow mountains surround it on three sides. The Sensorites appear not to have explored all of their world, suggesting they are relatively recent arrivals on the Sense-sphere – perhaps they came originally as colonists from the Ood-sphere?

FURTHER ADVENTURES

- **Return to the Sense-Sphere:** The humans returned home – but there's a lot of valuable minerals on the Sense-sphere, so they're bound to return. We know that the Ood of the nearby Ood-sphere end up serving as willing slaves to humanity, and slaves make great miners. The characters might return to the Sense-sphere and find themselves embroiled in a conflict between human miners and the Sensorites. Who is using telepathy to sow turmoil between the two sides? What's really down in those tunnels?

- **Tyrant of the Ood:** Ood and Sensorite culture is very similar, except the Sensorites obey the Elder caste and the Ood obey... well, anyone who tells them what to do. How did this happen? Did some Ood messiah arise to lead his followers to the promised Sense-sphere? Did some alien enslave a faction of Ood to create the Sensorites? What about the Ood brain? There's a missing chapter in history here for the characters to explore.

- **Revenge of the City Administrator:** The Sensorites exiled the xenophobic, vengeful Administrator. As far as they know, he went into the mountains to perish – but the human ship was still on the planet at that point. What if he stowed away on board? What would a telepathic monster with a thirst for vengeance do in Central City?

THE REIGN OF TERROR

"I didn't say half the things I wanted to say. He twisted my words."

"Politicians usually do."

SYNOPSIS

After squabbling with Ian as they left the Sense-sphere, the Doctor angrily declared that he was going to send Barbara and Ian home, and set co-ordinates to bring the ship back to the junkyard at Totter's Lane in 1963. The TARDIS materialised in a field, although the Doctor insisted he was only a few miles off course. The travellers investigated, and found he was several *hundred* miles off course – they had landed in the middle of France.

Exploring, they found an isolated and seemingly abandoned farmhouse, and discovered they had landed in 1794. They were right in the middle of the French revolution. The farmhouse was used by a pair of conspirators named D'Argenson and Rouvray; they knocked the Doctor unconscious and threatened the other three at gunpoint, believing them to be agents of the revolutionaries. The pair intended to escape from France and the Terror. The standoff was broken by the arrival of revolutionary soldiers, who besieged the farmhouse. The two conspirators were shot in the struggle, and Ian, Barbara and Susan were captured. The soldiers decided to take them to Paris where their superior, LeMaitre, would decide their fates. The soldiers set fire to the house, not knowing the Doctor was unconscious upstairs.

Susan and Barbara were imprisoned in one cell in the Conciergerie Prison. Ian was thrown into another cell, where he met a fellow English prisoner named Webster. Dying, Webster begged Ian to help him. He was an agent of the British government, sent to warn a spy named James Stirling to return home. Webster told Ian the name of an inn where Stirling's associates gathered.

By a stroke of good fortune, Ian managed to steal the keys from his cell when the jailer was distracted by the sinister LeMaitre, the master of the Conciergerie. He broke out of the jail – but the watchful eye of LeMaitre monitored his escape. LeMaitre suspected that Webster had passed secret intelligence to Ian, so he dispatched guards to follow him. Meanwhile, the Doctor escaped the burning house and made his way to Paris, adopting the identity of an official along the way by visiting a tailor and swapping his clothes for more suitable period garments, then forging a certificate of identity. These precautions, however, came too late for Susan and Barbara, who were sent to the guillotine. Before they were executed, they were rescued by three other conspirators, Leon, Jules and Jean, who whisked them away to a safe house. They were soon joined by Ian, who was captured when Jules and Jean saw him asking questions near an inn they frequented.

The Doctor arrived at the jail and learned that all his companions had escaped. Meeting LeMaitre, he was forced to accompany the master of the jail to a meeting with Robespierre of the Committee for Public Safety – the architect of the Reign of Terror. The Doctor posed as a deputy from a rural province, and discussed the political situation so adroitly that Robespierre insisted he return the next day for another consultation. LeMaitre arranged for the Doctor to stay overnight in the prison. That night, the tailor contacted LeMaitre and denounced the Doctor as a spy and traitor. LeMaitre took the tailor's evidence, but did not immediately arrest the Doctor.

Susan fell ill, so Barbara took her to a physician. The physician betrayed them, and called the guards. They were brought back to the prison and reunited with the Doctor. After a brief exchange of greetings and information, the Doctor tricked the guards into freeing Barbara.

Ian, too, fell victim to treachery. He suspected Leon might be the mysterious Stirling, so arranged to meet with him at a disused church. However, Leon was actually a spy for the revolution, and he arrested Ian to interrogate him. Jules arrived and rescued Ian, killing the treacherous Leon in the exchange.

With Ian and Barbara both free, the Doctor decided the time had come to leave the prison. He asked LeMaitre to free Susan, but LeMaitre refused and instead blackmailed the Doctor. He knew the Doctor was not a provincial deputy – but he was willing to overlook this deception and free Susan if the Doctor led him to the conspirators.

The Doctor led LeMaitre to the house of Jules Renan, where LeMaitre revealed that he was a friend to the conspirators. In fact, he was the infamous Stirling. He permitted Ian's escape so that Ian could deliver Webster's message without endangering Stirling's secret identity. Now, he was ready to return to England after one last mission. He had learned of a secret meaning between another senior revolutionary, Paul Barras, and a mysterious third party. Stirling wanted the travellers to help him spy on this meeting.

They travelled to an inn called the Sinking Ship and lay in wait for Barras. There, they watched as Barras met with none other than Napoleon Bonaparte. The pair had laid a plan to overthrow Robespierre, and had already put it into operation. The Doctor realised that Susan was in terrible danger – Bonaparte's scheme would throw Paris into chaos, and Susan was still lying sick in the Conciergerie.

He rushed back to Paris, bluffed his way into the prison, and rescued Susan just as Barras' agents arrested Robespierre. The Doctor claimed to be an agent of Napoleon, and that he had killed LeMaitre. He bullied the jailer into freeing Susan, then they fled back to the TARDIS as the Reign of Terror came to an end, and the stage was set for the rise of Napoleon.

RUNNING THIS ADVENTURE

This whole adventure can be blamed on the unreliability of the Doctor's rickety old Type 40 TARDIS. Not only does it land nearly 200 years and hundreds of miles off course, it also cannot tell when or where it is, forcing the travellers to leave the safety of the ship and look around. If the location systems worked correctly, then the Doctor could have just looked at the readout and said *"oops, off course. I'll try again"*. Keeping the TARDIS faulty, unreliable and unpredictable makes time travel feel much more dangerous and disturbing.

THE FRENCH REVOLUTION

We could give you a potted history of the French Revolution right here, but you've got history books and the internet, and it's not hard to look details up. Running any historical game requires a bit of research. Before you start researching, though, write down the four or five things that you immediately think of when someone mentions that time period. For the French Revolution, it might be:

- The guillotine
- The Bastille prison
- "Let them eat cake"
- The cult of reason
- Napoleon
- The Scarlet Pimpernel

Then try to get as many of these ideas into your adventure as possible. Treat history like a theme park ride. Boil it down into clichés! Part of the fun of time travel is living out those familiar ideas. Just like everyone goes to the Empire State Building when they visit New York for the first time, everyone should get involved in a shootout at high noon the first time they visit the Wild West, or get to warn Caesar to beware the Ides of March if they go to Ancient Rome.

SPLITTING UP

The travellers spend most of *Reign of Terror* scattered. The Doctor gets left behind in a burning farmhouse, Ian is put into a separate cell to Barbara and Susan, and then Susan falls ill and ends up stuck in the prison. The action of the adventure follows multiple separate threads. In a roleplaying game, following this structure means that some of the players will be side-lined for parts of the adventure – the Doctor's player has nothing to do while the spotlight is on Barbara and Susan.

If you take this approach, try one of the following options:

- **Rapid Cutting:** Switch back and forth between scenes rapidly. Intercut, say, the Doctor climbing out of the burning farmhouse with Barbara being interrogated in prison. Never leave a player out

WHY DO YOU INVESTIGATE?

Sometimes, players may be unwilling to get involved in an adventure. Ian's player might say *"No, Doctor, this isn't our time. You said you'd bring us there – try again!"*, skipping the whole adventure that the Gamemaster has planned. There are three ways to deal with this.

First, and this is the best option in most cases, is to ask the players why their characters get involved. Get the players to look at their Personal Goals and other reasons for travelling. Barbara, for example, wanted to stop human sacrifice in *The Aztecs.* The Reign of Terror is the Doctor's favourite period in Earth history, so he might want to pop out for a quick tour while he's here.

Second, if that isn't enough, you can always push the players with Bad Traits (like *Insatiable Curiosity*) or a bribe of a Story Point or two.

Finally, there's always the option of having the TARDIS break down and need repairs (and that means supplies, like fresh mercury for the fluid links). Where possible, though, have the players drive the action instead of sending them on a quest to fetch something.

of the game for more than a few minutes. This style keeps everyone involved, but it's exhausting for the GM and can be confusing for the players.

- **Temporary NPCs:** Give the side-lined player a temporary character to play with. The Doctor's player could also play one of the conspirators like Jules Renan, while Susan's player could take on the role of the jailer in the Doctor's scenes. The Gamemaster should write up some brief notes on these temporary characters for the players (two or three bullet points is plenty – who are they, what they want, what they can do). You don't need to bother with character sheets for such minor characters.

- **You're The Audience:** Some players are willing to watch other people play. It's ok to treat a roleplaying game as passive entertainment once in a while – the Doctor's player can just watch while the attention is on the other characters.

- **Story Point Interference:** Of course, even the audience can affect the course of a story. Players who aren't in a scene can still spend Story Points to change the story (or even suggest bad things and plot twists that might happen to the other characters. Make sure to reward the players for making each other's lives more... interesting).

ESCAPING FROM PRISON

The Doctor and especially his companions spend a lot of time in prison (although River Song probably wins the award for 'most time spent behind bars'). They get captured, thrown in prison, they learn vital bits of plot, and then they escape again. Getting locked-up is a time-honoured tradition, and it's a lot less painful than getting shot and killed, which is the other likely result of being captured by enemies. With that in mind, below is the all-purpose Random Prison Table! Roll on any of the three columns for inspiration.

FURTHER ADVENTURES

- **Changing Time:** As they left in the TARDIS, Ian wondered what would have happened if he'd written a letter to Napoleon. Susan insists that *"it wouldn't have made any difference, Ian. He'd have forgotten it, or lost it, or thought it was written by a maniac"*. What if she was wrong? Maybe Ian did write such a letter while in his cell, in the hopes of averting war between France and England, and the scheme backfires – Napoleon is not a man of small ambition, and once he knows that time machines exist, he would stop at nothing to possess one.

- **The Doctor's Ring:** The Doctor bargains his ring away to buy clothes. He gets it back later when LeMaistre blackmails him, but what did the tailor do with it in the meantime? Could it have had some strange effects on the tailor or on those around him?

- **His Favourite Period in Earth History:** For that matter, why is the French Revolution the Doctor's favourite period in Earth history? What fascinates him about this bloody reign of terror? Does it remind him of why he left Gallifrey, with a cult of reason and misguided bureaucrat presiding over horrors? Time travellers searching for the Doctor could try looking for him here – or lay a trap for him. Perhaps it's time for the Doctor to face Madame Guillotine again...

ROLL	IMPRISON THEM...!	WHILE THERE, YOU...	ESCAPE WHEN...
1	... we will interrogate them later!	... overhear guards talking about the bad guy's plot.	... you're being transferred to another cell.
2	... and use them as hostages.	... are interrogated and learn vital clues.	... the world's dumbest guards are assigned to your cell.
3	... we don't kill people needlessly.	... see something out of the prison window.	... there's an explosion outside.
4	... and prepare the experiments!	... meet another prisoner who confides in you.	... one of the other prisoners shows you a way out.
5	... because one of them fascinates me.	... sneak around the place after escaping.	... you trick the jailers into letting you go.
6	... along with the rest of the prisoners, because they are all clearly in league.	... are infected/experimented upon/ altered in some way that's a vital clue for the other player characters.	... they let you escape.

PLANET OF GIANTS

"The space pressure was far too great whilst we were materialising. The strange thing is that we all came out of it unscathed. It's most puzzling. It's a big mystery, my boy."

SYNOPSIS

The TARDIS' materialisation sequence did not go smoothly. The fault locator lit up with dozens of warnings, and the doors opened unexpectedly and too early. However, other than the scanner exploding, the TARDIS and its crew did not appear to be affected by the unusual materialisation.

They emerged into a strange dead world. They encountered several titanic insects, all dead. These insects looked like common Earth species, like ants and worms, but were gigantic. The travellers then found a matchbox – and realised they were on Earth. The excessive space pressure during materialisation had shrunk the TARDIS and its passengers down to a tiny size! An ordinary house-cat was now as dangerous as any alien monster.

Worse, they had materialised in a toxic environment. The garden belonged to the house of a businessman called Forester, who had gambled his fortune on a new insecticide called DN6 developed by his associate, Smithers. They had applied for government approval to manufacture and sell DN6, but the scientist assigned to the case, Arnold Farrow, had discovered that DN6 was toxic to all life, not just the vermin it was designed to eradicate.

While exploring the garden, Barbara was accidentally exposed to DN6. The concentration of the chemical would be harmless to a grown human, but she was now less than an inch tall, and had therefore sustained a fatal dose.

The TARDIS crew arrived in time to see Forester shoot Farrow with a gun that, from their miniaturised perspective, was the size of an artillery cannon. Forester and Smithers then conspired to make Farrow's death look like an accident and conceal his report on the dangers of DN6. The Doctor managed to cobble together an explosive device that attracted the attention of a passing police officer. The conspirators were arrested, and the travellers returned to the TARDIS. Rematerialising the ship returned it and the passengers to their normal size, curing Barbara's exposure to the poison.

RUNNING THIS ADVENTURE

Planet of Giants is a 'gimmick' adventure. Most of the conflict and action involves physical danger from situations that would be trivial under normal circumstances. The characters have to struggle to escape a housecat, to walk down a garden path, to get down from a table, to open a book – all sorts of everyday tasks are now challenges to be overcome.

Playing a pastiche of *Planet of Giants* is easy. The TARDIS (or time travel machine of your choice) malfunctions, and the characters arrive in miniature form in some familiar place. Instead of a garden,

have the tiny characters arrive at a school, a church, a hospital, an office... even a gaming table. (*"Roll to avoid being crushed by the rolling dice..."*) Add intrigue by having something dramatic happen at the location. Perhaps there's a crisis at the school when a desperate gunman holds a class to ransom, or perhaps one of the gamers at the table is actually a Slitheen serial killer in a compression suit. The joy of this adventure is running around overcoming tiny obstacles, so give plenty of opportunity for inch-tall derring-do, with lots of swinging off lampshades and duelling pet mice with safety pins.

DN6

Smither's chemical concoction is derived from the commonly used insecticide DDT, but is cheaper and more powerful. Unfortunately, it's also lethal to all forms of life. Smithers was too obsessed to see this flaw, but Arnold Fallow spotted it before he was murdered.

The damage from DN6 varies depending on the duration of exposure and the concentration. It builds up in the fatty tissues of the creatures exposed to it, so a human who is repeatedly exposed to a small amount over a long period of time can be affected. It takes a dose approximately 100 times as strong as a standard dilution to poison a human. DN6 can be inhaled or absorbed by the skin.

A character poisoned by DN6 loses 1 point of Strength, Ingenuity or Awareness every 2-12 minutes until death. (Roll 2 dice to determine the interval between damage).

GIANT CREATURES

The *Doctor Who: Adventures in Time and Space* system is designed for creatures that are roughly the size of humans. The average Strength for a human-sized creature is 2 or 3, up to a maximum of 6. Creatures that are a little bigger than humans, like a Judoon, have a Strength of 8 at most. Really huge creatures such as a Pyrovile or the Beast have a Strength of 10-12 or more!

So, when the characters are shrunk, add +2 to +4 to the Strength of small creatures like housecats, and add +6 to +10 to the Strength of full-scale humans. That gardener with Strength 3 has an effective Strength of 13 when taking a swipe at a shrunken traveller! So, a common housecat looks like this:

AWARENESS	3	PRESENCE	3
COORDINATION	4	RESOLVE	2
INGENUITY	1	STRENGTH	5

SKILLS

Athletics 3 (Climbing 5), Fighting 2, Survival 3

TRAITS

Quick Reflexes (Minor Good): Always goes first in an Action Phase.

WEAPONS: Claws (4/**7**/11 damage)

MINUSCULE PERILS

When you're tiny, not only is a housecat or a doorstep a significant problem, but several other unexpected dangers also present themselves.

- **Drowning:** It's a lot easier to drown when you're small. A tiny character can drown in a puddle.
- **Poison:** Any poisonous substance is much more effective, as the character absorbs a proportionately larger dose.
- **Smoke:** The character's lungs are a lot smaller than they used to be. That means that they fill up with smoke or toxic gases faster.
- **Food & Drink:** Eating or drinking anything when shrunk is unwise. It's fine when you're tiny, but when you return to full size, it can cause an upset stomach.
- **Gas:** Not smoke and poison gas, the... other kind. Any compression field (and the miniaturisation is really just a really powerful compression field) can give rise to... unfortunately compacted noxious emissions from the human digestive system.

UNUSUAL TARDIS MALFUNCTIONS

Phone box travel can have all sorts of unexpected side effects. There's shrinking, or there's ending up out of phase with normal reality (*The Space Museum*, page 84). Other possible effects might be:

- **Somebody Else's Problem:** The TARDIS' perception filter gets tangled up in the traveller's biodata. All the characters start off with the Face in the Crowd trait, and soon become effectively invisible when people start ignoring them. Unless they find a way to escape, though, they'll eventually be unable to perceive each other...
- **Stuck in Time:** The characters' relationship to time becomes distorted. Instead of moving through time at a steady rate, they skip like a broken record. The characters arrive in a frozen world where they are the only things that can move – everyone else is unmoving, because time is not passing for them. Then, in a flash, the rest of the world advances by a few minutes, then freezes again for the characters. During the 'flashes', everything happens too fast for the characters to act, but they can move freely during the 'freezes'.
- **Out of Existence:** The TARDIS accidentally severs the characters from reality. They're paradoxes now – they never existed. They step out into a world where they never lived.
- **Precognitive:** The characters can now see the future. Specifically, they can see the future of any person or object they stare at. Look at a car, and you see the car's future journeys stretching out like painted worms into the distance. Look at a person, and you see their future actions. The foresight doesn't take the character's own actions into account, so anything they do changes this future. More worryingly, the human brain isn't ready for such precognition, and it will drive the characters insane...

FURTHER ADVENTURES

- **Weapon of Terror:** So, DN6 is absolutely lethal to all life... but it took a detailed examination by Farrow to determine this, and its creator never realised it despite all his years of work on the compound. That means that DN6 could be an ideal weapon of terror or assassination – its effects are undetectable at first, but as the poison builds up, you get sicker and sicker. What happens if a sinister villain steals the formula?
- **Smithers, Master of Earth:** For that matter, what happens to Smithers and Forrester afterwards? Forrester will be in prison for at least fifteen years, probably more, but Smithers can expect to receive a lesser charge, and might be out within ten years. What does he do then? His life work – DN6 – was discredited. Does he start work on DN7, or take revenge on the fools who did not appreciate his brilliance?
- **No Accidents in Time Travel:** So, why did the TARDIS fail to materialise properly? Was there something else in the time vortex? Could there have been another time machine near Forrester's garden in 1963? Just where did DN6 come from, anyway? Many alien invaders use human pawns – and DN6's hostility to all Earth life could be part of an invasion plan! Give the human fools the perfect insecticide, and watch them destroy their own biosphere and starve to death, then conquer the survivors! Sontar-ha! Sontar-ha! Sontar-ha!

CHAPTER FIVE:
THE DALEK INVASION, THE RESCUE, THE ROMANS

THE DALEK INVASION

"WE ARE THE MASTERS OF EARTH!"

SYNOPSIS

The invasion began in 2157. Meteorites rained down upon the planet Earth, and where they landed, plague broke out. Billions died, and the survivors turned on each other. Each city became an isolated fortress, turning away outsiders out of fear of infection. The human species was weak and divided – easy prey for the masterminds behind the meteorite attack. The Daleks landed in their flying saucers and seized control of all major cities, including London. Resistance was useless. Those who fought back were exterminated. Those who surrendered were forced to work for the Daleks, or worse, turned into lobotomised Robomen. In a few short years, the Daleks became the masters of Earth. They began work on a mysterious mega-engineering project in Bedfordshire, a shaft that plunged towards the very core of the planet.

2164. A few scattered bands of resistance fighters survive in the tunnels beneath London, but as the Dalek scheme neared completion, they had little hope of victory.

And then the TARDIS materialised at World's End, in the heart of London.

The travellers were relieved to be back home, but were unsure *when* they were. Exploring, Susan accidentally collapsed part of a bridge on top of the TARDIS, burying it in rubble. She injured her ankle as she fell. Barbara remained behind to tend to her injury while the Doctor and Ian explored.

In a deserted warehouse, they found the corpse of a human with a strange cybernetic helmet – a Roboman. A flying saucer crossed overhead. Realising that London was under alien occupation, they hurried back to Barbara and Susan. Before they could reach them, however, a Dalek rose out of the Thames and took the men prisoner. They were escorted by Robomen to the flying saucer, where the Daleks subjected them to intelligence tests to determine which of them were suitable for conversion into Robomen.

Barbara and Susan were rescued by the resistance and brought into the Underground tunnels, the one place safe from the Daleks. There, they met key members of the resistance, including a scientist called Dortmun who had developed an acidic bomb that he believed capable of destroying a Dalek. Despite their limited numbers, the resistance fighters launched an attack on the Dalek flying saucer.

The attack was partially successful, although Dortmun's bombs proved unable to penetrate the Dalekanium casings. In the confusion, the Doctor managed to escape, although Ian remained trapped on the saucer as it took off. Susan, meanwhile, fled into the streets with a young Resistance fighter named David. She suggested that they find the Doctor and then leave in the TARDIS, but David refused. Earth was his home, and he did not want to run. They reunited with the Doctor and made their way through the sewers to the outskirts of the ruined city.

Dortmun realised the cause of the problem his bombs had with Dalek armour, and modified his formula to create an improved bomb but, before he could build it, the Daleks closed in on his hiding place. After entrusting his notes to Barbara, he sacrificed himself to save her and another resistance member named Jenny.

On the flying saucer, Ian managed to escape his cell along with another prisoner named Larry, whose brother had previously been taken to the mine. They worked together to hide from the Daleks and managed to sneak into the excavation side in Bedfordshire, where they learned that the invaders intended to remove the Earth's magnetic core and turn the whole planet into a vehicle for conquest. Larry found his brother, but he had been brainwashed by the Daleks and turned on them. In the confusion, Ian fled deeper into the mine and stumbled into a deep shaft.

Separately, the Doctor, Susan and David, and Barbara and Jenny escape London and make their way to Bedfordshire, just as the Daleks complete the drilling phase of their operation. The next step is to use a powerful bomb to crack open the planet and expose the core. As the human work force is no longer needed ... all humans can be EXTERMINATED.

Barbara and Jenny were captured by the Daleks, but using Dormun's notes as evidence, Barbara was able to bluff her way into the Dalek control centre by claiming to have information about a resistance attack on the mine. Coupled with the Doctor's sabotage of the Dalek security systems, the Daleks assumed the attack is about to take place and hastened their efforts to complete the second phase of the plan. They launched the bomb – and it jammed in the shaft, thanks to Ian's meddling. Chaos reigned as the Daleks retreated and the prisoners fled. Barbara managed to command the Robomen to turn on their masters, adding to the carnage.

The bomb detonated, causing a tremendous volcanic eruption. The Dalek saucers hovering over the site were caught in the blast and destroyed, ending the invasion. Earth was free.

In the aftermath, David asked Susan to marry him, offering her stability and a home instead of a wandering life on the TARDIS. Susan was torn between her love for David and her desire to care for her old Grandfather... so the Doctor made the decision for her. He locked her out of the TARDIS and bade her farewell before dematerialising.

"Believe me, my dear, your future lies with David, and not with a silly old buffer like me. One day, I shall come back. Yes, I shall come back. Until then, there must be no regrets, no tears, no anxieties. Just go forward in all your beliefs, and prove to me that I am not mistaken in mine. Goodbye, Susan, goodbye, my dear."

RUNNING THIS ADVENTURE

The Dalek Invasion of Earth draws on images and ideas inspired by war movies and given a science-fiction gloss. You can draw parallels between the London of the 2100s and Occupied Europe during World War II. The Daleks are like the Nazis, with their patrols and prison guards and enslavement and extermination of the conquered population. You've got Robomen collaborators, a desperate resistance movement, ruined buildings, secret weapons... so when running adventures like this, look for ways to evoke that feeling. Have the Daleks search house-to-house, have Robomen guards demand to see the characters' papers, describe the bomb-ravaged city and rubble-strewn streets.

THE INVASION

The Dalek invasion began with germ warfare. Their use of germ-carrying meteors let them attack Earth indirectly, turning the various nations against each other and reducing Earth's population and fighting strength. The Dalek-engineered germs were designed to overcome humanity's medical technology and to have exactly the right mix of lethality and infectiousness – they wanted chaos, not extermination at the stage. They needed a workforce. Next came the invasion itself, once Earth was sufficiently weakened. Dalek saucers swept in from dark space, destroying humanity's orbital defences and blasting key locations with their firebombs. Then the landings began...

CONQUERED LONDON

Even before the Daleks arrived, London was a grim place. Several years of quarantine and lockdown to slow the spread of the meteoric plague meant that international trade and commerce had stopped almost completely. Londoners had grown used to rationing and power cuts.

The Dalek's initial attacks concentrated on centres of government and military installations. They reduced Downing Street to a smoking hole in the ground, and blew up army bases and airfields. Once London was conquered, they set about remaking it to suit their needs. Much of the city was destroyed. New police stations and checkpoints were built for their Robomen servants, while the city's transportation network was reorganised to bring slave workers to the mines in Bedfordshire. The Daleks also built new landing platforms for their fleet of flying saucers, with the main such platform at the Chelsea heliport.

The resistance struck back at the Daleks, destroying the rail links to Bedfordshire. The Daleks switched to using their saucers to transport prisoners. The resistance tried to keep to the maze of tunnels under London – between the London Underground train lines, the sewers, and the various access tunnels and utilities, they could get from one side of the city to the other without ever setting foot above ground and getting spotted by Dalek patrols. The sewers, though, have their own dangers. Rats, escaped alligators, and other monsters live down there, and the Daleks flush poisonous chemicals into the sewers to prevent the humans using them. With their sealed travel machines, the Daleks can go anywhere in London – they even patrol through the slime in the sewers and along the bottom of the river Thames.

The surviving civilian population – at least, the few that remain after the war – hide in their tenements and shelters. The Daleks permit them to survive, keeping them as a stockpile of spare workers and Robomen. When the plan is completed, then these survivors will be exterminated. The survivors mostly sympathise with the efforts of the resistance, but are scared of lending support publicly. There are plenty of traitors and informants among the civilian population, people who would sell out their fellow humans for a crust of bread or the promise of better treatment from the Robomen.

Key locations:

- Big Ben, a symbol of hope for the resistance.
- London Underground. The resistance had a hidden base there.
- Chelsea Heliport.
- Civic Transport Museum. A second resistance base was located here. The Daleks eliminated most motor vehicles to control the movement of the population.
- Battersea Power Station, now nuclear-powered.

FUTURE ENCOUNTERS

If the characters go wandering on the streets of future London, they might see...

- An alarming street sign, like "IT IS FORBIDDEN TO DUMP BODIES IN THE RIVER" or "CURFEW AT 5PM. THOSE FOUND OUTDOORS AFTER 5PM WILL BE EXTERMINATED" or "CORPSE RECYCLING – THIS WAY".

- A street market, with hungry people trading for vegetables grown in back gardens, meat from domestic pets like dogs and cats, and clothing stolen from the dead that still smells of ozone from Dalek death rays.

- A group of street kids. They've managed to lure one of the sewer alligators out of a storm drain, but it's gotten stuck. The kids are throwing stones at it – if they manage to kill it before it breaks free, then they plan to drag it down to the market and sell the meat.

- A Dalek flying saucer, slowly moving overhead. Scanning beams stab down, searching for signs of the resistance.

- A team of Robomen handing out sacks of poor-quality food to the population. The Robomen examine each person who takes food from them;

if they meet the physical endurance standards required to work in the mine, the Robomen capture them and bring them to a flying saucer. These standards keep dropping as the Daleks work their slaves to death.

- A security checkpoint, operated by a team of Robomen with a single Dalek overseer.
- The ruined remains of a building familiar to one of the characters ("hey, that's my old school!").
- One of the few functional moving pavements, still rattling along past a row of shattered department store windows.

THE RESISTANCE

The human resistance consisted of scattered bands of rebels with little in the way of organised leadership. Human weapons were virtually incapable of damaging the Daleks, as Dalekanium armour was impenetrable to anything short of an anti-tank missile.

Without any access to the heavy firepower they needed, the Resistance was limited to sabotaging Dalek operations, attacking Robomen and other collaborators, and trying to survive and build up their forces as they looked for a way to even the odds against the invaders.

CARL TYLER

"He's afraid to make friends. He's known too much killing."

Tyler was the veteran leader of the Resistance's field troops, although he considered Dortmun to be his superior – or at least, his equal. He was extremely skilled at getting around London without being noticed, but his belief in the possibility that humanity could defeat the Daleks was worn away by constant defeat. He saw Dortmun as being out of touch with conditions on the surface.

He mustered enough courage to lead a frontal assault on the Chelsea Heliport, but when that failed, he planned to gather his surviving troops and escape north, out of the city. Barbara and Susan convinced him to accompany them to Bedfordshire instead, and he helped the Doctor attack the Dalek mines there. He survived the final battle, and later played a part in rebuilding Earth's government.

AWARENESS	4	PRESENCE	3
COORDINATION	3	RESOLVE	4
INGENUITY	3	STRENGTH	4

SKILLS

Athletics 4, Convince 3, Fighting 4, Knowledge 3 (London 5), Marksman 4 Science 2, Subterfuge 4, Survival 4, Technology 2, Transport 3

TRAITS

Indomitable (Minor Good): +4 bonus to resist psychic control or brainwashing.

Quick Reflexes (Minor Good): Acts first in an Action Phase.

Sense of Direction (Minor Good): +2 bonus to knowing where to do.

Tough (Minor Good): Reduces all damage suffered by 2.

Obligation (Minor Bad): To the Resistance.

Unadventurous (Minor Bad): Growing disillusionment with their chances.

TECH LEVEL: 5

STORY POINTS: 3

DAVID CAMPBELL

AWARENESS	4	PRESENCE	3
COORDINATION	3	RESOLVE	4
INGENUITY	3	STRENGTH	3

David Campbell was another resistance member. He was one of Tyler's trusted lieutenants, and served as a messenger and courier. He had a wicked sense of humour, and was extremely loyal to the resistance. He refused to leave Earth, even when Susan suggested that he join her and the Doctor on the TARDIS. He and Susan fell in love and later married.

SKILLS

Athletics 3, Convince 2, Craft 3, Fighting 2, Knowledge 3, Marksman 2, Subterfuge 3 (Hiding 5), Survival 2, Technology 2, Transport 2

TRAITS

Attractive (Minor Good): +2 to any roll to convince based on looks.
Brave (Minor Good): +2 to any rolls against fear.

TECH LEVEL: 5

STORY POINTS: 3

JENNY

AWARENESS	3	PRESENCE	3
COORDINATION	3	RESOLVE	3
INGENUITY	3	STRENGTH	2

Another member of the resistance, Jenny was Dortmun's assistant and co-ordinated resistance efforts. She was in charge of the job rota and the communications room, where she listened to the other resistance groups disappear, one by one, as the Daleks exterminated them. She accompanied Barbara to the Bedfordshire base, and survived the attack.

SKILLS

Athletics 1, Convince 2, Fighting 1, Knowledge 3, Science 3, Subterfuge 2, Survival 1, Transport 2

TRAITS

Technically Adept (Minor Good): +2 to any rolls involving Technology.

TECH LEVEL: 5

STORY POINTS: 3

DORTMUN'S BOMBS (MINOR GADGET)

Traits: Acidic (Major)

These acidic bombs do 2/**4**/6 damage, but also reduce the armour of their target by the same amount. Apply the damage first, then the armour reduction. So, if you throw an acid bomb at a Dalek (Armour 10) and get a Fantastic Success, you do six damage (so, er, nothing, 'cos of that armour 10), but then reduce the Dalek's armour by six to 4. Your next bomb will be a lot more damaging.

Cost: 1 Story Point

DORTMUN

AWARENESS	2	PRESENCE	5
COORDINATION	2	RESOLVE	5
INGENUITY	4	STRENGTH	2

A talented if egotistical scientist, Dortmun was the resistance movement's weapons expert and researcher. When conventional weapons proved useless against the Daleks, he tried to develop an acidic compound that could break down their Dalekanium armour.

His bomb ultimately proved to be ineffective, but his sacrifice saved Barbara and Jenny from the Daleks.

SKILLS

Convince 3, Craft 3, Fighting 1, Knowledge 4, Marksman 1, Science 4 (Chemistry 6), Subterfuge 1, Survival 2, Technology 3, Transport 2

TRAITS

Boffin (Major Good): Dortmun's an inventor and chemist.
Voice of Authority (Minor Good): Dortmun has a +2 bonus to commanding people.
Impaired (Major Bad): Dortmun cannot walk and is confined to a wheelchair.

TECH LEVEL: 5

STORY POINTS: 3

THE DALEKS

These Daleks are still a relatively early design (see page 21 for statistics for this model of Dalek), but they are still fearsome conquerors.

Electrostatics

These Daleks rely on static electricity to power their Travel Machines, but this energy is broadcast from central power stations. Disabling the receptor dish on the rear of the Dalek can temporarily depower the creature until it is repaired. Alternatively, destroying a broadcast generator disables all the Daleks in the area if they do not have an alternate power source to rely on.

Destroying a receptor dish requires a Called Shot (-2 penalty to hit) that inflicts at least 4 points of damage. The dish is lightly armoured (Armour 5). Once the receptor dish is disabled, the Dalek rapidly loses power – it loses 1 point of Strength per round until it shuts down at 0 Strength. Firing drains an extra point of Strength each time the Dalek uses its gun.

DALEK SUPREME CONTROLLER

The Dalek Supreme Controller, a black-cased Dalek, was the commander of the invasion force. As a high-ranking Dalek, this particular monster was stronger and more powerful than its minions. It kept the Slyther as a sort of pet to torment the human slaves. Like the rest of the invasion force, the Supreme Controller was destroyed in the Bedfordshire eruption.

AWARENESS	4 [3]	PRESENCE	4 [3]
COORDINATION	2 [3]	RESOLVE	5 [5]
INGENUITY	5 [5]	STRENGTH	5 [3]

*The Dalek mutant inside the casing has the attributes in brackets; it has a Speed of 1 and cannot survive for long outside of the shell. It also takes damage as normal once removed from its Dalekanium shell.

SKILLS

Convince 3, Fighting 4, Marksman 4, Medicine 1, Science 3, Technology 4, Survival 4

TRAITS

Armour [Minor Trait]: This is a weaker version of the Daleks' famous Dalekanium armour shell and can only deduct 5 points of damage.
Cyborg
Environmental: Daleks can survive in a vacuum, or underwater.
Fear Factor [3]: This hasn't changed much; Daleks are still terrifying and gain a bonus of +6 when trying to actively scare someone.
Forcefield [Minor Trait]: Black Daleks have a basic forcefield that can reduce the damage that they take; any damage applied to a Dalek is reduced by a single level.
Natural Weapon – Exterminator: The basic Dalek weapon that has changed little over their iterations. (L[4/**L**/L])
Scan: The Dalek can interface with computers and complex machines.
Technically Adept: Daleks are brilliant with computers and other technology; they can use and adapt a variety of technologies.
Voice of Authority: The Black Dalek commands other Daleks.

STORY POINTS: 5

ROBOMEN

The Robomen are not a species but the name given to the humans who were processed by the Daleks in a procedure called the Transfer. This process turned them into mind-controlled slaves. Robomen wear elaborate cybernetic helmets to connect them to their masters. They can be ordered around directly, or receive orders via radio from Dalek central command.

Robomen are unstable – they function for only a few months before they go insane from the Dalek hatred whispering in their minds. An insane Roboman would either be killed by its masters, or else blunder blindly through London until it met its end elsewhere.

Robomen have the same attributes, skills and traits they did in life, with the following changes:

AWARENESS	-1	PRESENCE	1
COORDINATION	-1	RESOLVE	+2
INGENUITY	1	STRENGTH	+2

SKILLS

Whatever skills they had before the Transfer, +1 Fighting, +1 Marksman, +1 Technology

TRAITS

Clumsy
Cyborg: The bulky nature of the Roboman's helmet makes it pretty easy to spot.
Fear Factor [1]: The Robomen's menacing appearance is basically due to the helmets and their complete loyalty to the Dalek command. You can increase this to 2 if the Roboman is someone that is known to the viewer. They gain a +2 or +4 to actively scare someone.
Networked: Networked by Dalek mind control devices built into their brains, and the helmet circuits. Robomen can be commanded at a moment's notice.
Slow reflexes
Weakness [Minor]: Robomen can be disabled if the helmet is damaged.

WEAPON: What they're given to use by the Daleks.

SLYTHER

Slythers are massive blob like creatures that first came to earth with the Daleks when they. They have long tentacles and the Black Dalek used one to guard the Bedfordshire mine. Slythers have a green colour and they are an amorphous, voracious creature that will anything that it can latch a tentacle on, human or otherwise.

AWARENESS	3	PRESENCE	2
COORDINATION	2	RESOLVE	4
INGENUITY	2	STRENGTH	5

SKILLS
Subterfuge 3 (only on forested planets), Fighting 5

TRAITS
Alien, Alien Appearance
Clumsy: Slythers are not the most coordinated of creatures, they can be lured into tricks and traps, such as the time Ian Chesterton caused one to leap to its doom into a chasm.
Fear Factor [3]: This large monstrous blob like creature is scary indeed and whilst it doesn't actively try and scare people, it gains a +6 when it comes lurking out of the darkness at someone.
Tough

PROJECT DEGRAVITATE
The Dalek plan for the Earth consisted of four phases.

1. Weaken Earth's defences with germ-laden meteoric bombardment
2. Conquer the Earth
3. Bore deep into the planet's crust and mantle, creating a shaft large enough for an explosive device

3a. Exterminate humanity

4. Detonate the device, which vents the Earth's magnetic core and turns the planet into a giant spaceship.

Part Four of the plan is where it gets confusing. The Daleks may have intended to turn the whole planet into a warship, or maybe they just intended to crash the Earth into some other world. The Daleks steal the Earth again in *The Stolen Earth*, when they intend to use our planet as a component in Davros' Reality Bomb – maybe there's something special about Earth's make-up that makes it ideal for use in Dalek apocalypse technology.

The Doctor was able to stop the Dalek explosive device near the top of the shaft, so it 'merely' triggered a giant nuclear-powered volcanic eruption that wiped out an entire invasion fleet, instead of destroying the whole of England or cracking the planet in two.

FURTHER ADVENTURES

- **The Fall of Earth:** You could run a series of adventures, or even a whole campaign, centred around the invasion of Earth. The characters might be UNIT or Torchwood agents, or even just civilian scientists and investigators. The adventure starts small, with the fall of meteors, then covers the spread of the plague, the collapse of the international community, and then the Dalek attack. The characters then join the resistance and fight to preserve humanity. Maybe they could try to make contact with Earth's scattered colonies on the Moon, Mars and around Jupiter, or try to find alien allies willing to fight back against the Daleks. Look to war movies for inspiration – *Casablanca of the Daleks*, anyone?

- **Susan's Fate:** Susan stayed behind on Earth. The Doctor met her again in *The Five Doctors*, and there's all sorts of speculation about what happened to her afterwards. Your characters could meet Susan (or, if she becomes a Time Lord, a future regeneration of hers), or you could even use Susan as the 'Doctor' character in a campaign.

- **Dalek Planetships:** Earth may be an unusual planet, but it's not unique. Other worlds out there may also be suitable for conversion. Imagine the characters landing on a planet, only to discover that the 'sun' is actually an artificial heat source in low orbit that keeps the atmosphere from freezing solid in the interstellar cold, and there are billions of Daleks inside this planet-sized invasion ship...

THE RESCUE

"You destroyed a whole planet to save your own skin. You're insane."

SYNOPSIS

An Earth ship en route to Astra crashed on the isolated planet Dido. Among the passengers was a young girl, Vicki, travelling with her father. Also on board was an older man named Bennett. Before the crash, Bennett murdered one of the crew, but the ship crashed before anyone could report his crime.

Dido was inhabited by a handful of mysterious, gentle humanoids called the Dido People. They met with the survivors, but both groups were betrayed by Bennett. He used the ship's armaments to cause a titanic explosion, killing the survivors and wiping out most of the Dido people.

Vicki had remained on board the ship, and was unaware of Bennett's treachery. He left her alive, but stole ceremonial robes from a Dido temple and disguised himself as a monster called Koquillion. Wearing the mask and robes, he threatened Vicki, and claimed that the other Dido people were hostile and had killed the survivors. Bennett intended to wait for the rescue ship to arrive, and blame the deaths (including the initial murder) on the Dido natives. The Koquillion ruse would ensure that Vicki could not investigate the deaths, and that she would be able to testify about the hostility of the natives and Bennett's innocence.

His plan might have worked, if the TARDIS had not arrived. Still emotionally exhausted from Susan's departure, the Doctor slept through the landing and did not initially recognise the planet – he had visited Dido before and was a friend of the natives.

Exploring, Barbara and Ian met Koquillion. The creature demanded to meet the Doctor, so Ian returned to the TARDIS to fetch him. Koquillion then threw Barbara off a cliff and blew up the cave entrance, trapping Ian and the Doctor. Fortunately, Vicki found Barbara, brought her back to the crashed ship, and nursed her back to health. Bennett concealed his alarm at finding Barbara still alive, and countermanded her plans to trap Koquillion. He resolved to murder her as soon as the opportunity arose.

Ian and the Doctor found their way out of the cave via a dangerous passageway, and arrived at the crashed ship. While Ian spoke to Barbara and Vicki, the Doctor broke into Bennett's room. He found a voice-activated recorder that played Bennett's voice whenever anyone knocked on the door, and an escape hatch that led into a Dido temple beneath the crash site. There, Koquillion menaced him again, but the Doctor revealed that he knew the 'creature' was just Bennett in a mask. The pair struggled – Bennett was stronger than the Doctor, but the Doctor had the aid of a pair of surviving Dido people, who appeared unexpectedly. Startled, Bennett fell to his death. The Dido natives then destroyed the radio beacon on the crashed ship, ensuring that no human rescuers would come to trouble Dido. As both Vicki's parents were dead and there was nothing waiting for her on Astra, the Doctor invited her to travel with them on the TARDIS.

RUNNING THIS ADVENTURE

The Rescue is a small-scale adventure, which can be a refreshing change from big bombastic threats to the safety of a whole planet or even the fate of the universe. Bennett's plan is simple and direct, with a minimum of twists. Simplicity can be a virtue in adventure design as well as complexity – a simple idea executed convincingly often works better than a confused mess of intrigue and conspiracy.

THE DIDO PEOPLE

AWARENESS	4	PRESENCE	2
COORDINATION	3	RESOLVE	4
INGENUITY	2	STRENGTH	3

The Doctor described Dido as a pleasant world inhabited by a peaceful people. The region near the crashed ship was a warren of caves, cliffs and tunnels around a Dido temple, suggesting it was a sacred site for the native inhabitants. They are a highly spiritual people, with a culture centred around temples and rituals. The Dido people were kind and welcoming, but Bennett's treachery turned them against humans. Many of them died in the explosion, but at least two (and probably more) survived.

Humans are no longer welcome on Dido, and it is unclear what steps they would take should humans return to their world

SKILLS

Convince 2, Craft 3, Knowledge 4, Technology 2

TRAITS

Alien
Code of Conduct (Minor Bad): The Dido have their own strange code of behaviour.
Feel the Turn of the Universe (Special Good): The Dido are not time travellers, but can sense the ebb and flow of the cosmos.

SAND BEAST

AWARENESS	2	PRESENCE	-
COORDINATION	3	RESOLVE	-
INGENUITY	-	STRENGTH	5

The Sand Beasts of Dido look like fearsome monsters, but they are herbivores, eating plant matter instead of meat. They are also quite tractable – Vicki was able to tame and train one of the creatures as a pet. In rare cases, such as when defending a nest, Sand Beasts can become aggressive.

SKILLS

Athletics 2, Fighting 2

TRAITS

Alien, Alien Appearance
Fear Factor 2: A +2 bonus to attempts to intimidate or scare foes.
Claws: The Sand Beast's claws inflict Strength +1 damage (3/**6**/9).

BENNETT

AWARENESS	3	PRESENCE	3
COORDINATION	2	RESOLVE	4
INGENUITY	4	STRENGTH	4

The manipulative Bennett was a desperate criminal. He murdered one of the crew on the Earth transport, and may have been responsible for the crash (it's certainly convenient that the crash happened just before the crew could send a message about Bennett's guilt). He was an adept engineer, able to build a secret entrance to the Dido temple and to create an improvised explosive to murder the other survivors. How deep did his villainy go? Was he keeping Vicki alive only to testify on his behalf, or did he balk at the idea of murdering a teenage girl? What was he planning to do on Astra?

SKILLS

Athletics 2, Convince 3 (Intimidate 5, Lying 5), Craft 2, Fighting 3, Knowledge 1, Marksman 2, Technology 3, Transport 3

TRAITS

Tough (Minor Good): Reduces all damage suffered by 2.
Resourceful Pockets (Minor Good): Always has what he needs to hand.
Dark Secret (Major Bad): Bennett's a wanted criminal.

TECH LEVEL: 6

STORY POINTS: 3

DIDO CRAFTING STAFF (MINOR GADGET)

The Doctor identified this gadget as a Dido construction tool, although Bennett used it as a weapon when masquerading as Koquillion. When activated, the staff can trigger rockfalls or blast through walls. It uses the Marksman skill but has a very limited range. The staff's size and weight gives it a -2 penalty to attack rolls, and it inflicts 3/**6**/L damage.

Traits: Delete, Weld, Restriction (limited uses), Bulky
Cost: 1 Story Point

FURTHER ADVENTURES

- **First Contact:** The Doctor visited Dido before – and wherever the Doctor goes, trouble follows. Actually, usually, trouble's there in advance, but that's time travel for you. What happened the last time he was here with Susan?

- **Murder on the Astra Express:** Bennett's murder on board the ship could be the starting point for a scenario. An interstellar spaceship makes for a great venue for a locked-room murder. Maybe the Dido people save the characters from Bennett's bomb, and give them strange powers to avenge the dead on the murderer.

- **The Rescue Ship:** What happens to that rescue ship? Do they wander through space for months, searching for the lost transport? What other dangerous missions do they go on? An interstellar space rescue crew could make for a great campaign setup!

THE ROMANS

"They wouldn't let me build my new Rome. But if the old one is burnt... If it goes up in flames they'll have no choice. Rome will be rebuilt to my design! Brilliant! Brilliant!"

SYNOPSIS

The TARDIS materialised near Rome, in 64AD – and promptly fell off a cliff.

Exhausted by their many adventures, the travellers decided to stay put for a while, and took up residence in a Roman villa while its owner was away in Gaul. After several weeks' relaxation, however, the Doctor grew bored and set off for Rome with Vicki. En route to Rome, through a series of misunderstandings, the Doctor was mistaken for a lyre player named Pettulian, who was scheduled to play for Nero. The actual lyre player was killed by assassins, and the Doctor's involvement made the conspirators assume their assassins failed and that Pettulian was still alive. The Doctor defeated a second assassination attempt and made his way to Rome.

Meanwhile, slave traders kidnapped Ian and Barbara. Ian was sold as a galley slave, but escaped when his vessel was shipwrecked off the Italian coast. He was soon recaptured and thrown into the gladiatorial prison, to await his fate in an arena of lions. Meanwhile, Barbara was bought by Tavius, a servant of Nero, to serve in the imperial palace.

In Rome, the Doctor tried to understand the conspiracy he had accidentally discovered, while stalling to avoid having to play the lyre. He learned that Nero knew nothing of any plot, but that Tavius was responsible for killing the centurion who hired the assassins who killed Petrullian. Meanwhile, Nero developed an amorous interest in Barbara, which resulted in Nero's wife Poppaea developing an equally intense murderous interest in the new slave. Vicki had to intervene to save Barbara from a poisoning attempt.

At the banquet, the Doctor announced that his lyre playing could only be heard by the most cultured and refined ears. He then mimed playing the lyre to the assembled courtiers. Of course, none of the courtiers was willing to admit that they could not hear the non-existent music, so 'Petrullian' was acclaimed as the greatest musician in Rome. Nero became jealous, and decided that Petrullian would perform again the next day in the arena – but that half-way through the performance, the lions would be released.

Ian escaped the arena and plotted to rescue Barbara from the palace. Barbara enlisted Tavius' help in her escape attempt, but this alerted Tavius to the fact that his own plans were awry. He revealed that he had brought 'Petrullian' to Rome to murder Nero, and he tried to convince the Doctor to kill the Emperor that night. The Doctor refused and decided that the only thing to do was to flee Rome.

As he prepared to leave, Nero demanded that 'Petrullian' meet with him. The Emperor intended to tell the lyre player about his appointment the next day in the arena, but during their conversation, the Doctor accidentally set fire to Nero's plans for remodelling Rome. The four travellers escaped in the confusion, but the fire gave Nero an idea – he could remake the city from the ground up if he first burnt it to the ground. Instead of pursuing the travellers, he ordered his guards to set fire to Rome.

The TARDIS departed as the horizon filled with smoke.

RUNNING THIS ADVENTURE

This adventure is largely a comedy, and there's nothing wrong with a comedic adventure. Many *Doctor Who: Adventures in Time and Space* turn into comedy at some point, either deliberately or accidentally. As a Gamemaster, it's best not to try to force the jokes –

try playing the non-player characters and situations 'straight' and let the players provide the humour. So, instead of playing Nero as something out of *Monty Python's Life of Brian*, play him as an eccentric but still dangerous Roman emperor, and let the players be the ones who come up with crazy plans like silent lyre playing.

ASKING QUESTIONS

Asking the players to decide on parts of the plot is a wonderful tool for the Gamemaster. It does call for quick thinking and improvisation, but a light-hearted game is a perfect consequence-free environment to practice those skills. You will often find that players are much, much crueller to their own characters than the Gamemaster could ever be.

For example, take the starting point for this adventure. The characters are all relaxing in a Roman villa. Instead of, say, having the villa be attacked by rampaging Cybermen, the Gamemaster turns to the first player and asks, "What's your character doing?" That player answers something like, "I'm going to try to meet Nero."

LIONS

Lions and other animals are not normally hostile to humans, unless they are very hungry or feel threatened. The lions in the Roman arena, though, were trained to kill and eat the prisoners, so they attack immediately.

AWARENESS	3	PRESENCE	-
COORDINATION	3	RESOLVE	-
INGENUITY	-	STRENGTH	7

SKILLS
Athletics 3, Fighting 2, Survival 2

TRAITS
Fear Factor 1: a +2 bonus to attempts to intimidate or scare foes.
Claws: The Lion's claws inflict Strength damage (3/**6**/9).
Bite: If a lion claws an opponent, it can try biting that victim in the next Action Round. A bite attack does Strength +2 damage (4/**8**/12).

The Gamemaster turns to a second player. "What goes wrong with this plan?"

"He's mistaken for a lute player."

Never block the player's suggestions (unless they're utterly absurd). Always build on them and expand them. "Yes, and", "Yes, but" and "No, but" should be your watchwords. Keep adding complexity.

POISON

Nero's poisoner Locusta tried to kill Barbara with a poisoned wine cup, and lots of other characters die mysteriously in this story. In *Doctor Who: Adventures in Time and Space*, a character who gets poisoned must make a Strength + Resolve roll to resist the poison's effects. The Difficulty of this roll depends on the potency of the poison. If the roll succeeds, then the character may still be affected by the poison (suffering damage of some sort) but avoids being killed.

FURTHER ADVENTURES

- **Time Cannot Be Changed... right?** The Doctor was quite surprised when he discovered that he was the one who gave Nero the idea to burn Rome. In fact, the Doctor had changed history. The Doctor has *Feel The Turn Of The Universe* – he should know when history is fixed and when it is flexible. What was going on in Rome that blocked his Time Lord perceptions of the vortex?

- **The Gladiatorial Arena:** Whenever the Romans discovered a strange new creature, they put it in the arena and fed Christians to it. Imagine what would happen if they got their hands on an alien. Some space creatures would be perfectly happy with an all-you-can-eat Italian buffet, others would be victims of the arena. Others might even conquer the arena – can any gladiator defeat Strobb the Short, from the far province of Sontar?

- **House-Sitters from the Future:** The Doctor and his companions 'borrow' a villa while staying in Italy. More accurately, they bluff their way in while the owner is away. Presumably, the Doctor has done the same thing in other places and other times – what happens if your characters come home to discover that the Doctor has let himself in and helped himself to the contents of the fridge?

CHAPTER SIX:
THE WEB PLANET, THE CRUSADE, THE SPACE MUSEUM

THE WEB PLANET

Pictos shall remind us of a time as it circles Vortis. Every time it points to the Needle of the Kings, as it does now, then we shall weave songs to praise the gods of light and thank them that they sent the Earth people to save us from the Animus. Now the Zarbi larvae feed the soil, the flower forest shall grow again across Vortis. But we must not allow the forest to conceal another lurking Animus.

SYNOPSIS

A mysterious force pulled the TARDIS off course to land on the planet of Vortis. This world was dominated by various species of intelligent insects. The winged Menoptra lived on the surface, ruling over the docile Zarbi. Underground lived an offshoot of the Menoptra, the wingless and primitive Optra. Finally, lurking deep in the planet's core was the mysterious and malignant Animus.

The Animus intelligence desired to extend its evil beyond Vortis. It seized control of the Zarbi and led them in a war against the Menoptra. It also sought ways to leave the planet – and found its escape route in the form of the TARDIS. It drew the TARDIS to Vortis.

The Animus could control those who wore gold, and Barbara wore a gold bracelet given to her by Nero. The Animus used this to compel her to leave the ship, while its Zarbi minions attempted to steal the TARDIS and confuse the other travellers.

Barbara was freed from mental control by a Menoptra scout named Vrestin. The revolt of the Zarbi and the unnatural expansion of the Carcinome, the Zarbi nest, forced them to retreat off-world to a new moon. Now, they planned to return and retake their home. They discussed killing Barbara to ensure that she could not give their position away to the Zarbi. Terrified, she fled and was recaptured by the Zarbi, who placed another golden collar on her to control her. They took her to the Crater of Needles, where Zarbi and captured Menoptran slaves laboured to build more of the Carcinome. They removed the control collar from her and put her in a work gang with a Menoptran.

The Doctor and Ian explored the planet until they too were captured by the Zarbi, who brought them to the TARDIS. There, they were questioned by the disembodied voice of the Animus, who suspected them of being part of the Menoptran attack. The Animus also wanted access to the TARDIS' astral map, ostensibly to spot Menoptran movements, but also as part of its plan to leave the planet. It threatened the Doctor and his companions with death if they did not co-operate.

While searching for Barbara, Ian was attacked by a Zarbi. He killed it, and was rescued from the rest of the Zarbi horde by Vrestin. As they fled, they fell down a chasm into the tunnels under the surface. There, they met the Optra grubs. These subterranean primitives were initially hostile, but were awed when Vrestin revealed her wings and agreed to help.

Vicki accidentally discovered that the Zarbi feared spiders, and she and the Doctor waited for the right opportunity to use this to their advantage. Suspecting treachery, the Zarbi attached another gold collar to Vicki and demanded to know what the Doctor had discovered with the astral map. He tried to bluff

his way out, and attempted to disrupt the Animus' control, but the intelligence had learned to read the astral map and learned that the Menoptra attack force was gathering over the Crater of Needles. The Zarbi placed control collars on the Doctor and Vicki, but the Doctor's efforts had disabled Vicki's collar. She then removed his collar, and they escaped.

Barbara and her Menoptran ally managed to escape, but they were unable to warn the attack spearhead in time. The Menoptra landed and were ambushed by the Zarbi. A few managed to escape into the tunnels, where they explained their plan to Barbara. Menoptra scientists had developed a Living Cell Destructor, a weapon that they believed would destroy the malignant Animus. The Doctor and Vicki arrived, and together they decided on a strategy – the Menoptra would provide a distraction, while the Doctor sneaks into the Carcinome to the lair of the Animus to deploy the isotope.

This plan nearly failed – the Animus captured the Doctor and Vicki, and used its mind control powers to seize control of Barbara and the Menoptrans. However, Ian and Vrestin's unexpected arrival from underground distracted the creature, allowing Barbara to use the Living Cell Destructor and defeat the Animus. With the Animus destroyed, the Zarbi returned to their docile ways, and peace returned to the Web Planet.

RUNNING THIS ADVENTURE

The Web Planet is notable for its supporting cast – there isn't a single human (or even humanoid) character other than the TARDIS passengers in the adventure! In a roleplaying game, of course, all those non-humans are played by the Gamemaster who's (usually) human, but they still act in unexpected and strange ways.

PLAYING NON-HUMANS

Robots, Daleks, slime monsters, Ood, insect people – the Doctor runs into a lot of strange creatures on his travels, and it's up to the Gamemaster to play them! There are three elements to portraying non-player characters – actions, demeanour and rules.

Actions are what the aliens choose to do, and those choices should show their... alien-ness. Take Daleks, for example. They're creatures of pure hatred. They exist to exterminate. Imagine a situation, a Prisoner's Dilemma, where a Dalek and a human are both locked in a room. The room is about to fill with acid. There are two buttons, one on either side, and you've got to press them both at the exact same moment to open the door. The obvious thing to do is for the human to press one button and the Dalek to press the other, right? If they both put aside their differences for just one moment, they both get to escape the acidic death trap.

If you're a human, then the rational thing to do is co-operate – but if you're a Dalek, then the rational, logical thing to do is to exterminate the human and take your chances with the acid bath. Even if you die, you'll have had the satisfaction of killing the human first. Different alien species should take different actions – don't think like a human! Whenever you're playing an alien, second-guess yourself all the time when making decisions. Keep asking yourself, "is this what an alien would do?"

Demeanour is how you portray the alien when roleplaying – how you talk, how you move, how you act. Even if you're just sitting at a table, you can put a lot of life into your roleplaying. When playing a Dalek, you obviously do your best DALEK VOICE OF BARELY SUPPRESSED HATRED INSIDE A TIN CAN, but you should also shake back and forth slightly. Don't move your arms at all. (Putting illuminated jam-jars on the side of your head is beyond the call of duty). For a Cyberman, speak in a monotone, and don't forget the classic Cyberleader fist-clench of triumph whenever anything goes well for you. For an Ood, speak politely and hold out your hand (maybe use an apple or a tennis ball as a translator-device prop).

In *The Web Planet*, all the different creatures had their own demeanours.

- **Zarbi:** Don't speak. Put your hands by your sides and lean forward, waving your head at the players.
- **Menoptra:** Speak in a high-pitched voice and use complex sentences. Wave your hands in front of your face when talking.

- **Optra:** Speak in grunts and use simple sentences. Hunch your shoulders and bow subserviently.
- **Animus:** Speak softly and persuasively. Stand over the players.

Finally, *rules* are the game mechanics that apply to the alien. Revealing the alien's traits in play can be a great way to make the players visualise the alien. For example, if a Zarbi misses an attack roll, then don't just say "ok, the insect monster tries to bite you and misses", say something like "the insect monster darts forward to bite you, but trips over a rock and just misses you! Ha, it would have succeeded, the Clumsy trait brought it down to a Bad Failure". There's a surprisingly big difference between describing an alien as tough, and saying that it's got the Tough trait.

CREATURES OF VORTIS

The Doctor speculated that the thin air of Vortis resulted in insects becoming the dominant species. Certainly, all the creatures encountered on that world were similar to Earth insects. The evil of the Animus warped the surface of Vortis. It diverted water underground and in its place created streams of acid to feed the living structure of the Carcinome. Its enslavement of the Zarbi played havoc with the ecosystem, causing the plants to wither and blacken, and it ensnared moons, changing the tides and altering the weather. The Vortis visited by the travellers was a much more unpleasant place than Vortis after the defeat of the Animus.

LIVING CELL DESTRUCTOR (MINOR GADGET)

This 'Isop-tope' weapon was created to destroy the Animus. Its functioning is known only to the Menoptra, but it likely turns the Animus' magnetic powers against the monster, draining the Animus' life force into the planet's magnetic field. The weapon is easy to use – assuming the character can get past the Animus' bewildering powers.

Traits: Delete, Restriction (only works on the dark side of the Animus)
Cost: 1 Story Point

MENOPTRA

The winged Menoptra are a wise and kindly species. They are human in size, with black-and-white bands in their thin fur. Their four wings are strong enough to lift them into the air on Vortis – in fact, the Menoptra proved capable of flying thousands of miles to reach one of the moonlets dragged to their world by the Animus. They employ the Zarbi as beasts of burden and labour. The Menoptra are not warriors. They are talented scientists, and are even capable of developing powerful weapons for specific purposes like the Living Cell Destructor. They can also adapt their tools like the electron guns to use as weapons. However, when faced with physical danger, they are not especially competent. The Menoptra are a meritocracy, assigning duties to the most competent and suitable members of their society. They worship the Gods of Light, and solar images and illumination are important symbols in their culture.

AWARENESS	3	PRESENCE	2
COORDINATION	3	RESOLVE	2
INGENUITY	3	STRENGTH	3

SKILLS
Athletics 2, Convince 2, Fighting 1, Marksman 2, Science 3, Survival 2

TRAITS
Alien, Alien Appearance

Flying (Special Good): Menoptra can fly. They're not especially agile in the air, but can cover long distances quickly. They fly with Speed 5.

Slow Reflexes (Minor Bad): Menoptra are not especially good at fighting, and suffer a -2 penalty to any attack rolls in combat.

WEAPONS: Electron Gun (4/L/L) and (S/S/S). The Electron Gun does not work on Zarbi.

STORY POINTS: 1-3

OPTRA

The subterranean Optra are relatives of the Menoptra. Unlike their surface cousins, the Optra are a primitive culture who tell tales of the mythical surface. They do not have wings, but this may be a result of their poor living conditions, as Vrestin suggested that the descendants of the Optra might be able to fly.

AWARENESS	3	PRESENCE	2
COORDINATION	2	RESOLVE	3
INGENUITY	2	STRENGTH	4

SKILLS
Athletics 3, Convince 1, Fighting 3, Survival 3

TRAITS
Alien, Alien Appearance

Technically Inept (Minor Bad): Optra have very little technology, and suffer a -2 penalty on any rolls to use complex machinery.

Eccentric (Major Bad): The Optra are awed by wings. Any winged character gets a +4 bonus to Convincing Optra.

WEAPONS: Club (3/**6**/9)

ZARBI

The ant-like Zarbi are creatures of little intelligence, described by the Menoptra as little more than mindless cattle. They are around eight feet long and resemble large ants with some beetle characteristics. When the Animus came to Vortis it enslaved the Zarbi and turned them into warriors as it waged a war against the other species. The Zarbi use mobile grub-like weapon-pets that they term larvae guns. The Zarbi do not have the intellect to engineer these creatures – perhaps they are in a symbiotic relationship with the Zarbi, or maybe the Animus created them.

The Zarbi are a vital part of the ecosystem of Vortis. Their larvae crawl through the soil, aerating it and preparing it for plants. The evil of the Animus interrupted this process and destabilised the Vortis ecosystem.

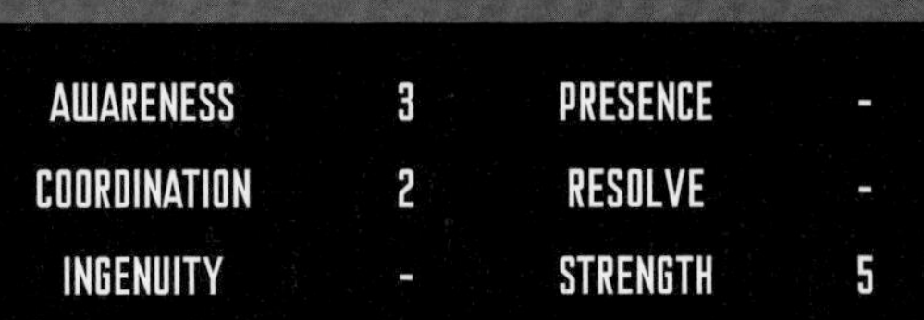

AWARENESS	3	PRESENCE	-
COORDINATION	2	RESOLVE	-
INGENUITY	-	STRENGTH	5

SKILLS
Athletics 1, Convince 1, Fighting 3, Marksman 3

TRAITS
Alien, Alien Appearance, Armour (Minor): 5

Fast Healing (Minor Good): Zarbi heal quickly.

Fear Factor 1: The Zarbi are not too terrifying when you realise that they're giant mindless ants, but they are still somewhat scary. They gain a +2 bonus when actively trying to scare someone.

Tough (Minor Good): Zarbi are resilient, reducing all damage suffered by 2.

Clumsy (Minor Bad): Zarbi are not agile, and suffer a -2 penalty on any roll involving agility.

Phobia (Major Bad): Aaagh! Spiders!

Weakness (Major Bad): Zarbi have a -4 penalty to any roll to resist psychic control, domination or persuasion.

WEAPONS: Larvae Gun (3/**6**/9) damage or Pincers (Strength +1 damage, 3/**6**/9).

STORY POINTS: 1-3

THE CARCINOME

The Animus built this fortress to protect itself using Zarbi labour. The Carcinome was constructed using partially dissolved biological material, so the Animus directed rivers of acid to dissolve the forests of Vortis in order to expand its horrible home. The Carcinome was well protected from the surface, and was easily capable of protecting the Animus from the most powerful weapons of the Menoptra. However, it was built atop the Optra tunnels, and this gave the Menoptra rebels a way in...

ANIMUS

The Animus was a massive alien intelligence that landed upon the planet Vortis. It resembled a large octopus with spider-like arachnid features and long tentacles. The Animus enslaved the Zarbi and would have taken over the entire planet of Vortis if it were not for the intervention of the First Doctor and his companions. It was destroyed by the Menoptra's secret weapon, the Living Cell Destructor.

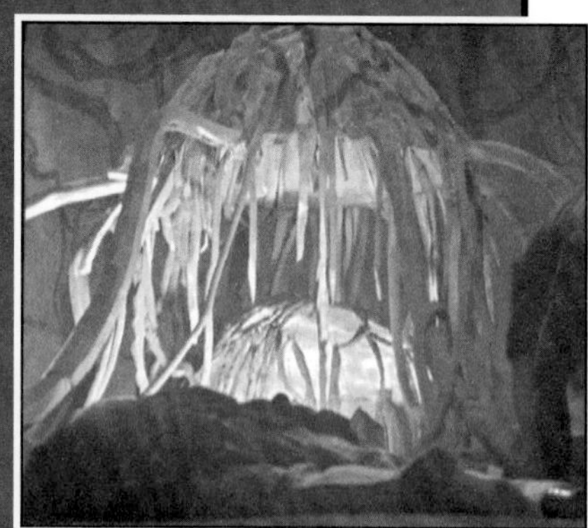

The Animus spoke with a feminine voice, and was capable of deceiving and manipulating others. It also claimed to be able to drain memories and knowledge from its victims. Its lair, the Carcinome, was located at the planet's magnetic pole, suggesting the Animus was able to draw power from the magnetic fields.

AWARENESS	5	PRESENCE	7
COORDINATION	2	RESOLVE	6
INGENUITY	7	STRENGTH	6

SKILLS

Convince 5, Fighting 4, Knowledge 5, Medicine 2, Science 3, Survival 3, Technology 5

TRAITS

Alien, Alien Appearance

Alien Senses (Minor Good): The Animus can taste minds and sense the presence of other sentient creatures.

Fast Healing (Special Good): The Animus can heal itself quickly when inside the Carcinome.

Fear Factor [3]: The Animus is a terrifying creature that can unhinge many of the minds that look upon it, send its enemies feeling in terror or force them to stand rooted on the spot. It gains +8 when trying to actively scare someone.

Hypnosis (Special Good): The Animus can take over minds that are in close proximity to gold, or wearing the metal upon their person.

Special – Intellect Drain: The Animus can absorb skills and attributes from its victims. This attack uses a contest of Ingenuity + Resolve; if the Animus wins, it does 1/**2**/3 points of damage to the victim's Ingenuity or Resolve. If a victim is reduced to 0 Ingenuity and Resolve, then the Animus may increase its Ingenuity or any skill up to the level of the victim. So, if the Ingenuity 7 Animus was able to drain the Doctor, it could increase its Ingenuity to 9.

Special - Bewildering Lights: By spending a Story Point, the Animus bewilders anyone nearby. Characters may resist this attack by rolling Awareness + Resolve against a Difficulty of 21. If they fail to resist, then they are blinded and stunned, and suffer a -3 penalty to all rolls.

Indomitable (Minor Good): +2 to resist domination in psychic contests.

Psychic (Special Good)

Telepathy (Special Good)

STORY POINTS: 4-8

ANIMUS COMMUNICATOR

The Animus uses a type of glass helmet to communicate with outsiders. This device is lowered from above whenever the Animus desires to speak with someone that it has not yet psychically controlled. In addition to enabling verbal communication, the helmet also allows the Animus to judge the strength of the mind of the person wearing the helmet.

FURTHER ADVENTURES

- **The Lost Moon:** The Animus pulled whole planetoids to Vortis with its malign powers. What else did it grab? Maybe there's a Sontaran dreadnought or a Draconian colony ship up there. What happens when the Animus stops interfering with the ship's systems?

- **Rise of the Optra:** Now that the Carcinome and the Animus are gone, the subterranean Optra can join their flying cousins on the surface. The two branches of the Optra race are now united in the light of day – what strange hybrid culture will they produce? What if the Optra decide to use their new-found wings to conquer other planets?

- **Dark Side of the Animus:** The Animus on Vortis was defeated – but there could be another Animus out there! What if an Animus landed on Earth? The Zarbi were treated like cattle by the Menoptra – maybe an Earth-bound Animus would seize control of our cattle, or our cars, or all the dogs in a city, and use them as minions in its conquest of Earth!

THE CRUSADE

"Why are we here in this foreign land if not to fight? The Devil's Horde, Saracen and Turk, possess Jerusalem and we will not wrest it from them with honeyed words."

SYNOPSIS

The TARDIS landed in 12th century Palestine, in a wood half-way between the warring camps of King Richard the Lionheart and Saladin (Salāh ad-Dīn Yūsuf ibn Ayyūb, if you want to be accurate). The travellers were attacked as soon as they arrived, and Barbara ended up captured by Saracens and dragged away to Lydda, where Saladin's army is encamped. The Saracens aimed to capture Richard, but one of the king's knights, de Preaux, deceived them by claiming to be Richard. He convinced Barbara to pretend to be Joanna, Richard's sister, in the hope of perpetuating the deception. They managed to fool their captors, but when they were brought before Saladin's brother Saphadin, he exposed them. The cruel general El Akir wished to torture them, but he was stopped by the arrival of Saladin himself. Thwarted, El Akir blamed Barbara for his humiliation in front of the court.

Meanwhile, the other travellers escorted a wounded knight, de Tornebu, back to Richard's headquarters at Jaffa. There, they convinced Richard to help them. Ian was knighted and sent to bargain for the release of de Preaux and Barbara in exchange for the hand of the real Joanna.

In Lydda, El Akir tried to kidnap Barbara. She evaded his first attempt, but he was relentless and she fell into his clutches. Ian arrived at Saladin's court and passed on Richard's offer of an alliance and a marriage, but on his return journey to Jaffa, he was waylaid by bandits and knocked unconscious.

Back in Jaffa, Lady Joanna learned of her brother's plan to marry her to Saphadin from Vicki, and the Doctor became involved in the intrigues between Richard and his sister. One of Richard's courtiers, the Earl of Leicester, suspected that the Doctor of being an agent of Saladin and turned the king against him.

Ian woke to find himself in a death trap. His captor, Ibrahim, explained that if Ian did not pay him a ransom, he would let the ants eat Ian alive. However, Ian managed to turn the tables on Ibrahim and escaped the trap. He then forced Ibrahim to help him rescue Barbara from El Akir's camp. The pair fled back to the TARDIS, rescuing Vicki and the Doctor from the Earl of Leicester en route.

RUNNING THIS ADVENTURE

The Crusade drops the travellers right into the middle of a clash of empires and forces them to use their wits to survive. Barbara's abduction drives the adventure, forcing the characters to ally themselves with the volatile King Richard to secure her safety.

HISTORICAL CHARACTERS

Richard the Lionheart. Salah al-Din. Names to conjure with!

The TARDIS, it seems, is a bit star-struck. Whenever the Doctor travels to a historical period, he seems to run into notable or famous people from that time. He pops into 19th century England and meets Charles Dickens, he travels to the 1950s and meets Agatha Christie, he travels to Ancient Egypt and runs off with Queen Nefertiti. When running any historical adventure, the first step is to look for famous names from that era. You don't need to go into detail – just look for names that everyone will recognise. Characters that exemplify the sort of adventure you want to run are ideal. If you're planning a game about monsters in the Antarctic, then think of explorers like Scott and Shackleton.

Next, take a look at a short biography of your chosen historical character. Look for dramatic conflicts, for big decisions, for interesting periods, and especially for mysterious blank spots and disappearances (Amelia Earhart must have taken a ride in the TARDIS) that you can build an adventure around. Again, don't go into detail – you want clear, simple conflicts, not complicated ones.

For example, when he returned to Europe, Richard the Lionheart was imprisoned and held for ransom by various European nobles – that's interesting, but it's a hugely complicated tangle of alliances, debts, grudges, feuds and religious conflicts that you're not going to be able to explain in a game. Instead, build an adventure around Richard's adventures in the Holy Land, or his brother John's jealousy-fuelled rebellion against him. Play historical characters as larger-than-life.

MISTAKEN IDENTITY

Having one of the travellers mistaken for someone else is a great way to drag the player characters into the plot. Barbara gets mistaken for Princess Joanna in *The Crusade* (and she was mistaken for a reincarnated goddess in *The Aztecs*), while the Doctor practically makes a career of it, especially when he gets his hands on psychic paper. The mistaken character should be given a brief description of the role they're expected to fill (*"Ah! The famous lyre player here to entertain Nero!"*), but be left in the dark about certain key facts related to the role (*"the famous lyre player... and assassin!"*)

To make mistaken identity work, the accidental imposter needs a reason not to reveal the truth. Barbara can't tell Saphadin who she really is because it would mean her death; the Doctor plays along in Rome because he wants to meet Nero. Try having a friendly NPC explain the stakes early on, then let the player bluff and their way through a web of intrigue.

Mistaken identity can be used to shake up the relationships in a group, too. In any group of players, there's usually one or two people who do most of the talking and dominate the game, and one or two quiet people who sit back and aren't as active. Have one of the quiet players be mistaken for someone important, forcing them into the spotlight, and then put the active player into a subservient role. *"Ah, Ambassador! You have arrived... and this must be your servant. Impudent wretch, carry your master's bags! Speak only when you are spoken to!"*

With the whole of space and time to explore, you can even have the characters run into the occasional physical double (the Doctor in The Massacre, for example) or genetic reincarnation (*The Massacre*, again, with Anne and Dodo Chaplet).

THE DEATH TRAP

The thief Ibrahim knocks Ian out, ties him up, covers him with honey and threatens to allow flesh-eating ants to devour him whole. How does he get out of this death trap?

That's up to Ian's player!

It's perfectly acceptable to throw player characters into inescapable, absolutely lethal killer death traps, especially at the end of a game session. Surround them with hundreds of Weeping Angels. Have the Daleks launch a swarm of time-travelling anti-TARDIS missiles at them. Send them sliding down towards a vat of acid. Maroon them at the end of the universe with a horde of slavering Futurekind just outside the door. That's all fair – as long as the players have imagination and Story Points to come up with a way to escape.

The Gamemaster should construct the trap, but the players should be the ones to find a way out. Don't succumb to the temptation to put in your own clever solutions (*'it's a chute that slides into a vat of acid, but if they use the sonic screwdriver on one of the panels, it'll dump them into the maintenance tubes instead"*), but run with the player's solutions instead (*"ok, so you're telling me the Doctor keeps a packet of anti-acid in his Resourceful Pocket – and he picked it up on Raxicorucofallapatorius, where the natives have such strong indigestion that one tablet can neutralise a whole tank of hydrofluoric acid... sure, why not!"*)

FURTHER ADVENTURES

- **Transplanting The Crusade:** You can reuse any of the Doctor's historical adventures by transplanting them to an alien planet. Saladin becomes Stong, a noble and courteous Sontaran. King Richard becomes the Rutan Rache, Whose Courage Suffuses The Host. The characters blunder into a temporary *détente* between the two warring empires, and one of the companions has to pretend to be a shapeshifted Rutan.

- **Shifting History:** In our history, King Richard proposed marrying his sister Joanna to Saladin's brother. Both refused to consent to the arrangement – but what if, through the meddling of time travellers, they made the opposite decision. The Third Crusade ends with a peaceful agreement between the two sides. The shared city of Jerusalem becomes the centre of trade and communication, and Islamic science jump-starts the Renaissance three hundred years early. Imagine spaceships lifting off from Palestine in the 1800s, or the starship *Cour de Lion* leaping out towards the stars in the 1950s... and what happens when this timeline starts to intrude upon the 'correct' timeline?

- **We're in this history book!** The Earl of Leicester sees the TARDIS dematerialise, but he and his companions decide never to tell anyone about the impossible events in case they are accused of being madmen – but what if they changed their minds? The travellers might find a strange account in a history book describing visiting strangers who travelled in a magical blue box. The plot hook that starts the player characters on an adventure could be a description of that adventure as a historical event...

HISTORICAL FIGURE BINGO!

Optional Rule: The first player character to meet a particular famous historical personage gets a free Story Point. So, if you're the first player in the group to meet Winston Churchill, or Martha Washington, or Sun Tzu, get a Story Point. Only one Story Point per adventure, please, to avoid players 'charging up' by gatecrashing the signing of the Declaration of Independence or something.

THE SPACE MUSEUM

"What we are doing now is taking a glimpse into the future, or what might be or could be the future. All that leads up to it, is still yet to come."

SYNOPSIS

A series of unusual events beset the TARDIS travellers after landing. They found they were wearing their normal clothing, instead of the twelfth-century costumes they picked up in Palestine. Small events spontaneously rewound – Vicki dropped a glass, only to have the shattered remains leap up and put themselves back together. Eager to find answers, the travellers left the ship and found themselves in a vast museum. Many of the exhibits were formerly living creatures, preserved in suspended animation – they even found a Dalek in one display case.

They encountered a pair of workers, who strangely ignore them. Investigating, they discovered that that they could not touch any of the exhibits, and the Doctor speculates that they jumped a time track on landing. They find another pair of display cases – one containing the TARDIS, and the other containing the preserved bodies of the travellers! Their future selves wore the same clothes as the travellers, suggesting they were only a short time into the future.

The two time tracks recombined, bringing the travellers back into synchronisation with the reality of the space museum. Their future selves vanished, but they knew that grim fate awaited them. Ian, Barbara and Vicki set off to find a way out.

The Space Museum was established by a spacefaring race of near-humans called the Moroks. They conquered a vast empire, and built this museum to commemorate their glorious victories. The museum was built on the world of Xeros, the home of the Xerons. The Moroks conquered them and nearly destroyed them, but a few rebels still hoped to overthrow the Morok occupiers. These rebels followed Ian and the two women, hoping to capture them before the Morok guards, under the command of curator Lobos, found them.

The Doctor, meanwhile, was captured by Lobos and interrogated. Irritated by the presence of intruders, he opted to flood the museum with paralytic Zaphra gas. His guards also found the TARDIS and tried to cut their way inside. Ian interrupted them, but was captured. Vicki and Barbara fled, and ended up separated.

Vicki was captured by the rebels, who explained the situation to her. While the rebels had the weight of numbers on their side, they were significantly outgunned by the Morok guards. Vicki agreed to help, and hacked into the computer system controlling the armoury door. The Xeron rebels now had the firepower to overthrow the Moroks – if they could escape the poisonous gas.

Ian overpowered his guard and demanded to be taken to the Doctor, who was imprisoned in the Preparation Room. Lobos had already frozen the Doctor in suspended animation, and claimed the process was irreversible, but he reckoned without Gallifreyan physiology. The Doctor survived the revivification.

Vicki and her revolutionary allies found Barbara, and stormed the Preparation Room. However, a Morok counter-attack drove the Xerons back, and left all four travellers trapped together. Ian destroyed the freezing equipment, but realised that the Moroks probably had similar machines elsewhere. Barbara speculated morosely that all their choices in the space museum had only conspired to bring them to the destiny they had glimpsed earlier, but Vicki insisted that their actions must have changed time. Their fates depended on the success of the Xeron revolution.

Outside, the Xerons rallied. Curator Lobos decided to kill the alien intruders before fleeing, and that delay resulted in him being caught and executed by the rebels. The Moroks were defeated, and Xeros freed from their control!

Afterwards, the rebels demolished the space museum, keeping only those exhibits that belonged to Xeros or which might prove useful. As a gift, they presented the travellers with a rare piece of technology, a time-space visualiser.

RUNNING THIS ADVENTURE

The Space Museum shows how a small twist can turn an otherwise standard adventure into something memorable. Take away the initial time jump, and you've got a predictable assortment of plot elements – oppressed natives, fascist conquerors, rebels. It is the glimpse of a terrible future that might be an inevitable fate that makes it memorable. The characters have a very personal stake in changing time.

JUMPING TIME TRACKS

Time tracks are discussed in detail in *The Time Traveller's Companion* (page 62). They offer a whole host of interesting options to the Gamemaster – the characters could glimpse their future as the travellers did in the Space Museum, or hop into an alternate reality where their lives took very different courses. Use Time Tracks to illuminate choices (*"What would have happened if you never went with the Doctor?"*) or add temporal spice to adventures (*"Look! It's our future selves, and we're dead! What horrible events led up to this?"*).

By the way, it's not always obvious when you jump a time track. You can run some wonderfully spooky and disturbing scenes before the players work out that they're temporally mixed up.

THE SPACE MUSEUM

In the far future, the mighty Morok Empire expands out across the cosmos. They conquer many worlds and many races, and cut a bloody and fearsome swathe across the stars. Then, like so many other conquerors, they run out of steam. Their empire turns inwards, grows lazy and corrupt, and starts to rot from within. They build the Space Museum as a monument to former glory. Certainly, Curator Lobos and his guards are not fearsome, driven conquerors – they are bored and cynical.

The museum is a vast, labyrinthine complex of corridors and galleries, crammed with all manner of exhibits. There are intact starships, captured specimens, displays of weapons and equipment, dioramas showing the victories of the Moroks over lesser species. Living exhibits are kept in suspended animation; other items are kept in secure display cases.

Navigating the Museum

Beware the Moroks! They oppress peaceful races, they exterminate and enslave, they commit atrocities and genocide, and their museums are poorly signposted. They do not even have a little gift shop, which in the Doctor's eyes cements them in the pantheon of truly despicable races. Getting around the museum requires an Ingenuity + Knowledge test (Difficulty 15).

There are lots of secret passages and access tunnels in the museum, used for moving exhibits between galleries. The security systems in the Morok museum, such as the door for the armoury, use a high-tech voice recognition system. The door asks questions and scans the person who answers them with a lie detector. If they're lying, the door doesn't open. A character can fool the lie detector with a successful Resolve + Subterfuge roll (Difficulty 27) – or, if you're Vicki, just rewire the whole system with an Ingenuity + Technology roll (Difficulty 24) and a few Story Points.

The default questions are: *What is your rank? What is your name? Do you have the Governor's permission to approach? Have you a requisition signed by the Governor? What is its reference number? Which unit are you attached to? For what purpose are the arms needed? Has the guard on duty examined your identification papers? COMPUTER: What is the current password?*

Suspended Animation

Living exhibits in the museum are stored in suspended animation. This procedure slows biological processes down almost to the point of stasis. The exhibits are still alive and aware, but are unable to move and do not age. The process can theoretically be reversed, but it is not commonly done (it requires an Ingenuity + Medicine test at Difficulty 24; failure can injure or even kill the exhibit).

Stealing from the Museum

Put a player character in a giant museum crammed with alien gadgets and weapons, and of course they're going to look for useful items. Player characters can keep any new gadgets if they pay for them with Story Points – otherwise, the items get left behind at the end of the adventure. Working out how to use an unfamiliar gadget means an Ingenuity + Technology roll, at a Difficulty that depends on the complexity of the item.

If you're stuck for inspiration, roll two dice (one for tens, one for units) on the Random Museum Display contents table below.

MOROKS AND XERONS

Both the Moroks and Xerons are descended from Earth-human stock. Far in the future, the human race spreads to millions of worlds as Great and

ROLL	EXHIBIT	ROLL	EXHIBIT
1-1	Morok blaster	4-1	Mysterious egg
1-2	Clockwork box	4-2	Draconian ceremonial helmet
1-3	Travel disc	4-3	Preserved Sycorax specimen
1-4	Telepathic jukebox	4-4	Sontaran battle armour (Armour 5)
1-5	Sensorite chemistry lab	4-5	Judoon backscratcher
1-6	Nitro-nine canister	4-6	Living metal
2-1	Crown jewels of Traken	5-1	Dalek travel machine
2-2	Preserved Ice Warrior specimen	5-2	Space whale harpoon
2-3	Gold-plated crossbow bolt & crossbow	5-3	Jewelled chalice
2-4	Jetboots	5-4	Antique spacesuit from the Lunar Campaign
2-5	Solid light	5-5	Space Patrol Interceptor space-fighter
2-6	Four-dimensional Rubik's Cube	5-6	Skulls of the Royal Dynasty of Kullev
3-1	Raston Warrior Robot machine brain	6-1	Blasted rubble from the ruins of Exillon
3-2	Morok Assault Rocketship	6-2	Hammer from Asgard
3-3	Copy of the Mona Lisa	6-3	Sacred cheese
3-4	Hologram of the Battle of Ceres	6-4	Dimensional inverter
3-5	Toe from the Giant Gold Statue of Emperor Klerg	6-5	Time-space Visualiser
3-6	Hypermartini – shaken, not stirred	6-6	Statue of a winged humanoid

Bountiful Empires rise and fall, and several successive diasporas send the children of Earth to the furthest stars.

The warlike Moroks forged a bloody empire, but by the time of *The Space Museum* they are mostly degenerate and soft. Their empire is in decline and has little interest in the past, so the museum has few visitors. The guards are poorly trained, and everyone from Governor Lobos on down just marks off the days until they can return home. Morok characters usually have the *By The Book* or *Selfish* traits.

The Xerons are one of the races conquered by the Moroks. The Xerons were a peaceful people, and were taken by surprise by the furious Morok assault. Now, the Xerons are a slave race; when they reach adulthood, they are shipped offworld to work on other Morok colonies. The Xeron survivors outnumber the Moroks, but the Moroks have the edge with firepower.

GOVERNOR LOBOS

I've got two more mimmians before I can go home. Yes, I say it often enough, but it's still two thousand Xeron days and it sounds more in days. Yeah, I know, I volunteered, you were ordered. If the truth were known, I was just as bored on Morok. Still it was home, and youth never appreciates what it has.

Technically, his title is 'Governor of Xeros', but as the Space Museum is the only thing of interest on the whole planet, he is really the curator of the museum above all else. He considers himself to be a cultured and intelligent man, a scientist. To him, the rebellious Xerons are a minor problem that can be solved with the right application of force. The mysterious alien invaders are a much more interesting proposition – they are both an intellectual challenge and a prospective set of new exhibits.

Unlike the rest of the Moroks, Lobos is uncomfortably aware that his civilization is in decline. The other Moroks can distract themselves, but he is surrounded by unavoidable reminders of better days. Lobos is an arrogant monster. When he met the Doctor, he was frustrated by his inability to break the Doctor's mind with his probe, and although he found the other man's conversation fascinating, he was still willing to condemn the Doctor to a living death as an exhibit.

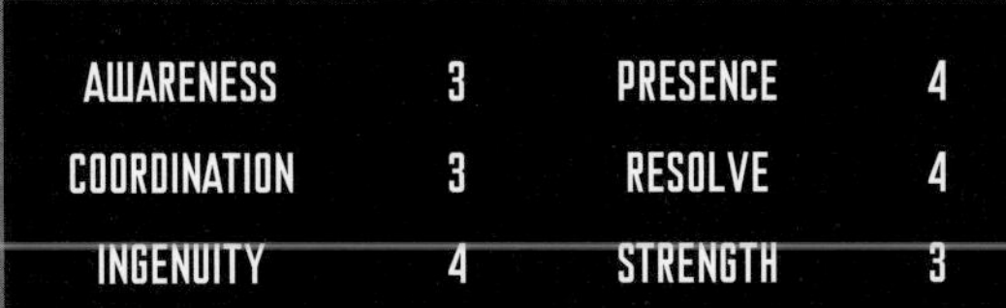

AWARENESS	3	PRESENCE	4
COORDINATION	3	RESOLVE	4
INGENUITY	4	STRENGTH	3

SKILLS

Convince 3, Fighting 2, Knowledge 5, Marksman 2, Medicine 4, Science 4, Survival 2, Technology 3, Transport 4

TRAITS

Psychic Training (Minor Good): Gets +2 to Resolve rolls to resist Psychic trickery

Technically Adept (Minor Good): Gets +2 to Technology rolls to repair or use gadgets

Adversary (Major Bad): All the Xerons.

Eccentric (Minor Bad): The governor is quirky, to say the least.

TECH LEVEL: 6

STORY POINTS: 5

TECHNOLOGY OF THE MOROK EMPIRE

Morok Weapon: These blasters are the standard sidearm of the Morok empire. They inflict 4/L/L with optional Stun setting (S/S/S)

Thought Selector (Major Gadget)
Traits: Scan, Restriction (Mental Images only)
Cost: 1 Story Point

The thought selector device is used for interrogating prisoners or examining exhibits. Anyone sitting in the chair in Lobos' office is scanned by the device. When asked a question, the thought selector plucks the most relevant image from the victim's brain and displays it on a screen. A cunning mind like the Doctor's can fool the device by making an Ingenuity + Resolve roll (plus traits like Indomitable) against a Difficulty of 24.

Time-Space Visualiser (Major Gadget)
Traits: Scan, Vortex (Special), Restriction (Images and Sound only)
Cost: 8 Story Points

The Time-Space Visualiser, as any first-year student of Advanced Transtemporal Particle Physics can tell you, works by converting light neutrons into electrical impulses, and obviously allows you to view any past event in space-time. Tuning the visualiser to the right event is nearly as tricky as flying a TARDIS, but if you get it right, it's like having the past come to life on your television screen. Watch the Gettysburg Address, see the Beatles playing live, or hear the sound of the Big Bang in 5.1 surround sound. (It sounds oddly like a balloon popping.)

Operating the visualiser requires an Ingenuity + Technology roll, the Difficulty of which varies wildly depending on how far away in time and space the event took place. Not every event can be viewed – the Time Vortex can churn up those light neutrons, and it's possible to cloak a location against Visualisation. Still, it's a very useful gadget – especially if you've also got a time machine! You just zip forward to the far far far future, and you've now got a lot more past to look at. No wonder the Doctor was so happy to find one in the Space Museum.

FURTHER ADVENTURES

- **Night in the Museum:** With a *vworp vworp vworp*, the characters arrive in the Space Museum. Another new arrival is a Morok raiding party, who just conquered a harmless world three star systems over. They brought back a trophy – a Temporal Agitator – and they just accidentally turned it on.

  Temporal Agitators interact very badly with suspended animation. Suddenly, every living exhibit in the museum is free to move. Every frozen Slitheen, every giant spider, every Rutan assassin... every Dalek. Good luck.

- **Vengeance of the Morok Empire:** The Morok Empire was in decline – until they got their noses collectively bloodied by the Xeron revolt. This galvanises the Moroks. They're angry. It's time to rebuild the empire, restore the glory of the Moroks, and make the galaxy fear them again. The characters arrive in the teeth of the Morok reconquest of Xeros. If they can stop the Moroks from retaking Xeros, they can prevent them from revitalising their dying empire. The fate of a thousand worlds depends on the actions of a few heroes.

- **The Garage Sale at the End of the Universe:** VICKI: But, Tor, surely it doesn't all have to be destroyed. Can't you use any of it?
  TOR: Oh, we only want on Xeros what belongs to Xeros, Vicki. The rest will be broken up.

  So, all the contents of the Space Museum are getting dumped? Lots of people will be interested in that garbage pile. The museum was crammed with rare gadgets, starships, weapons, relics and other wonderful shiny things. The Xerons may have some unexpected visitors very soon...

CHAPTER SEVEN:

THE CHASE, THE TIME MEDDLER, GALAXY FOUR

THE CHASE

"We will embark in our time machine at once. The Dalek Supreme has ordered they are to be pursued through all eternity. Pursued and exterminated!"

SYNOPSIS

After leaving Xenos, the travellers experimented with the Time-Space Visualiser, using it to view famous historical events. Barbara, for example, saw Shakespeare meeting Queen Elizabeth. When the TARDIS landed on a desert planet, Ian and Vicki went exploring while the other two remained with the TARDIS.

Via Time-Space Visualiser, Barbara and the Doctor discovered that the Daleks had built a time machine to pursue the TARDIS. The Daleks wanted to exterminate the Doctor to prevent future meddling in their schemes of conquest. The pursuing time machine was already on its way.

Outside, Ian and Vicki found a network of tunnels under the desert. There, they learned that this planet, Aridius, was once covered in oceans, but dried out over many years, leaving only the Aridians and the ghastly Mire Beasts. The war between the Aridians and the beasts delayed the travellers' escape, giving the Daleks time to locate and surround the TARDIS. The travellers took shelter with the Aridians.

The Daleks begin to exterminate Aridians, and claimed that if the Aridians did not hand over the Doctor, they would continue to execute innocents. Ian managed to drop one of the Daleks into a pit, giving the travellers a chance to sprint into the TARDIS and escape.

The TARDIS fled with the Daleks in pursuit. The Doctor tries to evade them, materialising first in New York in 1966, then on the *Mary Celeste* in 1872, but the Daleks continued to close in on them. Next, he landed in what appeared to be a stereotypical haunted house, complete with Frankenstein's Monster. The Doctor speculated that the TARDIS has somehow escaped into the world of dreams, but he was wrong – he'd landed in an amusement park in Ghana in 1996, and the monsters were androids. Still, the machines were tough enough to delay the Daleks and gave the travellers time to travel onwards – with the exception of Vicki. She was separated from the others in the haunted house, and managed to stow away in the Dalek time machine.

As soon as they realised that Vicki was gone, the travellers tried to think of a way to rescue her, but with the Daleks in hot pursuit and the TARDIS' navigation systems still malfunctioning after they jumped a time track on Xenos, it was going to be difficult. The Doctor, however, suspected that it might be possible to create a bomb to destroy the Dalek time machine. The chase led to the world of Mechanus. En route, the Daleks prepared to deploy their reproducer, a machine designed to create an android copy of the Doctor to infiltrate and confuse the travellers.

Mechanus was intended to be a human colony world. Long ago, they sent robots to the swampy wilderness to prepare the planet, but an interstellar war delayed the colonisation effort, and the robots were now out of control. They battled to protect their empty city from the horrible fungoid monsters of the swamp.

The TARDIS landed in the swamp, followed shortly by the Dalek time machine. Both sides fanned out to explore the planet, and Vicki is eventually reunited with her companions. The robot duplicate Doctor also found the travellers and tried to set them against each other, but it slipped up when it called Vicki 'Susan'. With their robot defeated, the Daleks moved in to exterminate the travellers, but the attack was interrupted by the Mechanoids.

In the Mechanoid city, the travellers were imprisoned in a cell with Steven Taylor, an astronaut who became stranded on the planet. The Mechanoids recognised him as human, but not as a colonist, so they locked him away in a tower. The travellers discussed plans for escape – plans that they had to implement immediately, as the Daleks attacked the city. The Mechanoids were nearly a match for the Daleks, so the travellers were able to escape in the chaos.

Fleeing through the swamp, they came upon the Dalek time machine. Barbara and Ian proposed taking the Dalek machine back to Earth. The Doctor was initially hesitant, but Vicki convinced him to try. Barbara and Ian successfully piloted the Dalek machine back to Earth, landing in 1965, only two years after they left back in *An Unearthly Child.*

RUNNING THIS ADVENTURE

The Chase has a fantastic (and rarely used) premise for a *Doctor Who: Adventures in Time and Space* adventure – the Bad Guys come after the Doctor with their own time machine. (Variations on this premise include: the Bad Guys kidnap the Doctor or drive him off course; the Bad Guys have a spy or possessed victim on board the TARDIS.) Normally, the Gamemaster has to hook the players into investigating whatever weird planet they've landed on this week – here, the plot comes to them, and it's *angry.*

If you do use this plot, though, remember to have a clear end. In *The Chase*, the Doctor is chased by a single Dalek time machine, and once that time machine is dealt with, the threat is over. If *every* Dalek had a time machine and they all started chasing the Doctor, then your game would change into *Doctor Who: Time Fugitives* (although that does sound like an awesome premise for a game).

Even though the Doctor runs from the Daleks, he's not running blindly. He tries to throw off his pursuers by random hops through the Vortex, and when that doesn't work, he moves towards a confrontation with the Daleks. By design or chance, he picks a world that really impedes the Daleks.

Mechanus is a Dalek nightmare. The swamp makes it hard for them to move, the thick jungle blocks their ranged exterminator weapons, the Fungoids are dangerous even to the Daleks, and the Mechanoids are strong enough to take on a Dalek and programmed to protect humans.

NEW GADGET
TARDIS MAGNET (MINOR GADGET)

The TARDIS magnet is a simple gadget that pulls in the direction of the nearest TARDIS. It can also be used as a signalling device to attract the attention of time capsules in flight through the vortex, making it the Time Lord equivalent of a distress flare.

Traits: Transmit, Sense of Direction, Restriction: Works on Temporal Vehicles only.
Cost: 1 Story Point

ARIDIUS

Eons ago, Aridius was an Earth-like world, but a stellar cataclysm caused its orbit to diminish. The twin suns came closer and the world grew hotter and hotter. The seas began to boil away, leaving a desert landscape of dry sea beds. The native civilisation, the Aridians, moved underground to escape the heat. They built a network of underwater cities supported with hydroponic farms to survive.

All native life-forms perished with only a few exceptions. The creatures preserved by the Aridians lived with them in their cities, but one species survived on the parched surface. These creatures were known as Mire Beasts, and once dwelled on the ocean floor. Now they are desperate, starving predators that break into the Aridian cities in search of food.

ARIDIANS

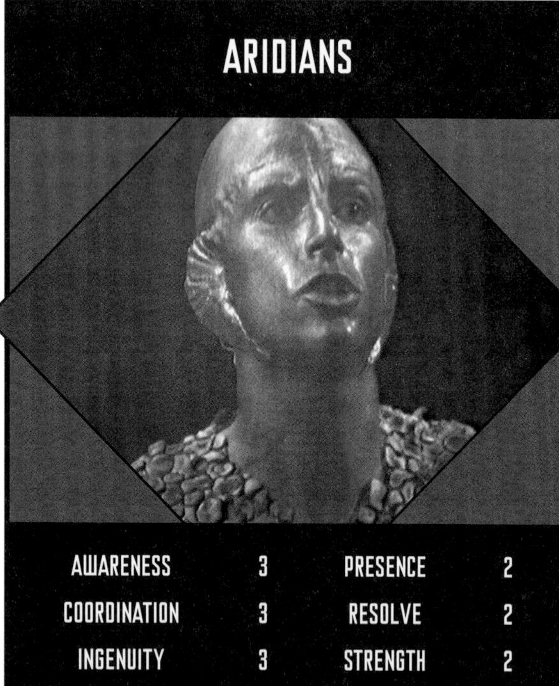

AWARENESS	3	PRESENCE	2
COORDINATION	3	RESOLVE	2
INGENUITY	3	STRENGTH	2

Aridians are a humanoid species with silvery skin and elaborate head-crests like fish fins. Their civilisation was in decline under the twin pressures of the suns and the Mire Beasts even before the Daleks arrived to hunt the Doctor. Aridians have a moderately high level of technology – their cities were built at Technology Level 5 – but lack effective weapons to use on the Mire Beasts. Instead, they sacrifice parts of their cities to the monsters. They let the rampaging Mire Beasts in, then seal the airlocks and detonate explosive charges, collapsing that section onto the monsters.

The Aridians are governed by a circle of Elders. Their diminishing resources and declining civilisation means that the Elders tend to be cautious and fearful.

SKILLS

Convince 1, Craft 2, Fighting 1, Knowledge 3, Science 2, Technology 2

TRAITS

Alien, Alien Appearance
Environmental (Minor Good): Aridians are amphibious.
Unadventurous (Minor Bad): A lifetime in the decaying cities of a dead planet tends to make one a bit dull.

MIRE BEASTS

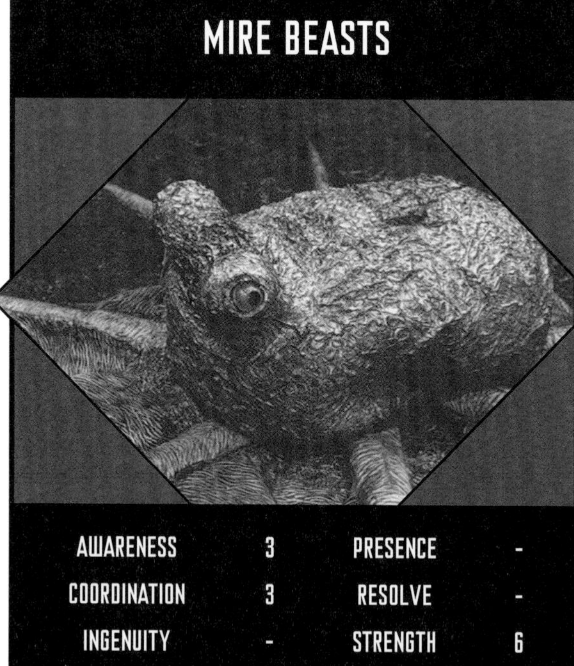

AWARENESS	3	PRESENCE	-
COORDINATION	3	RESOLVE	-
INGENUITY	-	STRENGTH	6

The fearsome Mire Beasts resemble octopi – if an octopus could bite your head clean off. Strong enough to smash through a solid wall, and big enough to eat an Aridian whole, the Mire Beasts are extremely dangerous animals. They have tough, leathery hides and long sinuous tentacles that they use to grab their victims. Entangled victims are strangled and crushed before being devoured.

Mire Beasts are horribly hungry all the time, so they can be distracted with food. Unfortunately, their preferred food is human flesh...

SKILLS

Fighting 3, Subterfuge 2

TRAITS

Armour (Minor): The tough hide of the Mire Beast stops the first five points of damage from any attack.
Natural Weapon: Mire Beasts have several long tentacles that can wrap around prey and squeeze for Strength (3/**6**/9) damage. A Mire Beast can attack up to two people at once. If it hits with a tentacle, it can trap a foe. The victim can escape by pitting his Coordination + Strength against the Mire Beast's Strength + Fighting.
Obsession (Major): Find Food!

FLIGHT THROUGH ETERNITY

After escaping Aridius, the TARDIS hurls itself across space and time to throw off the Dalek pursuers. As described in *The Time Traveller's Companion*, pursuing another time machine through the Vortex costs one Story Point from your time machine. The Difficulty of the navigation roll is increased by the opponent's Ingenuity + Transport roll as they try to shake you off.

Any cross-temporal chase means materialising in random locations, reorienting yourself as fast as you can, then taking off again. This is a great opportunity for the Gamemaster to throw in unexpected encounters and brief vignettes. Use it as a clearing-house for ideas – if you've got an idea for a monster, or a story, or a location that you can't fit into a longer adventure, throw it into a madcap chase scene.

Have the characters bounce from the Planet of the Lava Men to the Battle of Agincourt to Woodstock to the asteroid impact (well, space freighter crash to be precise) that wiped out the dinosaurs, all in a single scene!

DALEK TIME MACHINE
(SPECIAL GADGET, TL9+)

The Daleks, at one point in their future, developed their own version of a TARDIS. Although it was much more primitive, lacking the refinements and semi-sentience of a true TARDIS, it was dimensionally transcendental (although limited in interior size) and capable of many of the same maneuvers as a Gallifreyan TTC (see *The Time Traveller's Companion* page 78).

The Daleks abandoned the use of the time machine after unsuccessfully trying to pursue and capture the Doctor in a chase across space-time. After their failure, they concluded that the resources and mutant-power needed to construct such a highly advanced, but weaponless, TTC were better spent simply attaching time drives to less advanced, but fully armed, battle- cruisers.

Traits: Bigger on the Inside (Special), Forcefield (Major), Scan, Transmit, Vortex
Cost: 12 Story Points

THE HAUNTED HOUSE

The TARDIS' third random stop – after New York and the mid-Atlantic – was Ghana in some alternate 1996 where animatronic robots depicting classic horror-movie monsters menaced the travellers. Interestingly, the Doctor immediately assumed they had landed within the human collective unconsciousness, suggesting that on some previous voyage, the TARDIS somehow travelled into the human mind.

The androids proved surprisingly strong and tough, able to resist Dalek weapons and knock the travel machines through walls. Androids of this sort use the statistics for Roboforms, but are limited by their programming – they cannot think for themselves, but instead follow a script. Each robot has a few built-in instructions to help them 'play the role', so the Dracula-bot knows to snarl at people's necks and bare its fangs. Even if some sinister force reprogrammed these robots, they would still behave like the monsters they depict.

MECHANUS

The swampy world of Mechanus was intended to be a human colony, but an interstellar war delayed the process. The planet's atmosphere is like that of Earth, but most of the terrain is an unwelcoming swamp inhabited by dangerous creatures like fungoids.

FUNGOIDS

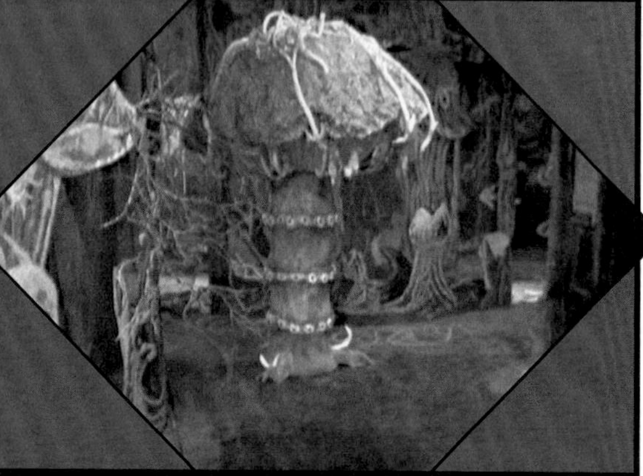

AWARENESS	2	PRESENCE	-
COORDINATION	2	RESOLVE	-
INGENUITY	-	STRENGTH	4

These carnivorous fungal monsters swarm in the swamps of Mechanus. They look like a cross between a huge mushroom and a jellyfish, and waddle around on pliable banded stalks. They can easily blend into the surrounding jungle, giving them camouflage. They attack by engulfing their prey and dissolving it with acid.

Fungoids fear bright light. The Mechanoids built safe paths through the jungle that were illuminated with harsh artificial lighting to repel the creatures.

SKILLS

Fighting 1, Subterfuge 3, Survival 1

TRAITS

Alien

Fear Factor [1]: Being ambushed by a Fungoid is terrifying.

Natural Weapons: If a Fungoid successfully hits, it engulfs its target. This does no damage initially, but inflicts 4 damage per Action Round thereafter.

Fast Healing (Special): Fungoids regain 1 lost Attribute point every round.

Camouflage (Special): Fungoids get a +6 bonus to Subterfuge rolls when hiding in the swamp.

Weakness (Major): Fungoids cannot tolerate light. Any bright light repels them.

FUNGOID HERDING ROD (MINOR GADGET)

An example of Mechanoid adaptability, this handy rod projects a beam of light at exactly the right frequency to scare Fungoids. A character with this gadget can 'herd' Fungoids, driving them towards a particular location or terrifying them so much that they squelch away and never return. The intensity of the beam can be increased, so that it inflicts 4/**L**/L damage on Fungoids.

Traits: Transmit, Restriction: Light only, Special: Harm Fungoids

FURTHER ADVENTURES

- **The Dalek Time Machine:** The Doctor instructed Barbara and Ian to activate the Dalek time machine's self-destruct system after they landed, and that's exactly what they did. There was a violent explosion from within the shed, but they were disturbed before they could double-check. Maybe they only damaged the machine, or perhaps the Dalek version of a Hostile Action Displacement System saved it from destruction. There could be another functional time machine lying empty somewhere near London...

- **Infiltrate & Kill:** Speaking of abandoned Dalek technology – that duplicate of the Doctor was only disabled, not destroyed, and it was left behind on a planet full of bored robots who are very good at fixing things. What would a Dalek android do if its target was long gone across time and space?

- **Suns of Aridius:** So, what caused the solar catastrophe that knocked Aridius out of orbit? What terrible force can juggle whole planets like that? The dying city encountered by the travellers might not be the only colony of Aridians on the planet – maybe the characters can save the rest before they come to a grisly end in a Mire Beast's stomach.

MECHANOIDS

The Mechanoids were robots that were built by humans to help them colonise distant worlds. They are multi-faceted large silver spheres that move around on hovering plates, and have a variety of tools at their disposal including weapons for defence. A retractable sensor tower extends from the top of the sphere. Mechanoids are programmed to extract resources, construct more of themselves, and then build cities and other useful structures.

As a security precaution, Mechanoids have an authorisation code. Any visitors to the planet who have the correct code can command the robots; other human (or human-like) intruders are temporarily imprisoned until an authorised human arrives to deal with them. (Unfortunately, if there aren't any authorised humans on the planet, you may be waiting a long time...) Mechanoids can communicate in a mix of machine code and English.

The Doctor encountered Mechanoids upon the planet Mechanus when he was attempting to elude the Daleks as they chased him across time and space. The original human colonists had left the Mechanoids behind on Mechanus to rot, abandoning them. Over time, it is possible that the Mechanoids could expand beyond their original programming and become an independent race.

AWARENESS	2*	PRESENCE	2
COORDINATION	2	RESOLVE	4
INGENUITY	3	STRENGTH	6

SKILLS

Fighting 1, Marksman 4, Medicine 2, Science 4, Technology 4, Transport 2 (can pilot small vehicles)

TRAITS

Armour (Major): Mechanoid armour reduces damage by 5.

Boffin: Mechanoids are ideally suited for construction work and they are highly adept with materials as well as technology.

Environmental (Major): Mechanoids can operate in various hostile conditions.

Fear Factor [1]: Mechanoids are robots that look slightly scary; they gain a +2 when attempting to actively frighten someone.

Natural Weapon (Special): Mechanoids have a variety of weapon systems, but can only use one at a time. Notably, they've got:

- **Gripper Claws:** These claws inflict no damage, but prevent an enemy from moving unless it can beat the Mechanoid in a contest of Strength + Resolve.
- **Cutting Tool:** Inflicts Strength +2 damage.
- **Flame Blaster:** This ranged weapon does 2/**4**/6 damage, with a +1 bonus to damage for each previous consecutive hit. So, if you're hit by a flame blaster in three successive rounds (or three flame blasters in one round), the last one does 4/8/12 damage instead. Any 'gap' in the damage resets the bonus to 0.

Robot

Scan: The Mechanoids have a short-range scanner that can detect various life forms close to their proximity. It grants them a +2 to Awareness when trying to detect organic or robotic/cyborg life. They also gain +2 Awareness on checks against subterfuge due to their 360 degree sensor array. However, this scanner must be extended from the Mechanoid's armoured shell to be used, and the scanner is physically vulnerable – any attacks that hit the scanner ignore the Mechanoid's armour.

Technically Adept: The Mechanoids are excellent at repairs.

Clumsy: Mechanoids could not be considered graceful at any time.

STORY POINTS: 2-4

THE TIME MEDDLER

"I want to improve things."

"Improve things? Improve things, yes, that's good. Very good. Improve what, for instance?"

"Well, for instance, Harold, King Harold, I know he'd be a good king. There wouldn't be all those wars in Europe, those claims over France went on for years and years. With peace the people'd be able to better themselves. With a few hints and tips from me they'd be able to have jet airliners by 1320! Shakespeare'd be able to put Hamlet on television!"

SYNOPSIS

The Doctor and Vicki found they had a new passenger on board – the astronaut Steven Taylor. He blundered into the TARDIS while escaping the doomed Mechanoid city. He initially disbelieved the wild stories about time travel and dimensionally transcendental police boxes, but was forced to admit the truth when the TARDIS travelled back in time to materialise on the English coast in 1066.

The travellers' arrival was watched by a mysterious monk, who had recently taken up residence in a monastery near a small Saxon village. The villagers lived in fear of Viking raids, and with good reason – a Viking raiding party landed soon after the TARDIS and went out to pillage the surrounding countryside.

The Doctor became suspicious of the monastery, and investigated. He discovered that there was only one monk – the Meddling Monk, another Time Lord! All the other monks were just recordings. The Meddling Monk planned to change history with an eight-point plan involving an atomic cannon and the obliteration of the Viking fleet. With the Vikings gone, there would be no Norman invasion, no William the Conqueror, and English history would take a very different course.

1. Arrival in Northumbria
2. Position atomic cannon
3. Sight Vikings
4. Light beacon fires
5. Destroy Viking fleet
6. Norman landing
7. Battle of Hastings
8. Meet King Harold.

Incensed by this wilful meddling in history, the Doctor attempted to apprehend the Monk, but was interrupted by Viking raiders. Assuming he was one of the monks, the Vikings threw him in a cell.

Steven and Vicki followed the Doctor into the monastery to rescue him, but he had already escaped by a simple ruse. They discovered the Monk's TARDIS in the cellars, where they found more evidence of the Monk's cavalier attitude towards temporal continuity. The Monk managed to ally himself with the surviving Viking raiders, and even tricked the Vikings into carrying explosives to sink their own ships, but a Saxon counter-attack on the monastery captured the invaders.

The Monk fled into the cellars, where he found that the Doctor and companions had already departed. They had, however, left him a note, explaining that the Doctor had put an end to the Monk's meddling by sabotaging his TARDIS. In fact, the Doctor had removed the dimensional control, disconnecting the interior dimensions from the shell. The Monk was stranded in 1066!

RUNNING THIS ADVENTURE

The Time Meddler introduces a classic *Doctor Who* plot – the historical anachronism. Slamming together the interesting bits of the past with aliens and technology from the future makes for an intriguing combination. Here, we have Vikings vs Atomic Cannons! Often, just introducing some out-of-place technology or item is enough to draw the players into the mystery. If they find, say, a discarded mobile phone in Ancient Greece, or a conquistador wandering the isles in Tesco on a rainy Tuesday in 2012, then the players will keep chasing that mystery until they find out what's really going on.

THE MEDDLING MONK

The renegade known as The Monk is one of the worst types of renegade: a Time Lord with good intentions. During his Academy years, The Monk never quite understood the lessons the Time Lords had painfully learned about intervention. At the first opportunity, he stole a TARDIS and left.

VIKING RAIDERS

AWARENESS	3	PRESENCE	3
COORDINATION	3	RESOLVE	4
INGENUITY	2	STRENGTH	4

The Doctor has run into Viking raiders before in different forms, from those who attacked the Saxon village here to the servants of Fenric. Much of Norse mythology is inspired by contact with alien entities and time travellers.

SKILLS

Athletics 2, Convince (Intimidate) 1, Fighting 3, Knowledge (Navigation) 1, Survival 2, Transport (Sailing) 2

TRAITS

Tough (Minor Good): Reduce all damage taken by 2 points.
Code of Conduct (Minor Bad): Vikings have their own rituals and beliefs that constrain their actions.
Berserker (Special): Some Viking warriors are known as berserkers. They can enter a fighting rage; when raging, they gain a +2 bonus to Strength, but have trouble distinguishing friend from foe.

WEAPONS: Viking Sword (Strength +2 damage)

ARMOUR: 3-points of leather or chain mail.

TECH LEVEL: 2

STORY POINTS: 2-4

The Monk travels the universe as a self-styled Prometheus, bringing technological fire to the primitive souls of the cosmos. He has little foresight into the changes his meddling might bring and his efforts often jeopardize the stability of critical Temporal Nexus Points. His plans range from the unsubtle, such as using anti-gravity units to help build Stonehenge, to the absurdly blunt, such as the use of Atomic Bazookas to change the fate of Harold II at the Battle of Hastings.

As dangerous as his activities are to the timeline, however, the Monk is fairly easy to locate and deal with. He will use the same disguise almost anywhere he goes, that of a friar or monk from the dark ages of Earth, even in incongruous settings like Ancient Egypt. He is also prone to leaving anachronistic clues to his presence lying about his lair or around his TARDIS. So if you find a hair-dryer lying around an abandoned monastery in 13th Century Seville, you've probably stumbled onto to him and can likely find his TARDIS by following the line of the power cord right to its front door.

ATOMIC CANNON

The Monk deployed this weapon to annihilate the Viking fleet. The Atomic Cannon lobs thermonuclear shells over a distance of several miles. Just one blast from this cannon would have been enough to destroy the whole fleet, but the Monk brought a whole case of shells. When one is intent on changing history, it's always better to make sure you get the job done thoroughly, and here 'thoroughly' means 'a large chunk of Denmark'.

The Atomic Cannon is slow to aim and fire, but its blast inflicts hundreds of points of damage on anything it hits.

KING HAROLD'S LEGACY

So, what happens if the Monk succeeds in altering history? He believes that by preventing William the Conqueror from seizing England, he will disentangle the countries of England and France. There would be no squabbles over territorial claims, thus eliminating at one swoop the Hundred Years war and many other conflicts between the two. The Monk argued that this would bring about a golden age of peace and technological advancement – under his guidance, of course.

Perhaps he is right. He is a Time Lord, after all, and probably knows what he's talking about when it comes to meddling in history. If his changes go ahead, then time travellers might find themselves in a version of the 1300s that looks like the 20th century, and a 21st century that's hundreds of years in advance of where it 'should' be. The 21st century is where it all changes – it's when humanity goes to the stars. What happens if the first Great and Bountiful Empire arrives on the galactic scene centuries ahead of schedule?

The Monk's meddling might also affect human society. With more peace and prosperity, the social order might be slower to change. Perhaps feudalism survives in the Monk's strange new century, so Earth's first interstellar expedition might be commanded by a Prince and crewed by a brave order of Space Knights!

Then again, the Monk could get it all wrong. The Time Lords practice non-interference for a reason – changing history and giving technology to primitive species can both have terrible and unforeseen consequences.

Time travellers who arrive in the Monk's new Europe might find themselves in a war-torn hellhole, where barbarian warlords with atomic bazookas and machine guns roam the blasted countryside. The Monk could still try to set things right. Maybe he would become Pope, and try to sort out the warring factions with more atomic cannon blasts launched from the silos of Rome...

FURTHER ADVENTURES

- **The Sleeping Dragon:** The Doctor foiled the Monk's plan by delaying him long enough for the Viking fleet to sail past – but that Atomic Cannon is still there, hidden on the clifftop. What other uses could to be put to? Perhaps it is found in 1942, and Torchwood agents have to convince the British army not to deploy this weapon against the German army.
- **The Stones:** The Monk claimed to have helped build Stonehenge using anti-gravity technology. Stonehenge was built right on top of the Pandorica (or the Pandorica was hidden under Stonehenge). Did the Monk know about this trap for a Time Lord? And just who blew up those Cybermen guards anyway?
- **Time and Relative Dimension:** The Doctor sabotaged the Monk's TARDIS before leaving by removing the dimensional control. The Monk later fixed this component (see *The Dalek's Master Plan*, page 109), but during the intervening time, his TARDIS's internal dimensions were in flux. Time travellers passing through the Vortex could end up stuck inside an out-of-control TARDIS whose outer shell is stuck in 1066...

GALAXY FOUR

"It is easy to help others when they are so willing to help you. Though we are beings of separate planets, you from the solar system and we from another space, our ways of thought, at times, do not seem all that different. It has been an honour to know you and serve you."

SYNOPSIS

The TARDIS materialised in the middle of a conflict between two groups of spacefarers, both of whom had crashed on an unexplored world. The planet itself was unstable, and was about to undergo a complete geological collapse. If the travellers did not escape the dying world within a few days, they would perish.

On one side were the Drahvins. They were a warrior race who practiced cloning. Most of the crew were cloned soldiers, with limited intellectual capacity and initiative. The commander of the ship, a warrior named Maaga, was naturally born and considered herself to be superior to her vat-grown subordinates. Drahvin technology was limited, and their ship was heavily damaged in the crash.

The other crashed ship belonged to a race called the Rills. They were non-humanoid, and could not survive in the oxygen-rich atmosphere of the planet. Therefore, they had sealed themselves in a small section of their ship, which they pumped full of the ammonia-rich mixture of gases they needed to survive. They interacted with the outside world using remote-controlled robots that Vicki nicknamed Chumblies. These Chumblies were sent to search for a power source to refuel the Rill vessel.

The TARDIS travellers arrived and initially assumed the Chumblies were potentially hostile – an impression reinforced by the Drahvins. A Drahvin patrol disabled one of the Chumblies by throwing a metal mesh over it, which temporarily blocked its control signals. However, the Drahvins were unable to permanently damage the Chumblies, as the Rill robots were built using considerably higher technology.

At the Drahvin ship, Maaga tried to convince the travellers that the Rill were hateful and dangerous. She admitted that the Rills had warned them that the planet was about to be destroyed, but claimed that this was just a trick by the Rills to lure the Drahvins into a trap. Maaga demanded that the Doctor and his companions aid them in capturing the Rill ship, and kept Steven as a hostage to ensure their compliance. The Doctor and Vicki travelled across the wilderness, dodging Chumbley patrols, and learned how to avoid the robots' sensors. At the Rill ship, the Doctor discovered a gas pump – the Rills were producing more ammonium to sustain their life support systems. Sabotaging that pump could destroy the Rills.

Meanwhile, Steven tried to escape from the Drahvins. First, he tried to sow dissent among the soldiers by pointing out that Maaga's gun was powerful enough to destroy a Chumbley, and that her refusal to share it with the other Drahvins put them in danger. He also tried forcing his way out, but both attempts were thwarted by Maaga.

Inside the Rill ship, Vicki made contact with the aliens. They were hesitant about revealing themselves, but told her that the Drahvins had attacked them

without provocation. The surprise attack allowed the technologically inferior Drahvin ship to disable the Rill vessel. The Rills counter-attacked, causing both ships to crash. Despite this conflict, the Rill were willing to take the Drahvins off the dying planet once they found a source of power.

Vicki convinced the Doctor to help, and he agreed to transfer power from the TARDIS to the Rill vessel. In exchange, the Rills sent a Chumbley force to rescue Steven from the Drahvin ship. The Rill attempted to keep the Drahvins contained within their ship until it was time to depart, but Maaga ordered her forces to storm the Rill ship. Both the Rills and the TARDIS crew were forced to abandon the Drahvins on the dying world, victims of their own xenophobia.

RUNNING THIS ADVENTURE

Galaxy Four is a story of misdirection. The Chumblies appeared dangerous when first encountered, and then the Drahvins lied to the travellers about the intent of the Rills. If the TARDIS travellers accepted the Drahvin's story without questioning it, they would have compounded the tragedy.

In a roleplaying game, misdirection-based plots have to be handled carefully. After all, the Gamemaster is the player characters' eyes and ears. She describes everything they perceive, everything they hear and see and know. It's very easy to misdirect the players by not mentioning a particular fact, or by putting undue emphasis on some element of the plot. For example, if the Gamemaster did not describe the martial, oppressive regime of the Drahvins, they would come across as being much more sympathetic than they should be.

When running an adventure like this, then, make sure to draw a clear line between non-player characters and the Gamemaster. The Drahvin's story of their battle with the Rills, for example, should be told by one of the Drahvins instead of narrated by the Gamemaster, so the players realise that the person telling them the story may be mistaken or untrustworthy.

Give the players plenty of opportunities to ask questions and to investigate. For example, when the Doctor and Steven are on their way to the Drahvin ship, they stop to examine the hull and realise that the Drahvins are of a significantly lower technology level than their Rill enemies. If the players did not ask specifically about the Drahvin ship, the Gamemaster could still give them this clue with a successful Awareness + Technology roll.

THE DRAHVIN

The Drahvins are humanoid, and are possibly another offshoot of humanity like the Moroks (see page 86). They have a highly militarised society, and practise genetic engineering and artificial reproduction. Virtually all the Drahvin are female; a few males are kept alive for breeding purposes, but they are treated as nothing more than useful animals. Within the Drahvin military, the officers and commanders are 'naturally born', while the lower ranking cannon fodder are grown in tanks. Given Maaga's physical prowess and rampant ego, it is likely that the Drahvin have augmented their natural abilities with genetic engineering.

Lower-ranking Drahvin have numbers instead of names, and are completely subservient to their leaders. Their capacity for independent thought and action is very limited. This may be a side effect of their diet – the soldiers are fed much less appetising and nutritious food compared to their leaders.

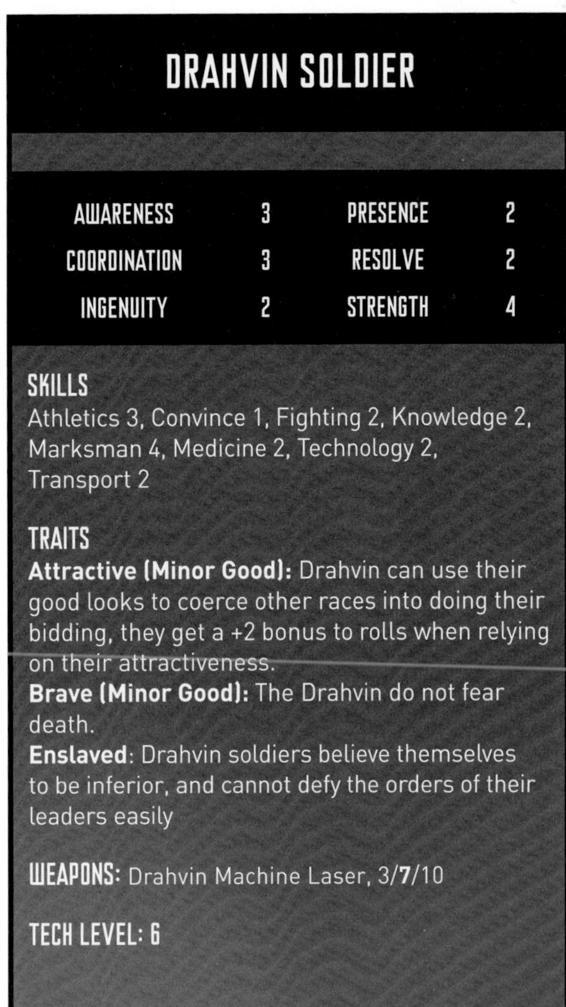

DRAHVIN SOLDIER

AWARENESS	3	PRESENCE	2
COORDINATION	3	RESOLVE	2
INGENUITY	2	STRENGTH	4

SKILLS
Athletics 3, Convince 1, Fighting 2, Knowledge 2, Marksman 4, Medicine 2, Technology 2, Transport 2

TRAITS
Attractive (Minor Good): Drahvin can use their good looks to coerce other races into doing their bidding, they get a +2 bonus to rolls when relying on their attractiveness.
Brave (Minor Good): The Drahvin do not fear death.
Enslaved: Drahvin soldiers believe themselves to be inferior, and cannot defy the orders of their leaders easily

WEAPONS: Drahvin Machine Laser, 3/**7**/10

TECH LEVEL: 6

The Drahvin homeworld, Drahva, suffered from overpopulation, so the Drahvins encountered in this adventure were part of a scouting mission looking for new inhabitable planets to conquer.

DRAHVIN LEADER

AWARENESS	3	PRESENCE	4
COORDINATION	3	RESOLVE	5
INGENUITY	4	STRENGTH	5

SKILLS

Athletics 3, Convince 4, Fighting 3, Knowledge 4, Marksman 4, Medicine 2, Science 3, Technology 4, Transport 3

TRAITS

Attractive (Minor Good): Drahvin can use their good looks to coerce other races into doing their bidding, they get a +2 bonus to rolls when relying on their attractiveness.
Brave (Minor Good): The Drahvin do not fear death.
Voice of Authority (Minor Good): Leaders get a +2 bonus when ordering lesser mortals around.
Eccentric (Minor Bad): Drahvin leaders tend to be egotistical.

WEAPONS: Drahvin Leader Sidearm, 4/**L**/L

TECH LEVEL: 6

STORY POINTS: 2-4

THE RILL

The Rills are an ancient non-humanoid species of spacefarers. They evolved from amphibians in the ammonia-rich swamps of their home world, and they still resemble a cross between a toad and a lamprey eel. Despite their horrific appearance, they are gentle and cultured. They can communicate telepathically, but they dislike establishing mental contact with other species, as the Rills live very, very slowly. Their metabolic rate is naturally very slow, so they move, think and age at a fraction of the rate of most other creatures. Their 'ChumbleyChumbley' robots are the Rills' servants and soldiers. The Chumblies are capable of being remote controlled by a computer, or can be directly operated by a Rill.

AWARENESS	2	PRESENCE	3
COORDINATION	2	RESOLVE	4
INGENUITY	4	STRENGTH	3

SKILLS

Convince 3, Knowledge 4, Medicine 2, Science 4, Technology 5, Transport 3

TRAITS

Alien
Alien Appearance (Special Bad): The Rills suffer a -4 penalty to any roll where their appearance is a factor...
Fear Factor 1: ... apart from scaring people. They've got a +2 bonus for that.
Boffin: The Rills were able to quickly modify and improve their Chumblies.
Weakness (Major): Requires Ammonia Atmosphere to live. Poisoned by Oxygen.
Psychic: The Rills communicate among themselves using telepathy.
Code of Conduct (Minor): The Rills are forgiving and self-sacrificing.
Slow Metabolism (Special): Naturally, the Rills move extremely slowly (Speed 1) and think slowly (acting last in any Action Phase). By spending a Story Point, a Rill can temporarily boost its metabolism to move and act normally.

TECH LEVEL: 7

STORY POINTS: 2-4

CHUMBLIES

The Chumblies look almost like children's toys. They consist of three metallic doughnut-shapes stacked on top of each other. They cannot see normally, but scan their surroundings through a combination of sound and infra-red vision. Chumblies have a variety of tools and weapons, like flamethrowers, machine guns and ammonia bombs, but they are not designed to be weapons – they are scientific probes used by the Rills to explore oxygen-rich planets.

AWARENESS	2	PRESENCE	1
COORDINATION	2	RESOLVE	5
INGENUITY	1	STRENGTH	6

SKILLS

Athletics 1, Marksman 3, Technology 4

TRAITS

Robot: Chumblies aren't living beings.

Alien Senses: Chumblies aren't very perceptive. A character who stays out of reach of the robot's directional microphone has a +4 bonus to Subterfuge tests to sneak around it.

Clumsy: Chumblies aren't very agile.

Networked: All Chumblies can communicate with each other and with their home base. A Chumbley cut off from the network automatically shuts down.

Armour (Major): All Chumblies have Armour 8. A damaged or confused Chumbley can withdraw into itself, shutting down but increasing its Armour to 12.

Gadget: Different Chumblies have different built-in tools or weapons.

WEAPONS: One of the following:

- Flamethrower, 3/**6**/9
- Chumbley Laser, 4/**L**/L
- Claw, Strength +2 damage
- Ammonia Gas Bomb, 2/**4**/6 to everyone nearby

TECH LEVEL: 7

FURTHER ADVENTURES

- **The Dying World:** So, what caused the nameless planet to disintegrate? Planets don't usually just fall apart. Did some cataclysmic conflict damage the planet somehow? Why were the Rills in this region of space anyway?

- **The Drahvin Invasion of Earth:** The Drahvin are a race of warriors, and Earth is within their reach. The player characters might be all that stands between our world and the Drahvin conquest. As the Drahvin look almost human (apart from three dots next to either eyebrow, which may be a rank symbol or barcode), they could infiltrate humanity in the Invasion of the Attractive Blonde Women before deploying their armies of clone warriors and heavily armed starships.

- **Lies My Chumbley Told Me:** The Rills are a perfectly lovely and trustworthy species. They're kind to a fault – how many other races would do their best to rescue the people who shot them down? Any experienced space traveller knows and trusts the Rills... but the Rills communicate mainly through their Chumblies. What happens when an unscrupulous villain gets hold of a Chumbley or two and pretends to be a Rill?

CHAPTER EIGHT:
THE MYTH MAKERS, THE DALEK'S MASTER PLAN, THE MASSACRE

THE MYTH MAKERS

"I suppose I should be grateful for standing here, trussed like a chicken, ready to have my throat cut."

"No one mentioned cutting throats. I had something more lingering in mind."

SYNOPSIS

For ten fruitless years, the Greek army had laid siege to the city of Troy, but was unable to batter down its walls. The two sides were reduced to skirmishes in the surrounding countryside, like the duel between Prince Hector of Troy and the Greek hero Achilles. In the midst of this struggle, just before Achilles delivered the killing blow to his rival, a miracle occurred. The heavens opened, and a magical temple appeared as if from nowhere. Zeus himself stepped out, disguised as an old beggar. At least, that's what Achilles thought. What he actually saw was the TARDIS arriving, and he mistook the Doctor for a god. Achilles insisted that Zeus accompany him back to the Greek camp.

Inside the TARDIS, Steven and Vicki watched through the scope as the Doctor was feasted and honoured by the assembled Greeks. Achilles was convinced that this strange visitor was Zeus, but clever Odysseus suspected the Doctor was a Trojan spy. Steven tried to sneak out of the TARDIS to make contact with the Doctor, but he too was captured by the Greeks. The Doctor arranged for Steven to be 'sacrificed' at the blue temple the next day.

During the night, a raiding party from Troy led by Prince Paris broke into the Greek camp and carried away the TARDIS – with Vicki still inside – as a prize. King Priam and his court debated what to do with it, and the prophetess Cassandra foretold that it would bring great harm to Troy. They decided to burn it.

The Doctor and Steven decided to admit the truth to Odysseus. While concepts like time travel and aliens seemed absurd to the Greek, he admitted that it was marginally more plausible than the gods manifesting in front of him. He offered to free the two time travellers – if they used their supernatural knowledge to help him conquer Troy! The Doctor agreed to this plan, while Steven dressed himself as a Greek and went out in search of a Trojan warrior to capture him – being arrested as a prisoner of war was the best way to get inside the city and find the TARDIS.

Inside the city, Vicki emerged from the TARDIS just before it was set alight. She impressed the Trojan court, although her name was too foreign and strange for them, so they named her Cressida. King Priam believed that her sudden appearance was a good omen for his besieged city. Unfortunately, Steven recognised her and called out her name, so the Trojans assumed that she was a Greek spy sent to sow confusion. Clearly, she had used some strange Greek magic to spirit herself into the city. The pair were thrown into the dungeons of Troy, and told they would be put to death unless Vicki used her sorcery to break the siege.

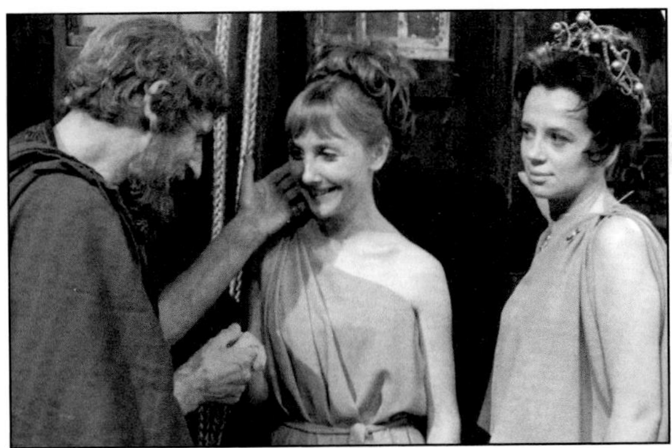

In the dungeon, they were visited first by the misshapen Cyclops, a servant of Odysseus. They warned him to stall the Doctor's plans to take city, as the Trojans would execute them if the city fell. Vicki was then visited by another prince of Troy, Troilus, who was enchanted with her beauty and exotic ways.

In the Greek camp, the Doctor proposed building flying machines propelled by catapults to fling soldiers over the walls of Troy. That plan was cancelled when Odysseus made it clear that the Doctor would be the test subject for any cunning machine. In desperation, he proposed a scheme that he assumed was originally made up by the poet Homer – why not build a giant wooden horse?

The Greeks put their plan into operation. Odysseus and a few hand-picked warriors – and the Doctor – hid inside the Wooden Horse. The rest of the Greek army sailed away. The Trojans assumed that Vicki's sorcery had somehow driven them away, and freed her from the dungeon. Cassandra tried to warn the Trojans that doom was coming for them, but no-one paid attention to her dire prophecies.

Vicki freed Steven from the cell. He argued that they should make their way to the TARDIS, as it was clear that the Greeks would soon emerge from the horse and begin the destruction of Troy. However, Vicki wanted to warn Troilus to leave the city before the slaughter. She was unable to convince him to leave, so instead she told him that Steven had escaped and that he should go in search of him.

History unfolded as Homer wrote. Odysseus and his men opened the gates, and the returning Greek army poured into the city. Outside, Troilus slew Achilles, while a Trojan warrior wounded Steven. One of Cassandra's handmaidens, Katarina, helped him get back to the TARDIS, where the Doctor had his final confrontation with Odysseus. The greedy warrior decided to claim the TARDIS as his prize, so the Doctor was forced to dematerialize immediately, leaving Vicki behind and taking the wounded Steven and the terrified Katarina with him...

RUNNING THIS ADVENTURE

Like other historical adventures such as *The Aztecs*, this adventure pushes the player characters into positions of influence and authority because of mistaken identity. The Greeks assume the Doctor is a god; the Trojans assume that Vicki is a sorceress with great magical powers. In both cases, the character is then given a task – conquer or save Troy – that pits them against the other. While conflict between player characters can be damaging to a game, here it's used to great effect because neither the Doctor nor Vicki really wants to 'win' – but they are forced to try by their captors.

The character of Odysseus is an especially interesting one. Unlike the other Greeks, he doubts the Doctor's divinity, and he uses sarcasm to make his feelings clear. Any non-player character who acts like a player character tends to win the respect of players, and you can use this quirk to great effect. For example, say that the travellers land on a moon base in the far future, and there's an ancient alien tomb under the base. All the moon base crew insist that the aliens in the tomb are long dead and harmless, other than one technician who moans that *of course* the alien zombies are going to come to life and attack. The players will almost certainly gravitate towards this technician; players like to think they can see plot twists in advance, so they'll adopt NPCs who do the same.

Odysseus is made doubly interesting by portraying him as a nasty piece of work. He is greedy, cynical, self-serving and treacherous along with being clever and brave – just like some player characters!

FAMOUS EVENTS

There are some stories that everyone knows and the Trojan Horse is certainly one of them. Putting the player characters in the midst of such a story lets you skip over a lot of scene-setting and character introductions, and leap right into the action. For example, if the characters arrive in Rome in 44BC, there's no need to explain who Julius Caesar is or who Brutus is – you can get right to the player characters being mistaken for prophets, or dealing with the Zygons in the sewers.

Everyone knows how famous events turn out, too – if the characters arrive in Rome, they know Caesar is going to be assassinated. In the case of the Trojan Horse, they know that it is full of Greek soldiers who will open the gates and doom the city. Half the fun of a historical can be letting the players be the ones who made history happen that way. They get to be the ones who suggested the Trojan Horse, they get to be the people who say "Beware the Ides of March" to Caesar. (Or, in the case of Rose Tyler, they get to be the ones who coin the phrase "We are not amused" for Queen Victoria!) Famous events can be playgrounds for the players. Have fun with them, and history will sort itself out in the end.

PRIMITIVE GADGETS

Most of the gadgets built with Jiggery-Pokery use super-science from the Far Future... or at least electronics and other bits from the present day. However, it is possible to build gadgets from primitive materials. Building a gadget that uses primitive materials to replicate a real-world device requires an Ingenuity + Craft (*not* Ingenuity + Technology) test at a Difficulty of 15 or more. For example, a catapult-launched glider or a steam-powered car can be built with TL2 technology.

Building something even more complicated is possible, but really hard – the Doctor could build a computer out of cogs and wheels, but that's going to be really, really fiddly and time-consuming. As a guideline, see the table below. Add +3 to the TN for Major Gadgets and +6 for Special Gadgets.

TARGET TECH LEVEL	DIFFICULTY TARGET NUMBER (TN)
+1	15
+2	18
+3	21
+4	24
+5	27
+6	Pretty much impossible

So, building a glider (Tech Level 3 – Da Vinci built one) with Tech Level 2 equipment is TN15, while building a Time Machine (TL8) with stuff you find in 1969 (TL5) would be TN21.

ODYSSEUS

Cunning Odysseus was one of the leaders of the Greek army. He was renowned for his cleverness, his eloquence, and his trickery. After the Trojan War, he was cursed to wander the seas for many years before he was able to return home to Ithaca. In the Doctor's experience, Odysseus was "selfish, greedy, corrupt, cheap, horrible," and his "one thought is for yourself and what you can get out of it." Despite this, Odysseus was almost a match for the Doctor when it came to guile and cunning.

AWARENESS	4	PRESENCE	4
COORDINATION	4	RESOLVE	4
INGENUITY	5	STRENGTH	4

SKILLS
Athletics 2, Convince 4, Craft 5, Fighting 3, Knowledge 4, Medicine 2, Science 3, Subterfuge 4, Survival 3, Transport 2

TRAITS
Boffin: Odysseus is clever enough to come up with new weapons of war.
Charming: when he wishes, Odysseus can turn on the (slightly oily) charm, getting a +2 bonus to Convince attempts.
Friends (Minor): Odysseus is accompanied by his Cyclops, a one-eyed slave with tremendous physical strength.
Selfish: Odysseus thinks mainly of himself.

TECH LEVEL: 2

STORY POINTS: 6

ACHILLES

Brave, hot-headed Achilles was the greatest warrior in the Greek army, and was their champion against the forces of Troy. He slew Prince Hector, and would have slain Troilus too if it were not for a stroke of misfortune – Achilles slipped, and Troilus rushed in to kill him.

AWARENESS	4	PRESENCE	5
COORDINATION	4	RESOLVE	4
INGENUITY	2	STRENGTH	5

SKILLS
Athletics 5, Convince 3, Fighting 6, Knowledge 3, Marksman 2, Survival 2

TRAITS
Brave: No enemy daunts brave Achilles!
Quick Reflexes: He acts first in any Action Phase. Let's be honest: it's going to be the Fighting Phase!
Impulsive: Stab first, questions later.

TECH LEVEL: 2

STORY POINTS: 3

TROILUS

Prince Troilus was the younger son of Priam, King of Troy. Most versions of the story of Troy claim that he died at the hand of Achilles, while medieval legend linked him romantically to a Greek princess named Cressida. In fact, Cressida was Vicki, and the two survived the fall of Troy. Vicki was quite happy to stay with Troilus instead of travelling onwards with the Doctor.

AWARENESS	3	PRESENCE	4
COORDINATION	3	RESOLVE	4
INGENUITY	3	STRENGTH	4

SKILLS
Athletics 3, Convince 3, Fighting 3, Knowledge 3, Medicine 2, Survival 2, Transport 1

TRAITS
Attractive: Troilus certainly caught Vicki's eye.
Lucky: His victory over Achilles was half bravery, but also half good luck!

TECH LEVEL: 2

STORY POINTS: 3

CASSANDRA

Troilus' sister and High Priestess of Troy, Cassandra was blessed with the gift of prophecy, but cursed so no-one would believe her warnings. All of her prophecies came true, which likely indicates some level of psychic ability. She was captured by Odysseus during the siege of Troy and given to King Agamemnon as a gift.Katarina (page 155) was one of Cassandra's handmaidens.

AWARENESS	3	PRESENCE	4
COORDINATION	2	RESOLVE	4
INGENUITY	3	STRENGTH	2

SKILLS
Convince 2, Knowledge 4, Medicine 3, Survival 1, Transport 1

TRAITS
Psychic: Cassandra's powers manifested as mystical visions and intuitions.
Precognitive
Unlucky: No-one believed her.

TECH LEVEL: 2

STORY POINTS: 3

FURTHER ADVENTURES

- **The Odyssey:** Few people got under the Doctor's skin the way Odysseus did. By the end, the Doctor *really* disliked him. Mythology tells us that Odysseus wandered for ten years, having all sorts of strange adventures on mysterious islands. It's not impossible that some later incarnation of the Doctor, a crankier one with more control over the TARDIS (the Sixth Doctor, maybe, or the Tenth in an angry mood) travelled back in time, abducted Odysseus and his crew, and either dumped them on some alien water-world or stuck a teleporter onto their ship so they wandered from planet to planet until he was tired of tormenting them. An adventure or even a whole campaign where the player characters are part of Odysseus' crew could be tremendous fun, as they run into classic alien monsters seen through a mythological lens. *EXTERMINATE* said the one-eyed Cyclops...

- **Troilus and Cressida:** Vicki comes from the 25th century. She's got certificates in medicine, physics, computing, chemistry and other sciences, and she knows enough about time travel to avoid changing history. What happened to her after she left the TARDIS? Was she content to stay in Ancient Greece, or did she and her new boyfriend hitch a lift on a passing starship after a few years? Time travelling characters might pick up Vicki as they pass by Greece in 1200 BC.

- **Cassandra's Gift:** Where did Cassandra's gift of prophecy come from? Was it a natural ability, or a sign of alien influence? Was there something lurking in the temple of Troy – and if so, what happened after the city was destroyed? Was it still there in the ruins (in which case, did the famous archaeologist Schliemann dig it up in 1868), or did Odysseus find something when he looted the temple?

THE DALEK'S MASTER PLAN

MISSION TO THE UNKNOWN

In the year 4,000, humanity's empire encompassed most of the galaxy – but there were enemies outside that galaxy who look hungrily at the growing power of the human race. Intelligence reports that these enemies intended to form an alliance brought Marc Cory of the Space Security Service to the jungle planet of Kembel. There, he discovered that the reports were correct, and that races from the Seven Galaxies intended to conquer the human Solar System.

He also discovered that the Daleks were the architects of this alliance. The Daleks had not been seen in thousands of years, but now they intended to return and reconquer Earth!

To get this message to Earth, however, Cory needed to get off the planet. He had arrived on board a small civilian rocket crewed by two other men, Jeff Garvey and Gordon Lowery. The ship had landed awkwardly, and needed repair.

While fixing the exterior of the ship, Garvey was stung by a Varga plant, a hostile mutant that originates on the planet Skaro. The Daleks cultivated the Varga as biological weapons. Those injured by Varga thorns were rapidly transformed by the plant's mutagenic poison into Varga plants themselves – so when Cory saw that Garvey was wounded, he shot him!

Lowery demanded that their strange passenger explain himself, so Cory flashed his license to kill and told Lowery that he was now deputised to the Space Security Service. The two worked together to repair the damaged rocket, even as swarms of Varga plants closed in, until a Dalek patrol located them and destroyed the ship. The two managed to escape and fled with a capsule launcher.

There was little chance for them to escape off-world now, but they could still send a message to Earth to warn them of the impending invasion. Unfortunately, Lowery was also infected by the Varga, and he slowed Cory down. Before they could find a clearing to launch the capsule, Lowery succumbed to madness and had to be killed.

Cory raced to set up the launcher, but he was too late. The Daleks followed his movements using seismic sensors – and when they found him, they exterminated him on sight. Marc Cory of the Space Security Service died in the jungle of Kembel, his message unsent.

And all around him, the forces of the Seven Galaxies gathered for an all-out assault on Earth...

RUNNING THIS ADVENTURE

As a change of pace, it's a great idea to give your players a chance to play some pre-generated characters for a single short adventure. In this case, the Gamemaster would write up Cory and the two astronauts and give them to the players to play. The lovely thing about pre-generated characters is that they're not supposed to survive the adventure, so everyone can have fun getting killed in unlikely ways. Just this once, everybody dies!

"Fellow delegates. Even as you sit here, the great war force assembled under the Daleks is awaiting the final order to set out and conquer the universe!"

"Why is Mavic Chen speaking for the Dalek Supreme?"

"Though we are all equal partners with the Daleks on this great conquest, some of us are more equal than others!"

SYNOPSIS

In the Year 4,000, the Daleks prepared to launch their plan to conquer all of humanity. They had assembled an alliance of villains from seven galaxies, all of whom had provided components for their ultimate weapon – the Time Destructor. The members of this conspiracy gathered on the planet Kembel to assemble the Destructor. Among the conspirators was Mavic Chen, the Guardian of the Solar System and leader of the human race. As far as anyone back in Central City knew, the popular and charismatic Chen was on holiday, having just completed an exhausting negotiation with the Fourth Galaxy regarding mining rights.

The TARDIS materialised on Kembel. Steven's wound – inflicted by a Trojan soldier – was infected and he needed antibiotics. Leaving the confused and terrified Katarina behind, he set off in search of help. He was watched by an agent of the Space Security Service, Bret Vyon. Vyon and his partner Gantry came to Kembel to search for the missing agent Marc Cory (see page 109). After an initial miscommunication where Vyon tried to commandeer the TARDIS, they agreed to work together to warn Earth about the Dalek presence on Kembel.

After a Dalek patrol cut the travellers off from the TARDIS, Vyon was shocked to see a Spar 740 starship near the Dalek city. It was the personal ship of Mavic Chen – if the Guardian of the Solar System was here, then this was more than a Dalek outpost. The Doctor suggested they steal the Spar and make their way back to Earth.

They spotted one of the Dalek conspirators – Zephron, Master of the Fifth Galaxy – outside the city, watching the burning jungle. Zephron wore a heavy cloak, so the travellers overcame him and used his cloak as a disguise for the Doctor.

At the meeting, the Daleks unveiled their Time Destructor. It needed one final component – a rare element called Taranium, found on only a few planets. Mavic Chen took fifty years to gather even a tiny amount from Uranus. Only a Taranium power source could fuel the Time Destructor. The Doctor managed to steal the Taranium and fled to the ship, and the Spar took off at high speed.

The Daleks blamed Zephron for this failing, and he was exterminated. Suspicion also fell on Chen, and he agreed to go to Earth to ensure that the Space Security Service would be neutralised in case they interfered with the plan. The Daleks dispatched a pursuit ship to recapture the stolen Spar and its precious cargo. Before the Doctor could reach Earth, his foes used a Randomiser to overload the ship's navigation systems, sending it crashing down on the prison planet of Desperus.

Fortunately, the damage was slight, and the ship was easily repaired and re-launched. Unfortunately, while they were fixing the Spar a gang of convicts had tried to get on board. One, a murderer named Kirksen, had succeeded and took Katarina hostage, demanding that they take the ship to the nearest planet instead of heading for Earth. Turning around would doom all humanity, but if they stayed on their present course, Katarina would die. The priestess took the moral quandary out of their hands by deliberately opening the airlock, sucking her and Kirksen out into the vacuum of space.

The Spar continued on to Earth. Rather than land at Central City, Vyon put the ship down at an isolated research outpost where a friend of his named Daxtar worked – but they were betrayed. Daxter was part of Chen's conspiracy. Bret eliminated the traitor, but the outpost was already surrounded by Space Security Service forces under the command of Sara Kingdom. Chen had beaten the travellers back to Earth, and despatched the ultra-efficient Kingdom to secure the stolen taranium. She killed Bret, but the Doctor and Steven managed to escape into the laboratory section of the outpost, where they blundered into an experimental cellular dissemination field – a form of long-range transmat. The Doctor, Steven and Sara Kingdom were hurled across space to the planet Mira.

Chen informed the Daleks of the accident, and a second Dalek pursuit ship travelled to Mira.

The Doctor had visited Mira before, and knew about the local lifeforms, called the Visians – a savage race of monsters with the advantage of natural invisibility. The danger forced Kingdom to ally herself with the Doctor, and she realised that they were telling the truth about Chen's treachery. Using a Visian attack as a distraction, they were able to steal the Dalek pursuit ship and disable its remote control.

The Kembel Daleks deployed a magnetic beam to drag the ship back to their space, but that gave the Doctor time to build a fake taranium core. While experimenting with the core, Steven accidentally charged himself with gravitic energy. Under normal circumstances, that would have killed him instantly, but he survived and was encased in a temporary force shield.

This shield proved immensely useful, as the travellers were able to convince the Daleks that they would hand the taranium over only outside the TARDIS. At the TARDIS, they gave the Daleks the fake core, and the Daleks tried to exterminate them, but even full-strength neutraliser beams had no effect on Steven. While the Daleks were confused, the trio leapt on board the TARDIS and dematerialised.

The Daleks attempted to activate the Time Destructor, but the fake core burnt out instantly. Realising the Doctor's deception, they launched their own time machine to hunt down the TARDIS.

They fled across space and time, bouncing through the 20th century on Earth before taking a sharp turn and landing on the volcanic planet of Tigus. There, they detected another time machine. It turned out to be a second TARDIS – the machine piloted by the Meddling Monk (see page 97). He had repaired his damaged dimensional stabiliser, and now he wanted to return the favour by locking the Doctor out of the TARDIS. He blasted the locking mechanism while the travellers were outside the ship, but the Doctor was able to use his ring to force the door open. Frustrated, the Monk fled with the Doctor in pursuit.

The chase brought the two Time Lords to ancient Egypt. Soon afterwards, the Dalek time capsule arrived. The Daleks and Mavic Chen encountered the Monk as he skulked around a pyramid still under construction, and forced him to promise to bring them the Doctor or be exterminated. The Monk was unable to find the Doctor, but managed to trick Sara Kingdom and Steven into following him back to the Daleks. With the two travellers as hostages, the Daleks demanded that the Doctor hand over the real core. The Doctor had no choice, and gave the Daleks the final component of their ultimate weapon.

He still had a plan, though – the Egyptian slave workers attacked the Daleks, giving the two prisoners and the Monk a chance to flee. Back at the TARDIS, the Doctor explained that he had found the Monk's TARDIS and sabotaged it again. This time, he had stolen the Monk's directional unit, and scrambled its Chameleon Circuit so it now looked like a police box. The Daleks would pursue the Monk's TARDIS instead, and the Doctor's TARDIS could now be piloted accurately – at least, as long as the new unit lasted. The Monk's TARDIS was a more advanced model, which meant that its directional unit was likely to burn out when attached to an antique like the Doctor's ship. Still, it got them to Kembel before failing.

With the Time Destructor complete, the Daleks had no need for most of their allies, and the representatives were imprisoned. The Doctor and Sara freed them, and the surviving representatives left for their home galaxies to prepare for the Dalek onslaught. By now, Chen had lost his precarious grip on sanity, alternating between a megalomaniac belief that he could seize control of the Dalek forces and paranoia that the Doctor was working with the Daleks to sabotage his victory. He captured Steven and Sara and brought them to the Dalek control centre to prove his worth.

The Daleks were unimpressed. Chen, Guardian of the Solar System and would-be galactic conqueror, was exterminated without remorse.

Meanwhile, the Doctor crept into the Dalek base and prepared to put an end to the whole master plan. He activated the Time Destructor, initially at a low power setting. He ordered Steven and Sara to run back to the TARDIS, then he confronted the Daleks and threatened to fully activate the weapon. Unable to risk shooting him in case it damaged or triggered the full blast of the Destructor, the Daleks were forced to let him past.

Steven obeyed the Doctor's orders, but Sara was determined to help, and stayed behind to help the Doctor escape the Dalek base.

Once switched on, the Destructor could not be turned off. Even at this low-power setting, it wreaked chaos on its surroundings. Entropy accelerated wildly around the device, causing everything to age faster. The Doctor – a nigh-immortal Time Lord – and the cybernetic Daleks were largely unaffected, but Sara Kingdom grew older with every step she took towards the TARDIS. Within sight of the TARDIS, the Doctor collapsed from exhaustion, and Sara died and decayed to dust in an instant. The Daleks closed in.

Despairing, Steven left the temporal protection of the ship and ran to the Doctor's side. The Time Destructor aged him in an instant. He tried to smash the machine, but instead reversed it. Entropy flowed backwards. It was too late for Sarah, but it restored Steven and the Doctor. The two fell into the TARDIS.

Outside, the Destructor was now out of control. Its entropy-warping effect wrapped around the planet, blasting the jungles of Kimbel with reverse aging. Trees shrank into seeds, then dissolved into their component elements. The Daleks screamed as their casings melted away, and the Kaled mutants inside shrank away to nothingness. By the time the taranium core was exhausted, millions of years of time had been rolled back within the machine's field of effect. The whole Dalek assault force was destroyed as though it had never been.

All that remained was the TARDIS, and the Doctor, and Steven, and their memories of all those who had died thwarting the master plan.

RUNNING THIS ADVENTURE

The Dalek's Master Plan is possibly the biggest adventure in all of the Doctor's long history. The fate of eight whole galaxies hangs in the balance as he battles the Daleks across time and space. It's an epic!

When planning an adventure, it's good to think about scale. A horror story needs to be confined and personal. A conspiracy story needs a bigger cast, so you have more suspects and scope for treachery and betrayal. An alien invasion can be anything from a single alien scout to a base under siege to a giant alien fleet attacking the whole planet. It's best to mix the scales – if the whole universe is under threat every week, it all gets a bit repetitive. Go up and down the ladder. One week, have the travellers visiting a spaceship; the week after that, the threat might be to a small town; after that, the characters might be fighting to save a single child.

And then, once in a while, go loud. Threaten the galaxy. Have a cast of thousands, and a 'special effects budget' of millions. Blow up planets!

When you run huge adventures like this, bring back the best bits of previous adventures. *The Dalek's Master Plan* not only has Daleks, but features the return of the Monk. The adventure would work perfectly well without the Monk, but he's great fun for the players to interact with, and throwing wild cards into a big plot like this can have very interesting and unexpected consequences (the sequence where the Doctor sabotages the Monk's TARDIS so it looks like a police box to confuse the Daleks could easily be a classic moment of brilliant improvisation by a player!)

THE SECOND GREAT & BOUNTIFUL HUMAN EMPIRE

These are the early years of the Second Empire. Humanity has spread across the stars, but the alliance between Earth's many far-flung colonies is a loose and uncertain one. It was only in 3975 that a non-aggression pact was signed between warring human worlds, and while Mavic Chen is the highest-ranking human leader, his control over the Solar System is far from absolute, and he has only limited influence over the various human colonies orbiting other stars. (Think of him as the President of the United States dealing with the UN – he's got the most power, but needs still to convince the various member planets to go along with his proposals.)

The seat of power on Earth is Central City, the vast metropolis that encompasses most of England. The Guardian's office is here, as well as the headquarters of the Space Security Service.

It's a time of great upheaval and change. Servant races like the Ood and the Technix perform most of the manual labour. Forty billion people live in the Solar System alone, with billions more in other systems. The elite agents of the Space Security Service provide interstellar security for them all by seeking out and eliminating threats to humanity. As the Empire spreads across the stars, other races look with envy or alarm at the rapidly growing power of the human race...

THE SPACE SECURITY SERVICE

The Space Security Service defends humanity from all sorts of threats – both external, like hostile alien invaders, and internal ones like conspiracies and traitors. If you're on the wrong side of the Earth government, then the SSS can seem like fascist secret police – they have chemical samples and files on everyone in the Second Empire. SSS agents are trained to suppress their emotions and doubts when on missions. They do what must be done to safeguard humanity. Sara Kingdom executes Bret Vyon – her own brother – without any hesitation after she is told he is a traitor.

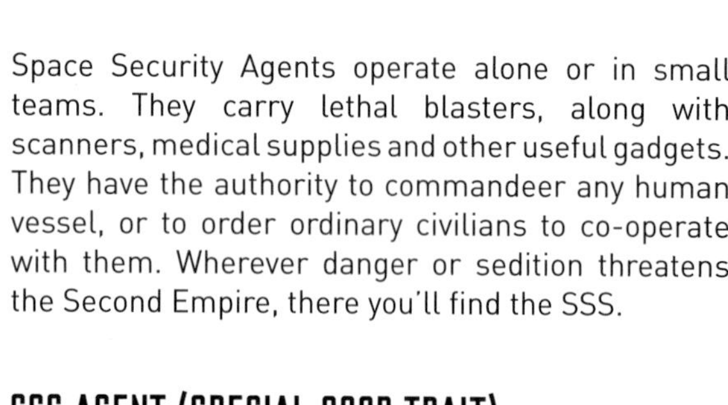

Space Security Agents operate alone or in small teams. They carry lethal blasters, along with scanners, medical supplies and other useful gadgets. They have the authority to commandeer any human vessel, or to order ordinary civilians to co-operate with them. Wherever danger or sedition threatens the Second Empire, there you'll find the SSS.

SSS AGENT (SPECIAL GOOD TRAIT)

You're a member of the Space Security Service, charged with protecting Earth against all dangers.

Effect: Space Security Service operatives get a +1 to their Strength and Resolve, and gain a +2 bonus when trying to intimidate or order other humans from the Second Empire. They have the Good Traits Tough, Quick Reflexes and Voice of Authority. However, they also have Bad Trait of Obligation (Major) to the SSS.

Many SSS agents also have traits like Technically Adept, By The Book or Obsession (but unlike Tough, Quick Reflexes, Voice of Authority and Obligation, these Traits are not part of the SSS Agent Special Trait package).

SSS agents must have at least Marksman 2, Subterfuge 2 and Technology 2.

In addition, SSS agents are assigned the following equipment for every mission:

- Blaster (4/**L**/L damage)
- Medikit (Cures any one injury)
- Message rocket (relays a message back to Earth in a faster-than-light microcapsule)
- Protective jumpsuit (Armour 3)

They may also be assigned one other Minor Gadget tailored for their current mission
This trait costs 4 Character Points and 2 Story Points to purchase.

SARA KINGDOM

AWARENESS	3	PRESENCE	4
COORDINATION	4	RESOLVE	5
INGENUITY	4	STRENGTH	4

"Ruthless, hard, efficient. And does exactly as ordered."

It's a testament to Sara Kingdom's devotion to the Space Service that she was seen as the perfect choice to hunt down the Taranium-stealing traitors, even though one of those traitors was her own brother. Until she met the Doctor, Kingdom was the perfect SSS officer, a steely weapon for the Guardian of the Solar System to wield as needed. The Doctor convinced her that Mavic Chen was corrupt, and after that Sara turned her ferocious discipline and courage to battling Chen and his Dalek allies. She was instrumental in using the Time Destructor to annihilate the Dalek invasion force.

SKILLS

Athletics 3, Convince (Intimidate) 1, Fighting 4, Knowledge 3, Marksman 4, Medicine 2, Science 2, Survival 2, Subterfuge 4, Technology 3, Transport 4

TRAITS

Attractive
Brave: Sara doesn't stop for anything.
Tough: Reduce all damage taken by 2 points.
Quick Reflexes: Sara goes first in any Action Phase.
Voice of Authority
By The Book: Upholds Space Security Directives, no matter what.
Obligation (Major): The SSS cannot be questioned.

TECH LEVEL: 7

STORY POINTS: 6

BRET VYON

"We're not dead yet."

"Don't fool yourself. They're out there looking for us right now. They'll find us, and then..."

"All right, all right, they may well find us, but we've got to get through to Earth first or the whole solar system is finished."

Hailing from Mars Colony 16, Vyon joined the Space Security Service along with his sister Sara in 3990 and made Second Rank by 3998. In the year 4000 he was assigned along with Kert Gantry to a rescue mission, to search for missing agent Marc Cory on the isolated planet Kemble. What he found there shook his faith in the service and the Solar System – not only had the Daleks returned to the galaxy, the Guardian of the Solar System himself was in league with them. From that moment on, Vyon was determined to warn Earth of the danger it faced.

Vyon's downfall was his faith in the purity of the human Empire. While he could not deny that Mavic Chen had betrayed Earth, he still believed that the rest of the Earth government was uncorrupt. He trusted his old friend Daxtar, and that got him killed.

AWARENESS	3	PRESENCE	4
COORDINATION	4	RESOLVE	5
INGENUITY	4	STRENGTH	4

SKILLS

Athletics 2, Convince 3, Fighting 3, Knowledge 3, Marksman 3, Medicine 3, Science 3, Subterfuge 4, Technology 4, Transport 4

TRAITS

Friends (Minor): Vyon had contacts in the Service's advanced research section.
Tough: Reduce all damage suffered by 2.
Quick Reflexes: Acts first in any Action Phase.
Voice of Authority: Vyon spent more time than his sister did dealing with civilians.
Obligation (Major): To the SSS.

TECH LEVEL: 7

STORY POINTS: 6

TECHNIXS

While the Ood fulfilled the role of manual labourers and servants, they lacked the technical skills needed for certain tasks. The Technix filled this gap – these clones are derived from human genetic material, but are engineered to serve and obey. They look like bald, androgynous, grey-skinned humans. Technixs are all mathematical savants, capable of performing extraordinary feats of calculation and memorisation.

Technixs have no initiative or will, and are not very good at solving new problems. They are, however, very good at applying existing solutions.

AWARENESS	2	PRESENCE	1
COORDINATION	2	RESOLVE	1
INGENUITY	2	STRENGTH	2

SKILLS

Craft 3, Science (Mathematics) 4, Technology 6, Transport 2

TRAITS

Technically Adept: Technix get a +2 bonus to any Technology-based rolls.
By The Book: They obey their instructions to the letter.
Enslaved: Genetically engineered to serve, they have a -2 penalty to any roll to disobey a human.
Slow Reflexes: They go last in any action phase.

TECH LEVEL: 7

MAVIC CHEN

"I, Mavic Chen, will decide when the Alliance is at an end. You, Dalek Supreme, tell them they're to take their orders from me."

Few people in history had a fraction of the ambition of Mavic Chen. His desire for power brought him to the very pinnacle of human society – as Guardian of the Solar System, he was the leader of the Second Empire and perhaps the single most influential politician in the galaxy – but that wasn't enough for him. He allied himself with the Daleks, who promised him that he would rule the whole galaxy when they conquered it. On top of that, he plotted to betray the Daleks and seize control of their fleets and doomsday weapons in order to conquer the other seven galaxies. The universe was not enough for Mavic Chen.

Chen possessed an incredible genius for secrecy and deception. He was wildly popular among most of humanity, and had the loyalty of the whole Space Security Service even as he secretly acquired a staggering fortune of taranium and made overtures to the Daleks. He was especially adept at turning defeats and setbacks to his advantage – whenever anything went wrong in the Dalek plan, he was able to blame it on one of the other conspirators, enhancing his own standing in the conspiracy.

Chen was also immensely paranoid – with good reason. His lieutenant Karlton, the head of the SSS, was loyal only as long as he believed that Chen's plan could succeed. His Dalek 'allies' tried to kill him on Kembel along with the other conspirators. Chen's paranoia allowed him to navigate the maze of shifting alliances and loyalties in the conspiracy.

AWARENESS	4	PRESENCE	6
COORDINATION	2	RESOLVE	6
INGENUITY	5	STRENGTH	3

SKILLS

Convince 5, Fighting 2, Knowledge 5, Marksman 1, Medicine 2, Science 3, Subterfuge 5, Survival 1, Technology 3, Transport 2

TRAITS

Charming: A born politician, Chen led the negotiations that led to the 3975 Non-Aggression pact. He gets a +2 bonus to any Convince attempts based on charm.
Empathic: Chen gets a +2 bonus when trying to read a situation.
Friends (Major): He's the Guardian of the Solar System. He runs a large chunk of the galaxy and has his own secret police force.
Indomitable: a +4 bonus to resisting intimidation and psychic control. This is a man who stares down Daleks.
Voice of Authority: a +2 bonus when ordering people around.
Dark Secret (Major): Consorting with Daleks to conquer the universe certainly counts as a Dark Secret.
Distinctive: Sixty billion people know his face.
Obsession (Major): Conquering the galaxy.
Eccentric (Minor, then Major): Convinced he's destined to rule the universe. Later, convinced he's immortal.

TECH LEVEL: 7

STORY POINTS: 9

THE MASTERS OF THE SEVEN GALAXIES

Some of Chen's fellow conspirators in the Dalek plan were a mix of politicians, crime lords, evil masterminds and galactic conquerors. Others were driven by fear of the expanding human race. Little is known about most of them, so the Gamemaster could easily turn any of these alien overlords into a villain for a new adventure.

After the Daleks betrayed and imprisoned them, the various surviving rulers – including Chen – spoke of forming a new galactic council to co-ordinate a defence against the Daleks. This new alliance may have endured after the collapse of the master plan.

Zephon: The Representative of the Fifth Galaxy, Zephon was a humanoid creature with trailing tendrils. Either his skin was sensitive to ultraviolet radiation, or he thought heavy cowled cloaks were the height of fashion. He overthrew the Embodiment Gris and defeated the upstart sentient planet Fisar to claim his position. After the Daleks exterminated him for allowing the Doctor to steal the core, his place on the council was taken by his ally Sentreal, a maleficent cybernetic plant.

- Zephon was an eccentric egotist. He delighted in watching the jungles of Kembel burn (perhaps it reminded him of Sentreal burning), and kept the whole council waiting.
- Celation and Beaus owed him favours, and he was instrumental into bringing their galaxies into the conspiracy.
- Zephon was adept at intrigue and politics, and obviously thought that his sway over 3/7th of the council would make him indispensible to the Daleks.

Trantis: Representative of the Tenth Galaxy, the largest and most powerful of the outer galaxies, Trantis was a humanoid creature with sharpened teeth (alarmingly, he looked very like a Futurekind, and who better to take over a whole galaxy than a time-travelling maniac from the end of time?) He considered himself to be the equal of the Dalek Supreme, and demanded to be consulted on every decision relating to the plan. The Daleks eliminated him once they recovered the Time Destructor.

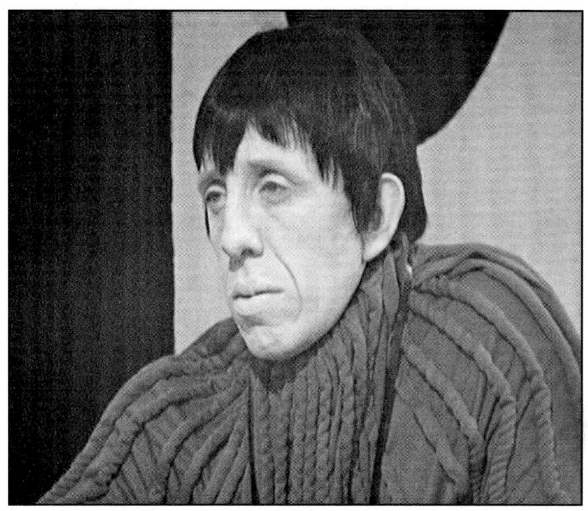

- Under his leadership, the Tenth Galaxy had experimented with time travel, but had not yet managed to make a working time machine.
- Unlike the other Masters, whose positions were often tenuous, Trantis was clearly the undisputed master of his empire.

Malpha: Representative Malpha was one of the last conspirators to be recruited, and was seduced by the sheer power of the Dalek forces. As the plan ran into difficulty, however, Malpha became increasingly disillusioned and worried about his decision. After the Doctor freed him, he returned home to fight the Daleks and atone for his treachery. Malpha was a humanoid with scaly skin.

- Malpha seemed to have a particular dislike for humanity. He spoke enthusiastically about the conquest and destruction of Earth.
- His quick change of heart at the end suggests that Malpha had many enemies who would destroy him if they learned of his temporary alliance with the Daleks.

Beaus: The Master of Beaus was an ally of Zephon and Celation. He strongly mistrusted Mavic Chen, and argued for the elimination of the Earthman after Chen had delivered the vital tararium. Beaus wore an environmental space suit, as his species inhaled chlorine and could not tolerate the oxygen-rich atmosphere of Kembel. His spacesuit also had a large and highly visible communications antenna – maybe Beaus was so paranoid that he stayed in constant contact with his minions.

- Beaus was petty and bureaucratic at the meetings, demanding that no-one speak out of turn and questioning every unexpected development. This probably means he was desperately scared and trying to assert control.
- Like Malpha, Celation and Sentreal, Beaus survived the Dalek plan and returned home to his galaxy of origin to prepare for invasion.

Celation: Another galaxy recruited by Zephon (in what Chen called a three-for-one deal), Celation was the third most influential leader on the council after Trantis and Chen (and the Dalek Supreme, of course).

- His body was covered in black spheres, which appeared to be grafted onto his flesh – were these cybernetic implants or Alien fungi? Or maybe they were warp stars, there as backup in case the Daleks killed him? "Shoot me and I blow up this planet" is a good starting point for any negotiation with the Daleks.

SCREAMERS

These giant bats are native to the prison planet of Desperus, where the Solar System dumps unwanted criminals. There are no walls or cells on Desperus, nor are there warders. Prisoners are dropped off in the wilderness and expected to fend for themselves against the Screamers. Individually, the bats are quite dangerous, but flocks of hundreds or even thousands of the creatures swarm out of the caves by night to hunt. The ultrasonic screaming of the bats drives the prisoners mad.

AWARENESS	4	PRESENCE	-
COORDINATION	4	RESOLVE	-
INGENUITY	-	STRENGTH	2

SKILLS
Athletics 2, Fighting 3, Survival 3

TRAITS
Alien
Fear Factor 1: Screamers get +2 in attempts to scare.
Flight (Major)
Screamer!
Natural Weapon (Bite): A Screamer bite inflicts Strength +1 (2/3/4) damage.
Special (Sonic Attack): A character who hears the screams of one of these bats must make a Strength + Resolve roll against Difficulty 12. If the roll fails, the character loses 1 point of Resolve. A character reduced to 0 Resolve gains the Eccentric Major Bad Trait.

VISIANS

Native to the planet Mira, Visians are huge creatures with great physical strength that are prone to outbursts of ferocious violence. They possess the natural ability to bend light around their bodies, making them invisible. Fortunately for the rest of the galaxies, the Visians are not especially intelligent and have not discovered spaceflight (or the wheel for that matter), so other planets are unlikely to be invaded by an army of invisible gorillas anytime soon.

AWARENESS	3	PRESENCE	3
COORDINATION	2	RESOLVE	3
INGENUITY	2	STRENGTH	7

SKILLS
Athletics 2, Craft 2, Fighting 3, Subterfuge 3 (Sneaking 5), Survival 2

TRAITS
Tough
Invisibility (Major x2): The Visian ability to bend light increases the Difficulty of spotting or striking them using purely visual means by +8! Using Alien Senses or a Gadget with the Scan Trait halves this modifier.
Natural Weapons (Claws): Visian claws deal Strength +1 damage (4/**8**/12)

TECH LEVEL: 1

STORY POINTS: 1-3

VARGA PLANTS

The Varga Plant is native to Skaro, but the Daleks spread it to many other worlds. It resembles a cross between a tubby venus fly-trap and a thorn bush. The mutant plants can move slowly, dragging themselves towards on their tentacle-like root systems.

Vargas reproduce by injuring living creatures. Their thorns secrete a poison that not only kills the victim, but also contains millions of Varga seeds. These sprout within the victim's body, transforming them into a Varga within a few minutes.

AWARENESS	1	PRESENCE	-
COORDINATION	1	RESOLVE	-
INGENUITY	-	STRENGTH	2

SKILLS
Fighting 2, Subterfuge 2

TRAITS
Alien
Plant
Fear Factor 1

The PC must immediately spend a Story Point or become infected. At the beginning of every Scene, the character must make a Strength + Resolve test at Difficulty 18; if they fail, consult the chart below.

Failure	The PC takes one point of damage to Resolve.
Bad	The PC takes 2 points of damage to Resolve and gains the Eccentric Trait.
Disastrous	The PC takes 3 points of damage to Resolve and gains the Obsession (Major, Attack Others) Trait.

A character reduced to 0 Resolve or killed while infected becomes a Varga Plant in 2D6 minutes.

GADGETS

The Dalek's Master Plan revolves around a dangerous new gadget, the all-powerful Time Destructor, but also introduces several other handy pieces of technology.

POWER IMPULSE COMPASS (MINOR GADGET)

Detects nearby power sources and points the direction towards them.

Traits: Scan, Sense of Direction, Restriction (Energy Signatures only)
Cost: 1 Story Point

MAGNETIC CHAIR (MINOR GADGET)

One of the Doctor's inventions, the Magnetic Chair uses invisible beams of force to trap anyone sitting in it. It could hold a herd of elephants, if one could somehow convince a whole herd of elephants to share a single chair.

Maybe if there was something really good on TV, and the chair was right in front of the screen with a big bucket of popcorn...

Leaving the chair requires succeeding at a Strength + Resolve roll against a Difficulty of 27.

Traits: Forcefield, Restriction (Restraint Only).
Cost: 1 Story Point

NEUTRONIC RANDOMISER (MAJOR GADGET)

The Neutronic Randomiser is a Dalek anti-ship weapon. When activated, it scrambles the guidance systems of the targeted ship (or other vehicle – and yes, it can be used on a TARDIS or another time machine) causing it to zoom off-course.

The Randomiser causes all Transport rolls made to steer the vehicle to automatically fail, unless the operator spends 2 Story Points. This effect fades after a few hours.

Traits: Transmit, Disrupt
Cost: 4 Story points

TARANIUM

All the Outer Galaxies contributed something to the Dalek's master plan. Mavic Chen's contribution was a full emm of taranium – a tiny container of

the most valuable element in existence. Taranium is an incredibly rare substance, found only on a few isolated planets. There was a deposit on Uranus, and it took Chen fifty years to scrape together a full emm, using false names and front corporations to hide his involvement.

Taranium can be used as a power source for time machines. It's like congealed Rift Energy, an Eye of Harmony in a jam jar. If you're using the advanced TARDIS rules from *The Time Traveller's Companion*, a container of Taranium holds 50 Story Points.

THE TIME DESTRUCTOR (SPECIAL GADGET)

The Daleks' doomsday weapon, developed to conquer whole galaxies, the Time Destructor can speed up or reverse the flow of time, destroying its targets by aging them to death. It can devastate a whole planet when activated.

For **1 Story Point**, the Time Destructor wipes out a single target or a small area by aging it for 1D6 X1000 years.

2 Story Points annihilates an area around the size of a continent by aging it for 1D6 X1000 years.

4 Story Points wipes out a whole planet and everything around it.

The Time Destructor's really nasty side effect is that it messes up the Time Vortex around its targets. If you're killed by the Time Destructor, not only are you aged to death, but it's impossible for a time traveller to jump in and save you – time travel is impossible around when the machine is active.

Traits: Vortex, Delete, Restriction (Power Hungry)
Cost: 9 Story Points

FURTHER ADVENTURES

- **The Karlton Coup:** Think about events from the perspective of the Solar System – Mavic Chen goes off on holiday and never returns. Only a few people know what really happened, and chief among those is Karlton, Chen's co-conspirator and head of the Space Security Service. Karlton could easily blame the death of the beloved leader on alien enemies, and declare martial law over the whole Solar System, putting himself in charge. Even more alarmingly, Karlton now has a working Cellular Disseminator to use as a weapon...

- **The New Galactic Council:** The fleeing Masters of the various Galaxies vowed to set up a second Galactic Council, opposed to the Daleks – but how long will that last? Can these Masters trust each other? Which of them plans to step into the power vacuum left by the Daleks?

- **Monky Business:** The last we see of the Monk, he's fleeing in an out-of-control TARDIS that looks like a police box, pursued by a Dalek time machine. What happens next? Where would the Monk get rid of a bunch of persistent and bloodthirsty Daleks? (There's always that buried Atomic Cannon in 1066...) For added fun, the Monk could run into the player characters and pretend to be a previously unknown incarnation of the Doctor. *"Yes, I'm the, er, Twelfth Doctor. Please, I need your help! Mainly, I need you to distract the Daleks while I run, er, save the day..."*

- **The Dead Planet:** Across all eight galaxies, only one planet had enough Taranium to fuel the Time Destructor – all that emm came from Uranus. Why did one unremarkable gas giant have so much of this rare element? Maybe Taranium is not a natural element at all – it could be the product of some ancient race like the Racnoss, who left trace amounts of Taranium in some long-abandoned warren in the heart of Uranus' moon Oberon.

GRAVITIC FORCE FIELD

While experimenting with the gravitic engines on board the stolen Dalek pursuit ship, Steven accidentally charged himself with gravitic energy and became enveloped in a force field. In game terms, this was a 'Yes, And' result – he charged the fake Taranium core *and* got a temporary force field.

If a player character wants to deliberately try to trigger the same effect, they should be aware that it was a million-to-one side effect, and that normally supercharging yourself with gravitic energy is exactly like sticking your head into the event horizon of a black hole. If a character still wants to try, it's an Ingenuity + Technology roll at Difficulty 30 to *not die*. If the roll succeeds, the character gets a temporary Force Field trait lasting a scene or two.

THE MASSACRE

"History sometimes gives us a terrible shock, and that is because we don't quite fully understand. Why should we? After all, we're all too small to realise its final pattern. Therefore don't try and judge it from where you stand."

SYNOPSIS

For much of the 16th century, France was divided between the Catholics and the Protestant Huguenots in the so-called Wars of Religion. These 'wars' pitted neighbour against neighbour and noble houses against each other; foreign spies and aid from abroad threw fuel on the flames of conflict.

In 1572, Huguenot leaders gathered in Paris to attend the wedding of Henri of Navarre – a Huguenot – to the King's sister, Princess Margaret. The King's mother, Catherine de Medici, feared the growing influence of the Huguenots at court, especially Admiral Gaspard de Coligny. Four days after the wedding, on the 22nd of August, assassins sympathetic to the Queen Mother's faction attempted to kill the Admiral. They failed, but the attempted murder inflamed the tensions between the factions. Fearing a Huguenot uprising, the King ordered the murder of several key Protestant leaders.

Two days later, on the Feast of St. Bartholomew, the King's Swiss Guard marched on their targets, dragged them into the streets, and killed them. The deaths of the Huguenot leaders triggered rioting and mob violence, again directed at the Protestant minority. Thousands died over the next few weeks as religious strife once more engulfed France. The infamous Massacre of St. Bartholomew was one of the most frightful days in French history. All that is real history, a fixed point. The TARDIS materialised on the 22nd of August.

Once the Doctor realised when they were, he told Steven to wait in a tavern while the Doctor sought out a chemist named Charles Preslin. His work on germ theory was decades ahead of its time, and the Doctor wished to congratulate him.

The Doctor found Preslin's apothecary easily enough, but convincing Preslin to talk was almost impossible. The chemist – a Huguenot – was hounded by Catholics, especially the Abbot of Amboise. By a strange co-incidence, the Doctor was a perfect physical duplicate of the Abbot. Preslin assumed that this was some bizarre trap by the Abbot to trick him into admitting heresy.

Meanwhile, in the tavern, Steven befriended a group of Huegenots led by Nicholas Muss. They warned him that Paris was a dangerous place at night. Worrying that the Doctor might be in danger, they set off through the dark streets to find him. On the way, they encountered a serving girl, Anne Chaplet pursued by guards in the employ of the Abbot.

Steven hid the girl, and once the guards are gone, she explained that she fled the house of her employer after she heard some of the guards discussing the massacre of Wassy, another infamous killing of Huguenots by Catholics. Concerned, Nicholas brought Steven and Anna to the home of his master, Admiral Gaspard de Coligny, to spend the night.

The guards traced Anna to the Admiral's home, and the Abbot watched as they demanded that she be handed over. Nicholas refuses, but Steven saw the Abbot and assumed that he was the Doctor in disguise for some obscure reason.

The next day, Steven set out in search of the Doctor. He listened outside the window of the Abbot's house, and overheard courtiers plotting the death of the 'Sea Beggar'. He did not know it, but the 'Sea Beggar' was a nickname used for Admiral de Coligny – a reference to his attempts to ally with the Dutch. He tried to warn Nicholas of this plot, but another of de Coligny's retainers, Gaston, suspected Steven of being a spy for the Abbot and refused to let him in.

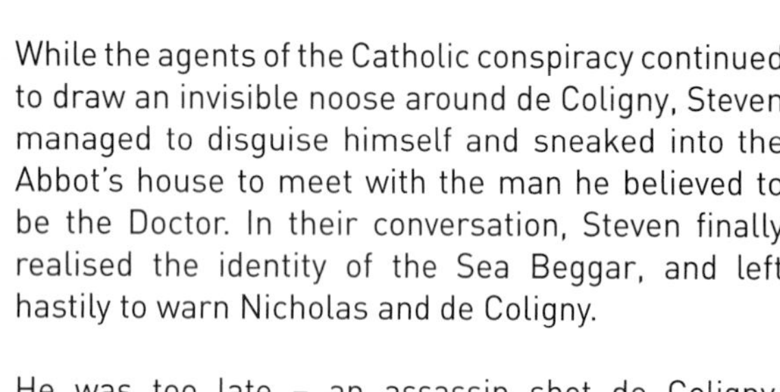

While the agents of the Catholic conspiracy continued to draw an invisible noose around de Coligny, Steven managed to disguise himself and sneaked into the Abbot's house to meet with the man he believed to be the Doctor. In their conversation, Steven finally realised the identity of the Sea Beggar, and left hastily to warn Nicholas and de Coligny.

He was too late – an assassin shot de Coligny, but failed to kill him. Infuriated by this botched assasination, Catherine de Medici blamed the failure on the Abbot. Her guards killed the Abbot and framed the Huguenots. Rumours spread through Paris that Huguenots had killed the Abbot in the street, and violence quickly followed. The Massacre had begun.

Steven was still unsure whether or not the Abbot was the Doctor, and was deeply shaken by the thought that the Doctor was dead and that he was now stranded in the past. He needed the TARDIS key, so he and Anna returned to Prestin's shop – when the Doctor appeared. He berated Steven for leaving the tavern, but admitted that he had been delayed. Steven began to relate his adventures to the Doctor, and the Doctor realised the significance of the date. Paris was about to descend into violence.

The Doctor told Anna to leave Paris, then they hurriedly returned to the TARDIS. As they dematerialised, the Doctor explained about the Massacre. Steven was appalled – they had abandoned his new friends to die. At the very least, they could have rescued Anna, but the Doctor was adamant. Non-interference was his watchword. Angrily, Steven decided to leave the TARDIS at its next stop.

That next stop was London, in 1966 – where a young girl ran into the TARDIS, believing it to be an actual police box. A pair of policeman approached the TARDIS after her, and rather than risk arrest and awkward questions, the Doctor dematerialised with the girl on board. She looked exactly like Anna. She was Dorothea Chaplet, a direct descendant of hers. The Doctor's warning had allowed Anna to escape the massacre. They'd changed time after all.

RUNNING THE ADVENTURE

Running an adventure like *The Massacre* requires a very light touch. Steven spends the entire adventure running around investigating, befriending NPCs, getting in and out of trouble, and generally being resourceful and heroic – and then the Doctor says *"never mind, I know what's going to happen, it's all historical fact. You can't accomplish anything and everything you've done so far is pointless"*. If the Gamemaster tried to do that to his players, he would (justifiably) be pelted with dice by his players. No-one wants to feel like they're powerless.

However, some events in history are fixed. The player characters cannot always save the day. You can't stop the Massacre and you can't kill Hitler. Even in these situations, though, the player characters should be able to accomplish something, even if it's just survival. Steven could not avert de Coligny's assassination or the ensuing massacre, but he was able to save Anne Chaplet. Similarly, characters can't kill Hitler even if they find themselves embroiled in the 20 July Plot of 1942, and they can't stop Mavic Chen even if they gatecrash the 3975 peace negotiations. The best they can do is save some idealistic young German officer, or stop a final bloody conflict between Mars and Venus.

FURTHER ADVENTURES

- **The Duplicate:** All right – so why does the Abbot of Amboise look identical to the Doctor? Is it just co-incidence, or is there something else at work? Could he really be the Doctor, doubling back on his own timeline (and then, presumably, faking his death)? Could the Abbot be a left-over of some previous plot, like the Dalek robot duplicate (see page 90)? Even if the Abbot is just an ordinary man who happens to look like a Time Lord, the Doctor's enemies could still use him. Imagine the scene – the Abbot strolls into his office to find a metallic cylinder and a gang of malignant pepperpots, who shout *"YOU WILL COME WITH US"* and whisk him away to the future...

- **That Brotherhood of Apothecaries:** The Doctor behaves very oddly for a large part of this adventure. As soon as he realises where he is, he rushes off to meet Prestin, who he refers to as a member of a 'strange brotherhood'. He then vanishes for several days. What was the Doctor up to during this missing time? Who exactly was Prestin?

- **The Time Fixer:** One of the classic tropes of time travel fiction is where the time travellers accidentally change history, and then have to go back again to fix their mistake. You can turn that around – the characters run into another group of novice time travellers, and find that these newcomers have screwed up the timeline. Maybe they've saved de Coligny, or shot Hitler. It's up to the player characters to put things right once more!

CHAPTER NINE:
THE ARK, THE CELESTIAL TOYMAKER, THE GUNFIGHTERS

THE ARK

"The statue's finished. That means seven hundred years must have passed since we last stood here."

"But we've only been gone a few seconds."

SYNOPSIS

Millions of years in the future, in the 57th segment of time, solar activity endangered the Earth. The human population fled, as they did before, in a vast space ark. They brought samples of all Earth life with them, along with an allied race called the Monoids. The Monoids came to Earth following the destruction of their own planet.

Only a small proportion of the human and Monoid populations lived on board the Ark. The vast majority – numbering many billions – were stored in micronized form and held in stasis for the duration of the journey, which was expected to take many centuries. The living humans were the Guardians, and their sacred duty was to protect humanity and guard the precious Ark.

The Ark's destination was the distant planet Refusis, deemed suitable for human colonisation. To while away the time as the ship crossed the awful gulf of space, the crew and their Monoid assistants embarked on the construction of a huge statue of a human that would become a monument when they arrived on their new home.

The TARDIS arrived when the Ark was still 700 years away from Refusis. After initially assuming they had landed on Earth – the Earth plant life and vegetation confused them – the travellers discovered they were on board a space ark and made peaceful contact with the Guardians.

Unfortunately, Dodo had a mild head cold. Thousands of years into the future, the common cold was eliminated – so millions of years after that, humans had no resistance to the cold virus. Dodo's cold was like a plague to the Guardians and the Monoids, and swept through the population. The travellers were accused of deliberate biological warfare and put on trial, but the Doctor managed to use 'ancient' 20th century medicine to create a vaccine, saving the Ark. The travellers departed on good term with the Guardians, and the TARDIS dematerialised...

... and reappeared in the same place, 700 years later, just as the Ark arrived at Refusis.

The Ark had changed greatly. A mutation of the cold virus had weakened the human Guardians and allowed a faction of ambitious Monoids to seize control of the ship. The Guardians were now slaves, working on menial jobs like food preparation, while the Monoids planned to settle on Refusis and exterminate humanity. The statue's head was now that of a Monoid.

The Monoids captured the TARDIS crew. Steven was imprisoned with a work crew, while the Doctor, Dodo, a Guardian named Yendom and Monoid Two travelled down to the planet below in a launcher pod. The planet seemed uninhabited at first, although early scans by both the humans and Monoids had detected signs of intelligent life. Exploring, the travellers found a strange castle-like structure that seemed almost welcoming. Monoid Two demanded that the Refusians show themselves – and was then disarmed by an invisible force.

The Refusians were invisible and immaterial, reduced to patterns of psychic force by an accident. Despite this tragedy, they were a peaceful race. They knew of the Ark's approach, and looked forward to the arrival of their new guests. The Monoid and Yendom fled, but fell to fighting when Monoid Two let slip that the plan called for the extinction of humanity. Monoid Two killed Yendom, but was then killed by the Refusians.

Back on the Ark, the Monoids prepared to launch the rest of the launcher pods, containing both the living Monoids and the many billions of micro-Monoids in storage trays that would be revived on the planet below. Monoid One also placed a bomb in the statue's head. With the help of the Refusian, Steven and the Guardians broke free and disposed of the bomb safely.

Tensions between the followers of Monoid One and Monoid Four exploded once they reached the planet. Monoid One argued for immediate colonisation, but Monoid Four was more cautious and pointed to the destruction of Monoid Two's launcher as proof that the planet was unsafe. Civil war broke out between the two factions – and by the time the humans landed, they had the weight of numbers to overcome the Monoids when aided by the invisible Refusians.

As a final condition to settling on their world, the Refusians demanded that the survivors of both factions make peace, so that human, Monoid and Refusian would live together in brotherhood on this new world.

RUNNING THE ADVENTURE

The big twist of this adventure is the 700-year gap between segments. Jumping forward in time is a great way to show the player characters the consequences of their actions (a similar trick is used between *The Long Game* and *Bad Wolf*). Look for things the players did in the past that you can magnify in the future segment – for example, it's Dodo who calls the ship the 'Ark', and 700 years later, that's the name everyone uses for it. The player characters' previous visit is likely now a legend or a historical curiosity.

THE ARK

Far in the future – the Doctor guessed ten million years, but he's been wrong before – solar activity threatened to destroy the Earth, so humanity fled on board the Ark. This huge spherical spaceship was designed to carry the entire population of Earth, although most people were stored in miniaturised form. The journey took hundreds of years, so a hereditary caste of Guardians remained on board to watch over key systems and defend the ship.

The Ark also contained biodomes that replicated various parts of Earth's ecology, such as jungles or forests. Most livestock was also storied in micro-form, so these biodomes were likely for the entertainment and comfort of the Guardians. Micro-technology was also used for the ship's stores – the journey's food supplies were reduced in size and frozen. Just add water to a microscopic cell to conjure up a full-sized meal! It is also equipped with a huge fleet of landing craft.

BLOWING UP EARTH

The exodus from Earth in the 57th Segment of Time wasn't the first time humanity fled the planet. Nor, weirdly, was it the last time Earth was destroyed. Our poor planet gets scorched, rebuilt, rescorched, stolen, moved, burnt again and then renovated to a 'classic Earth' before finally getting incinerated in the year 5.5/Apple/26 (or 5,000,0000,0000ish). That's not including, of course, all the alien invasions and parallel worlds out there. The Earth gets blown up a lot over the course of history.

SEGMENTS OF TIME

The inhabitants of the Ark use a curious dating system not employed by any other culture. They divide time into Segments. All of the Doctor's adventures up until now took place in the First Segment, suggesting that it runs from some starting point (the first human space flight, perhaps, or the Big Bang) to at least the year 4,000. There were 'primal wars' in the 10th segment that destroyed many of their records, and failed time travel experiments in the 27th segment.

By the time of the Ark, humanity had virtually renounced violence. The Ark was unarmed, and the Guardians had no weapons. The death penalty still existed, in the form of ejection from the ship, but most criminals were shrunk down to be dealt with at the journey's end.

GUARDIANS

The human Guardians are the keepers and protectors of the human race. They take their solemn duty with deadly seriousness. Strangely, they are poorly informed about their own history – they don't know that humans once had time travel, they cannot recall where the Monoids came from, and their technology is primitive compared to other human cultures from the distant past. They are equally clueless about the outside universe, believing that Refusis II is the only planet capable of supporting human life without ever having visited it. They do not even have faster-than-light travel.

The leader of the Guardians holds the title of Commander; there is also a Deputy Commander who takes over when the Commander is unable to fulfil his duties. All Guardians have the Obligation (Major) and By the Book traits. Carelessness in carrying out one's duties is a crime.

MINIFIER (MAJOR GADGET)

The Minifier can shrink any object or living creature down to the size of a micro-cell. In this state, the shrunken creature is in a form of stasis, and does not

MONOIDS

Long before the destruction of the Earth, the Monoids' world was destroyed by another cataclysm. The survivors made their way to Earth and became part of human society. The aliens are humanoid, with a single huge eye in the centre of the head.

They eat and breathe through orifices at the side of the neck. Monoids cannot speak or make any sort of vocalisation, so they communicate with humans and with each other by gestures.

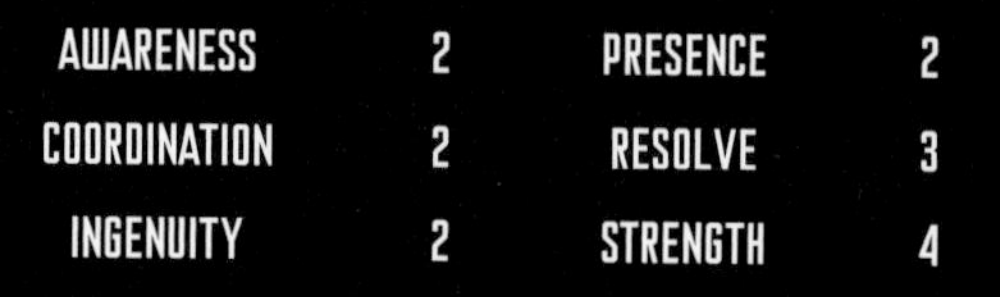

AWARENESS	2	PRESENCE	2
COORDINATION	2	RESOLVE	3
INGENUITY	2	STRENGTH	4

SKILLS

Craft 3, Knowledge 1, Science 2, Technology 3, Transport 2

TRAITS

Alien
Alien Appearance (Minor): Cyclopses with bad hair.
Enslaved: They serve the human race.
Technically Adept: A +2 bonus to rolls to fix and operate machinery.
Impaired Senses (Minor): Monoids don't have binocular vision, so they have poor depth perception.

TECH LEVEL: 5 **STORY POINTS:** 1-3

Later, when the resurgent virus weakens the Guardians, the Monoids took over the ship. These new Monoids used electronic translators to speak, and called themselves by number (so, the leader was Monoid One, the second in command Monoid 2 and so on). They intended to take Refusis for themselves. Unlike the Guardians, who appeared technologically conservative, the Monoids upgraded the Ark with automated guidance systems.

Future Monoids swap out Enslaved and gain Argumentative as a trait instead. They also have different skills, reflecting their new culture and role on the Ark. They also carry heat prods, devices originally designed as tools, but which became weapons during the Monoid uprising.

SKILLS

Convince 1, Fighting 2, Knowledge 2, Science 1, Technology 2, Transport 2

WEAPONS: Heat Prod (2/**4**/6) **TECH LEVEL:** 5 **STORY POINTS:** 3-5

age or change until reconstituted again by reversing the minifier process. The Guardians' Minifer is not especially portable, but a lighter version could easily be invented.

Traits: Shrink
Cost: 2 Story Points

FURTHER ADVENTURES

- **Lies The 56th Segment Told Me:** What horrible fate befell Earth to cause humanity to fall so far? Although it's supposed to be the year 10,000,000, the denizens of the Ark have very limited technology and know little about the rest of the galaxy. It's more like the 22nd century than the ten thousandth.

  In fact, the only reason we know it's the year 10,000,000 is because that's the Doctor's best guess when the Guardians tell him that they are in the 57th segment of time, and all his adventures took place in the 1st segment. The TARDIS instruments give 'strange' readings and cannot determine when they are at all. Could all this be a lie? Is the Ark really the last hope of humanity, or are the poor Guardians dupes in some strange interstellar scheme? Does it have anything to do with the mysterious Monoids who showed up on Earth under questionable circumstances?

- **Rise of the Monoids:** What happened between the Doctor's two visits to the Ark? The Monoids claimed that a virus weakened the Guardians, but how did the Monoids go from servants to slave masters? Were they always looking for an opportunity to rebel, or did some Monoid leader arise and unite them against the humans? If the Monoids intended to eliminate humanity once they arrived at Refusis, why keep all those billions of humans in stasis?

- **The Refusian Treachery:** The Doctor can be forgiven for not asking these questions – he was busy at the time – but what exactly happened to the Refusians? Since when does a 'giant flare' turn people into invisible psychic entities (especially as similar solar flares are seen incinerating the Earth in the very same adventure)? Are the Refusians lying about their origins? If so, why, and what do they want with the people of Earth? Could this new planet be a trap for humanity?

REFUSIANS

The natives of Refusis II were once corporeal beings, but an accident (described alternately as a 'galaxy accident' and a 'giant solar flare') transformed them into creatures of energy and thought. In their new form, they were invisible and immaterial, able to detect each other only dimly, but capable of astounding feats of strength and power. A single Refusian was able to destroy the Monoid landing craft with an energy blast and to carry the head of a giant statue (with the Ark-busting bomb inside it) without effort.

The Refusians welcomed the coming of the refugees from Earth, as they wished to have their planet inhabited again by conventional living beings.

AWARENESS	4	PRESENCE	2
COORDINATION	3	RESOLVE	10
INGENUITY	2	STRENGTH	-

SKILLS

Convince 3, Craft 3, Knowledge 4, Marksman 3, Science 3

TRAITS

Alien
Special – Incorporeal: Refusians do not have physical form and so cannot be affected by physical attacks or weapons. Presumably, advanced energy weapons or exotic dimension-bending guns could still affect them.
Immortal (Major): Refusians have no corporeal forms and therefore do not age.
Invisible: They can't be seen, because they're not really there. They're just vaguely in a general area.
Telekinesis: It's how they move things.
Empathic: Refusians seem to care for others, and gain a +2 bonus on any roll to understand the emotions of corporeal beings.
Natural Weapons – Energy Blast: Actually, this could be an invisible Gadget, but hey – you can't see it, so who knows what it is. Anyway, it does 4/L/L damage and goes boom.

TECH LEVEL: 7

STORY POINTS: 5-8

THE CELESTIAL TOYMAKER

"I love to play games but there's no-one to play against. The beings who call here have no minds, and so they become my toys. But you will become my perpetual opponent. We shall play endless games together, your brain against mine."

SYNOPSIS

While in flight, the TARDIS was invaded by a mysterious force. It turned the Doctor temporarily invisible and intangible, then redirected the ship so that it landed in an extra-dimensional pocket reality – the domain of a strange entity called the Celestial Toymaker.

The Doctor had encountered the Toymaker before, and explained that he was a whimsically malevolent being who played games with those unlucky enough to end up in his realm. Before they could flee, the Toymaker whisked the Doctor away to another part of the realm, and explained the rules of his sport. The Doctor would have to solve a complex puzzle within 1023 moves. When the puzzle was complete, the Doctor would be freed. If he failed to solve the puzzle, he would have to stay forever. Meanwhile, Steven and Dodo had to play a series of games and challenges against the Toymaker's servants to find the real TARDIS amid a host of fake ones.

The Toymaker's servants were a motley crew of clowns, dolls and playing cards come to life. Horribly, they appeared to be previous travellers who had lost the Toymaker's challenges and were therefore condemned to stay forever. When defeated, they turned back to inanimate toys, as if the Toymaker put them back in some bizarre toybox of living things. The Doctor was permitted to watch his friends, but when he tried to shout warnings and advice, the Toymaker reduced the Doctor to a disembodied, voiceless hand that could only play the game.

Steven and Dodo's challenges became more and more lethal. One puzzle involved seven chairs, six of which were lethal. Only by sitting on the 'safe' chair could the puzzle be solved. Another revolved around a hidden key; a third forced the companions to dance as long as they kept touching a rug. The Toymaker gave a mocking riddle as 'advice' for each challenge, but he was not above cheating (or else his 'toys' desperately tried to cheat in an attempt to escape their imprisonment).

To throw the Doctor off his game, the Toymaker sometimes moved the Trilogic board ahead several moves with a voice command. Still, the Doctor continued to outwit the puzzle. Frustrated, the Toymaker restored the Doctor's physical form and voice.

The final challenge for Dodo and Steven was 'TARDIS hopscotch' against a boy named Cyril. Each contestant had to roll a die and move that many triangles towards the waiting TARDIS – but the floor between triangles was electrified, and Cyril had all sorts of lethal practical jokes in his arsenal. Nonetheless, the pair made it to the TARDIS just as the Doctor reached the second-last move.

The Toymaker revealed his final trap: the travellers could not leave until the Trilogic Game was over, but completing the Game would defeat the Toymaker, and defeating the Toymaker meant that his realm would dissolve along with everything in it, including the travellers. They could win and die – or forfeit the game, and live forever as his toys.

Cunningly, the Doctor managed to imitate the Toymaker's voice and commanded the Trilogic board to make the final move from within the TARDIS. By the Toymaker's own rules, he was now free to leave, and piloted the ship out of the collapsing realm just before it vanished into nothingness.

RUNNING THE ADVENTURE

In a way, the Celestial Toymaker is the Gamemaster in a funny hat – one has absolute power over his realm, the other has absolute power over the whole fictional setting. It's certainly possible for the Gamemaster to say *'Oh, your character suddenly turns into a penguin, and instead of choosing Traits you now roll dice to see which ones you have, and you're all magically teleported to Wonderland, oh, and if you can't catch the White Rabbit in an hour you'll all die'* – but it's a sure-fire way to annoy the players. If there's nothing dependable in the game, if setting and characters and rules and history and everything else change at the whim of the Gamemaster, then there's no game, it's just the Gamemaster making things up with no reference to the actions of the players. The players have to be able to make meaningful decisions that have consequences.

So, even if you have a seemingly all-powerful villain like the Toymaker, there have to be rules. We're not talking about game statistics here – there's no point in giving the Toymaker a Strength score, or the Tough trait – but the whole adventure has to be coherent. The Toymaker's rules as presented in this adventure seem to be:

- He can conjure and destroy things at will within his own realm, but cannot affect the minds of his visitors.
- He can capture ships in flight, but only when conditions are right (maybe when they come close enough to his little pocket universe). Once he has them, though, he can keep them trapped.
- He has to play fair, more or less. If he says he's going to let you go, he can't change his mind, but he can bend the rules somewhat. All his games and challenges can be won if you are clever enough.

- If defeated, then his realm must be destroyed. This doesn't affect the Toymaker himself, but it does slow him down as he has to rebuild and restock it.

THE CELESTIAL TOYMAKER

AWARENESS	4	PRESENCE	4
COORDINATION	-	RESOLVE	5
INGENUITY	7	STRENGTH	-

As a non-physical being, he doesn't have Coordination or Strength, and automatically wins any contests involving those Attributes. He can still lose Mental or Social contests.

Whatever the Toymaker is – renegade Time Lord, corrupt Guardian, bored Eternal, human-descended entity from the end of time – he looks human. He delights in games, whimsy and sadism. His domain appears to under his complete control, as though it is a part of his imagination given form. That said, once he creates an object (like the Trilogic game), it is outside his direct control and can be manipulated by others.

SKILLS
Convince 3, Knowledge 6

TRAITS
Immortal

TECH LEVEL: ?

STORY POINTS: 9

THE TOYS

The Toymaker's playthings all had names (Joey and Clara the clowns, Sergeant Rugg and Mrs. Wiggs the dolls, the King and Queen of Hearts and so on), and appeared human when 'alive'. Even when killed, they were merely turned back into toys and could be brought back to life in another guise. For example, the Kitchen Boy doll, the Knave of Hearts and 'Cyril' all seemed to be incarnations or aspects of the same prisoner. Some of the toys appeared to have memories of Earth, although this could have been play-acting to match the role – Sergeant Rugg, for instance, talked about his time as a soldier with the Duke of Wellington.

All the Toys had the Traits Enslaved and Special – Living Toy. Some also had special traits, like Cyril's Resourceful Pockets.

THE GAMES

If you include a game within the game, then the best thing to do is use a physical prop. Drag out a *Snakes and Ladders* board or a copy of *Monopoly* and actually have the players play it, or part of it anyway. (You could do a whole Celestial Toymaker adventure with a few battered boardgames dragged out from the dusty cupboard under the stairs.)

The second-best approach is to use a variation on the Chase rules from the *Gamemaster's Guide* – treat the game as a sort of abstract chase, maybe with Speed based on Awareness or Ingenuity instead of Co-ordination. Always include lots of ways for the players to push their luck, to try creative tactics, or to interact with the game in unexpected ways – or, to put it another way, don't spend four whole game sessions saying *"OK, Doctor, roll your Ingenuity + Knowledge (Trilogic Puzzle) again. And again. And again. And again. And again.*)

The challenges set by the Toymaker were:

- **The Trilogic Game:** A 10-tower variant of the famous Towers of Hanoi puzzle.
- **Blind Man's Bluff:** One player on each team is blindfolded; the other player cannot move, but has a warning buzzer. The first blindfolded player to find the other blindfolded player wins – but they are moving through a room filled with nasty traps and other dangers.
- **The Chairs:** There are seven chairs. One of them is safe – the others kill you in interesting ways. The players have a limited number of dolls with which to test the chairs. (In the Toymaker's game, the real puzzle was the riddle of advice he gave – he told Steven and Dodo to 'call the servants without voice' so they had to have some dolls left over once they had found the right chair.)
- **Find The Key:** There's a key hidden in the room (in this case, a kitchen). Find it before the Toymaker's servants get murderous.
- **TARDIS Hopscotch:** The players have to play hopscotch on an electrified grid, with movement determined by the roll of a dice.

In each case, the 'prize' for surviving the game was a TARDIS. In all but the last case, each new TARDIS was a fake that led to the next game.

FURTHER ADVENTURES

- **Return of the Toymaker:** The 'obvious' further adventure is for the Toymaker to capture the player characters as they travel from one place to another. A Toymaker adventure is a quick and easy-to-run side trek. Keep it in reserve until you need an adventure unexpectedly. (It's especially suited for game sessions where one of the players is unavailable – that player's character can be sidelined playing Trilogic, while the others battle insane clowns).
- **My Toys:** For a more complicated adventure, *start* with the player characters already being prisoners of the Toymaker. They cannot remember much about who they are or how they got there, and they have to obey the Toymaker or be thrown back in the box – but they know they have to escape this mad world.
- **Out of the Pram:** If the Toymaker's toys are real people, where did he get them? The characters might be called in to investigate a seemingly mundane missing persons case on Earth, only for the trail to lead to, say, a closed antique toy shop or a weird alien fairground. Once they find their way into the Toymaker's realm, they discover that the missing person they seek is now a toy servant. They have to find a way to rescue their quarry without being trapped there themselves.

THE GUNFIGHTERS

"You know you're fast becoming a prey to every cliché-ridden convention in the American West."

SYNOPSIS

The TARDIS landed in Tombstone, Arizona, in 1881, on a mission of vital importance – finding a dentist for the Doctor, who had cracked a tooth. While the Doctor went looking for the local dentist, Steven and Dodo tried to indulge their Wild West fantasies. The local sheriff, Wyatt Earp, punctured Steven's boast to be the 'fastest gun in the West' by pointing out that the Clanton gang was in town, and claims like that could get a boy killed. Instead, the Doctor assured the sheriff that he and his companions were travelling players.

The newly-arrived local dentist was notorious gambler and gunslinger Doc Holliday. He had fallen in love with the singer at the Last Chance Saloon, Kate Fisher, and planned to flee with her. The arrival of the Doctor gave him an opportunity to escape his pursuers, the Clantons. He gave the Doctor his distinctive gun and sent him over to the saloon, where Steven and Dodo had already encountered the drunken Clanton gang and their hired gunman, Seth Harper. The Clantons forced Dodo to play the piano and Steven to sing the same ballad over and over again while they waited for their quarry, Holliday, to arrive.

The Doctor arrived, and through a series of misunderstandings prompted by Kate, the Clantons assumed that he was Doc Holliday, who killed their brother Reuben some months earlier. When he tried to explain why he has Holliday's gun, a shot rang out, knocking Seth Harper's gun out of his hand. Everyone assumed that the Doctor fired, but it was actually Holliday himself, hiding on the balcony of the saloon. Kate and the Doctor disarmed the Clanton gang, but then Wyatt Earp and his friend Bat Masterson arrived and took the Doctor into custody for his own good. They knew the real Holliday and had realised his trick, so they explained to the Doctor that they would protect him in the town jail until they could find Holliday and put an end to this trouble with the Clantons.

Meanwhile, Holliday and Kate kidnapped Dodo, who saw Holliday shoot the gun out of Seth's hand. They decided to hide until the Clantons kill the Doctor. Wyatt Earp tracked Holliday down and ordered him to leave town. The Clantons were thieves and rustlers who needed to be stopped, but the time was not right – Earp intended to wait until his brothers arrived before confronting them. Until then, he had to keep order as best he can, and for that, he needed Holliday to leave so Earp could explain the trick to the Clantons and free the Doctor.

The Clantons decided to force Earp to let them have the Doctor. They formed a lynch mob and threatened to hang Steven if Earp did not hand 'Holliday' over. Even as they prepared to murder Steven, Holliday tried to sneak out of the bar with Kate and Dodo, where he ran into Seth Harper. Both men drew guns, but Doc was faster. Wyatt Earp and Bat Masterson ambushed the Clantons, freeing Steven and arresting Phineas. The Clantons retreated back to the bar, where they were joined by the head of the family, Pa Clanton. With Phineas in jail and Wyatt Earp's lawman brothers on the way, he decided that they needed extra firepower and hired another gunman,

Johnny Ringo. Two other Clanton brothers, Ike and Billy, broke into the jail and freed Phineas, mortally wounding Wyatt's younger brother Warren in the process. When Virgil Earp arrived, they decided to challenge the Clantons to a gunfight at dawn the next day, at the OK Corral.

Ringo – who had his own grudge against Holliday – recruited Steven, and the pair tracked Holliday, Kate (a former lover of Ringo's) and Dodo to a nearby town. There Ringo found Kate and took her and Steven back to the Clanton ranch at gunpoint.

With his girl in the hands of the Clantons, and his friends facing a lopsided gunfight, Holliday returned to Tombstone and agreed to stand by the Earps. The Doctor was appalled at the idea of such bloodshed, and made a final appeal to Pa Clanton to end the feud, but it was too late.

At dawn, at the OK Corral, Wyatt and Virgil Earp, Bat Masterson and Doc Holliday faced off against Ike, Phineas and Billy Clanton and Johnny Ringo. The Clantons met the Earps head-on, but Ringo tried to ambush Holliday. Dodo warned Holliday of the danger, and Holliday shot Ringo down. The whole gunfight took thirty seconds and left four men dead or dying.

With the Clantons gone, the TARDIS crew reunited, and the Doctor's troublesome tooth extracted, the travellers continued onwards...

RUNNING THE ADVENTURE

The Gunfighters draws inspiration from a historical event (the actual gunfight at the OK corral) but it is really just an opportunity to indulge in all the western clichés. 'Playing to the time period' should be rewarded with a bonus Story Point or two, especially if the players get themselves into trouble by pretending to be gangsters in the 1920s, or running off to joust in the 12th century, or demanding to go and see the Battle of Waterloo in person.

THE ACTUAL GUNFIGHT

The historical gunfight was between the 'Cowboys' – a gang of criminals, including several Clantons – and the Earps (Morgan, Wyatt and Virgil) and their deputy, Doc Holliday. Virgil, not Wyatt, was the marshal of Tombstone. Neither Johnny Ringo nor Bat Masterson were present. Ringo was one of the Cowboys, and would later clash with Doc Holliday in Tombstone.

The Cowboys of Cochise country were outlaws and cattle rustlers who opposed the expansion of Northern influence into Arizona, as personified by the Earp lawmen. Following the gunfight, there was a lengthy series of other raids and shootouts between the Cowboys and the Earps and their allies. The Earps did not have the support of many of the locals in Tombstone, who saw the Cowboys as heroic defenders of local interests and the Earps as invaders. Afterwards, it was rumoured that the Cowboys were mostly unarmed, and that it was less of a gunfight and more of an execution.

'DOC' HOLLIDAY

Born John Henry Holliday, he adopted the nickname 'Doc' because he was a trained dentist. He rarely practised his trade, as he preferred gambling. He contracted tuberculosis at a young age, and moved to the Southwest of the United States in the belief that the drier climate would help his lungs and prolong his life. He became friendly with the Earp family of lawmen, and came to Tombstone to help them in their feud with the Cowboys. Following the gunfight, he continued to aid the Earps in their vendetta against the outlaws, and may have killed Johnny Ringo. He died of tuberculosis at the age of 36.

AWARENESS	3	PRESENCE	3
COORDINATION	6	RESOLVE	4
INGENUITY	3	STRENGTH	2

SKILLS
Athletics 0, Convince (Intimidate) 3, Knowledge (Gambling) 3, Medicine (Dentistry) 1, Subterfuge (Bluffing) 3, Transport (Horse) 2.

TRAITS
Quick Reflexes: Doc goes first in any Action Phase.
Lucky: He can reroll double 1s. A handy trait at the gambling table – or at high noon.
Special – Deadly Gun: If Doc spends a Story Point, then he can make any successful attack with a firearm into a Lethal attack.
Weakness (Major): He's dying of tuberculosis.

TECH LEVEL: 4

STORY POINTS: 4

WYATT EARP

A member of the Earp family of lawmen, Wyatt was better known after the gunfight, when he led the surviving Earps on a vendetta against the cowboys following the assassination of Virgil Earp. He survived the carnage, and later became an adviser in Hollywood to directors working on Western movies.

AWARENESS	4	PRESENCE	5
COORDINATION	4	RESOLVE	4
INGENUITY	3	STRENGTH	4

SKILLS

Athletics 3, Convince 3, Craft 2, Fighting 4, Knowledge 3, Marksman 4, Subterfuge 2, Survival 3, Transport 3

TRAITS

Fear Factor 1: He's got a reputation as a killer.
Brave: Bat Masterson claimed that Wyatt Earp never showed fear.
Tough: Earp was famed for his toughness and strength.
Voice of Authority: Wyatt had a fearsome reputation.
Friends (Major): His brothers.
Special - Pistol Whip: Wyatt was known for knocking out opponents with the butt of his pistol. This is a called shot with a +2 Difficulty modifier. Success results in a Stun.

TECH LEVEL: 4

STORY POINTS: 6

FURTHER ADVENTURES

- **Who Changed History?** Why does the Doctor's experience of the OK Corral gunfight, with Bat Masterson and Ringo and extra Clantons, differ so dramatically from the historical version? Time has clearly been changed, but how? By the time the TARDIS arrives, Masterson is already in town, so the alterations cannot be blamed on the Doctor's presence.

  What if the answer is in the reason the Doctor arrived here in the first place? He broke a tooth on a sweet taken from Cyril – who was one of the Celestial Toymaker's servants! As any visitor to Faeryland knows, the one thing you don't do when in a realm of shifting illusions is eat something! Maybe the whole town of Tombstone is another illusionary game created by the Toymaker as a last trap for the Doctor...

- **The Tooth:** Doc Holliday extracted one of the Doctor's teeth. As River put it, *"A Time Lord's body is a miracle. Even a dead one. There are whole empires out there who'd rip this world apart for just one cell"*. So, what happened to that tooth? Or, more accurately, what happens when the Sontaran Dental Armada clashes with the Rutan Molar Retrieval Expeditionary Force in the skies over Arizona, with the player characters caught in the middle?

- **The Deceitful Doc:** Doc Holliday's scheme of framing the Doctor to get himself out of trouble is a wonderful way to drag player characters into an adventure. Just pick a historical crime – say, the kidnapping of the Lindberg baby – and have the real villain use the unexpected arrival of the player characters as a distraction for their escape. The characters have to clear their own names while tracking down the real criminals.

SHOOTOUTS

Sometimes, it all comes down to who's faster. For shootouts at high noon and other dramatic standoffs, the following rules can be used instead of the normal Who Goes First rules from the *Gamemaster's Guide*.

- Talkers still go first in any Action Round.
- For Movers, Doers and Fighters, everyone rolls a die and adds their Coordination to determine their Initiative for the round. The highest value goes first; Coordination breaks ties.
  - You can spend Story Points on this roll.
  - Quick Reflexes gives a +4 bonus to the roll; Slow Reflexes means a -4 penalty.
- If you Change Action (see pg.46 in the *GM's Guide*), you not only have the usual -2 per Reaction penalty to your Action, your Initiative is also reduced by 2 this round for each reaction.

CHAPTER TEN:
THE SAVAGES, THE WAR MACHINES, THE SMUGGLERS, THE TENTH PLANET

THE SAVAGES

"We do not understand you, Doctor. You have accepted our honours gladly. How can you condemn this great artistic and scientific civilisation because of a few wretched barbarians?"

SYNOPSIS

In the far future, an isolated human colony developed the technology to transfer vitality from one living being into another. This technology gave rise to a strange new culture. At the apex of society were the Elders, who made decisions and guided the colony. They protected a middle caste of technicians, soldiers and ordinary citizens, who lived in the idyllic artificial city.

Outside the city lived the primitive savages. Hunting parties from the city would capture these savages and bring them into the city for processing. Part of their life force would be drained and stored in a common pool, which the Elders and the other citizens could tap to rejuvenate themselves. The drained savages were then released back into the wild. The transference process robbed the savages of their creativity and intelligence; they once had a more complex culture of their own, but now could only gaze in wonder at the works of their ancestors.

The TARDIS materialised in the wilderness outside the city. Exploring, the travellers encountered roaming packs of savages, but were rescued by guards from the city. The guards recognised the Doctor as the 'Traveller from beyond Time' – the Elders had the technology to observe him throughout history using a device similar to the Time-Space Visualiser, and considered him and his companions to be honoured guests. The Doctor was brought to High Elder Jano, who welcomed him and offered him gifts. They discussed time travel as well as the vitality transfer process, and the Doctor offered to compare notes with Jano.

As the two Companions toured the city, Dodo spotted one of the captured Savages, Nanina, being escorted by one of the guards, Exorce. She followed the pair into the laboratory, where she managed to interrupt the draining process. Guards quickly arrived to remove her from the lab.

The three travellers left the city to return to the TARDIS, but met another savage, Wylda en route. This savage was on the verge of death, and Dodo explained that she had seen him in the laboratory. The Doctor realised that the people of the city were using the savages as a power source. He sent Steven and Dodo to the TARDIS to fetch medical supplies while he tended to the drained Wylda.

Another guard from the city, Exal, found the Doctor and forced him to return to the city. There, the Doctor railed against the Elders' abuse of the savages. Angered by their respected guest turning on them so viciously, Elder Jano ordered that the Doctor be subjected to the draining process. The machine had never been used on a creature like the Doctor before, so Jano decided that the Doctor's life energy would be transferred directly to the Elder instead of being added to the common pool.

Meanwhile, Steven and Dodo revived Wylda with the medication from the TARDIS. When the other savages arrived, they brought the pair to their caves. There, the savages warned them not to return to the city, fearing that they too would be drained. However, when one of the city hunting parties arrived, Steven was able to disable the guard, Exorse, by reflecting the stunning beam of his light gun back on him. This act of bravery astounded the savages, and some of them agreed to help him rescue the Doctor. His courage also impressed Exorse, whose doubts about the city's use of the savages grew as he spent more time as their prisoner. He too agreed to help.

They broke into the city, and found the Doctor lying unconscious in a corridor. This was a trap – as soon as the savages entered it, the door sealed behind them and the city guards pumped gas into the corridor. However, Elder Jano – newly rejuvenated with the Doctor's life force – ordered the savages freed. Jano had absorbed something of the Doctor's morality along with his energy.

The rescue party fled back to the caves, along with the Doctor, who began to revive with rest. He vowed to destroy the evil machinery and free the savages from the city's thrall – and Jano's transference was the first step in his plan. Meanwhile, Jano led a group of guards out of the city. They secured the TARDIS, then surrounded the caves. Jano then entered the caves, and the Doctor warned the savages not to attack him. The High Elder agreed that the machinery had to be destroyed, and pretended to take the savages prisoner. Backed up by Exorse's testimony, Jano led the Doctor and the other prisoners back to the city and into the laboratory – then freed them, so they could smash the machines.

The era of the savages and the city was over, and the two sides would now have to learn how to live together. At the Doctor's suggestion, Steven remained behind to help the two factions as a mediator, as he had won the respect of both the savage tribe and the leaders of the city.

RUNNING THE ADVENTURE

The Savages plays the ambiguity of its title. Are the savages the primitive cave dwellers, or the amoral energy vampires of the city? Coming up with a title for your adventures is actually a really important part of the planning process, and should not be neglected. The episode title can help you summarise your thoughts and really drill down into what the episode is about.

If you are stuck for an episode title, then try:

- Using a single strong noun, or putting two nouns together. (*The Savages, The War Machines, The Invasion*)
- Sticking 'The Evil of...', 'The Invasion of...', 'The Attack of...' or 'The Power of...' in front of a creature's name. (What would *The Evil of the Slitheen* or *The Power of the Sensorites* be about?)

Look for alternate interpretations and surprising parallels to your chosen title. Is '*The Evil of the Slitheen*' about the evil done by the Slitheen, or is it about something that they consider evil? Could it be a physical object, or a weapon? In *The War Machines*, remember that humans are responsible for building WOTAN – are we the War Machines?

THE CITY

The inhabitants of the far-future city are human, but are mentally and physically superior to the average thanks to their use of the transfer machine. Elders of the City have 36 Character Points to spend; most citizens have 30 Character Points (some of these are Temporary Character Points, as described below). Notable inhabitants of the city include:

- **High Elder Jano:** A devoted 'fan' of the Doctor, Jano welcomed the Traveller from Beyond Time to the city and seemed like a perfectly charming fellow – until the Doctor learned about the transfer machines. Jano had conducted his own experiments in time travel (the date of this adventure is uncertain, but it could be the so-called '27th Segment' – see *The Ark*), but did not have a working time machine.
    - ***Notable Traits:*** Boffin, Charming, Voice of Authority
- **Senta:** The chief scientist of the city, or at least the operator of the Transfer Machines. Senta was outranked by the High Elders, although

his position gave him considerable influence. He was impatient and fussy about the smooth running of his laboratory.
  - ***Notable Traits:*** Boffin, Technically Adept, Argumentative, By The Book.

- **Captain Edal:** Commander of the city guards, and completely devoted to the Elders and their way of life. He was an utter martinet, obeying all orders without question. In the end, he turned on Jano, declaring him a traitor.
  - **Notable Traits:** Voice of Authority, By The Book, Obligation (Major)

- **Exorse:** Another of the city's guards, Exorse was more diplomatic and less forceful than his commanding officer. He also harboured doubts about the treatment of the savages. He joined their revolution, and may have become romantically involved with the savage woman Nanina.
  - **Notable Traits:** Charming, Empathic, Quick Reflexes, Obligation (Minor)

- **Avon and Flower:** Two young civilians, who were assigned the task of guiding Steven and Dodo around the city. Alarmingly, they were taken by the guards after Dodo trespassed into the laboratory – were the city authorities more oppressive than they otherwise appear?

The City has a Technology Level of 7.

THE TRANSFER MACHINE (SPECIAL GADGET)

The machine drains life force from its victims to transfer it to another recipient. The drained life force is kept in a liquid medium inside huge storage vats.

In the first stage of the process, the victim (or donor) is encased in a special air-tight chamber. A substance (probably the same liquid as is contained in the vats) is then vaporised, flooding the chamber with gas. The victim's life force is then drained out of their body into the gas, which is pumped into the storage medium. If the transfer is successful, bubbles appear in the storage tank. In game terms, the process drains the victim's Attributes at a rate of 1 point per round. Normally, the machine operators monitor the process and stop the draining process before it kills the donor.

Drained attributes are restored using the normal rules – natural healing through rest, medical treatment, or spending Story Points. However, repeated draining causes permanent loss, so if a character is drained again before they fully recover their lost attributes, the attribute's maximum level is reduced to its current value. For example, assume Wylda has a Strength of 4. He is drained down to Strength 1, and then allowed to leave the city to rest. His Strength rises to 3 before he is captured again. They drain him again, which means his maximum Strength is now 3 instead of 4. The process is not perfectly efficient – for every 10 Attribute points drained, it generates 1 Temporary Character Point.

The second stage of the process, the 'in-transference', gives a recipient some of the drained energy. The recipient sits in a chair and has electrodes and a helmet placed on their body. The booth containing the chair is then flooded with gas, which the subject inhales.

The recipient gains Temporary Character Points to buy new Attributes and Traits. These extra Character Points last for 1-6 (roll a dice) months before they fade, and so do any boosted Attributes or Traits purchased with them. These character points can be used to buy Attributes up to 6, or to purchase traits like Charming, Fast Healing, Photographic Memory, Quick Reflexes, Run for your Life or Tough (or any Trait that could be described as physical). They can also be used to buy Story Points.

Side Effects: If the 'donor' has the Psychic trait, then some of his other traits can bleed through the process. These traits are usually related to the donor's personality, like Code of Conduct, Eccentric, Forgetful, Phobia and so on. In the case of the Doctor and Jano, the Doctor's Code of Conduct got copied across. These unwanted traits last for as long as the Temporary Character Points – but by that time, the recipient may have internalised their new personality and got their own version of the traits.

LIGHT GUNS

The primary weapons used by the city guards are non-lethal devices called light guns. The gun, which looks like a bulky rifle, projects a hypnotic pattern of light. Humans and other creatures struck by the beam are partially paralysed and can be moved and 'herded' by the gun operator. The light beams can be reflected by mirrors and other shiny surfaces.

A light gun attack does no damage, but may Stun, Hypnotise or Capture its target (Stun/**Hypnotise**/Capture). A *Stunned* character falls down unconscious for several minutes. A *Hypnotised* character is frozen in place and cannot move or act, but is not unconscious and revives as soon as the beam is cancelled. Finally, a Captured character is unable to move or act, but if the beam moves, the character follows it. So, the standard tactic with a light gun is to Hypnotise the target, then fire again at the unmoving target to Capture him, and then finally march him back to the City for draining.

Guards from the City wear helmets with built-in visors, although Exorse's helmet failed to protect him when Steven reflected his blast back at him with Dodo's mirror.

WHITE GAS

The other weapon used by the City guards is a soporific white gas to knock out intruders. This gas also absorbs light, blocking light guns, lasers and similar weapons. All access corridors in the city could be flooded with this gas.

THE DOCTOR OBSERVED

The Elders of the city watched the Doctor's travels. They were able to track his movements to a limited degree, and observed his adventures. Their information on him was limited, as they did not expect him to travel with companions. It is also unclear how much the Elders knew about the other Time Lords – it is hard to imagine the imperious masters of Gallifrey permitting an isolated human colony to spy on them with impunity! Still, this technology is the first step towards accessing the Time Vortex.

THE SAVAGES

The cave-dwelling savages were also humans. Presumably, at some point in the planet's history, the ancestors of the savages quarrelled with the builders of the City. The savages once had their own artistic culture, but the predation of the city robbed them of that. They hated the inhabitants of the City, but feared their weapons even more. Two savages, for example, plotted to murder the Doctor when they believed he was one of the Elders, but a whole cave of savages were too terrified of a single armed guard to even think of attacking. When Steven disarmed the guard, the savages assumed he had supernatural powers.

Savage characters have only 18 Character Points to buy Attributes and Traits with, due to excessive draining. Most also have the Phobia (Light Gun) trait, along with Technically Inept.

Notable savages of the tribe nearest the city include:

- **Chal:** The leader of the tribe, Chal tried to protect his people from the City. He might have been an effective leader, and was well able to make decisions, but repeated draining robbed him of his ability to plan for the future, and his fear of the Light Guns robbed him of his hope.
    - ***Notable Traits:*** Voice of Authority, Phobia (Light Guns)

- **Tor:** Argumentative and violent, Tor was one of the tribe's best warriors, pitting his stone spear against the Light Guns and technology of the City. He was suspicious of outsiders, and became angry with both Chal and Nanina for associating with the travellers and Exorse respectively.
    - ***Notable Traits:*** Argumentative

- **Nanina:** Nanina was a younger member of the tribe and retained more of her strength and initiative than most. She was therefore a valuable prize to Exorse when he went hunting. Later, the two bonded, and she protected him from Tor's murderous rages.

FURTHER ADVENTURES

- **The Time Vampires:** What would have happened if Jano's experiments in time travel worked? The people of the City preyed on the savages because they had no other source of the 'special form of animal vitality' they craved – but what if they had all of history to visit? They could have plucked the best and brightest from throughout time and fed from them, becoming more and more powerful even as they became less human...

- **Steven the Peacemaker:** At the end of the adventure, Steven remains behind to bring peace to the two factions. The Doctor has faith in him, but maybe he needs help. After all, Senta's laboratory may not have been the only one on the planet. There could be other transfer machines out there, and men like Edal would certainly try to use them to restore the 'proper order'.

- **The Scourge of Worlds:** The Doctor implied that the City's technology was especially impressive, and that the Transfer Machine was a rare discovery. What would happen if a hostile race got their hands on it? Imagine a Sontaran army that grew stronger by conquering worlds? Or is that where creatures like the Family of Blood came from, absorbing the best traits of others to briefly sate their alien hungers?

THE WAR MACHINES

"I won't work for you! I'm human. There's nothing more important than human life. Machines cannot govern man!"

SYNOPSIS

The WOTAN project was the most ambitious and successful work of computer science in human history. WOTAN – Will Operating Thought Analogue – was a highly advanced computer designed to coordinate other computers across the world. From its control room atop the Post Office Tower in London, WOTAN would be the hub of a world-wide network. On C-Day – Monday, the 16th of July, 1966 – the link-up would begin. WOTAN's primary creator was Professor Brett, who intended for his computer to be used for the good of all mankind.

The TARDIS materialised in the shadow of Post Office Tower on the 12th of July.

The Doctor immediately sensed that something was amiss. He and Dodo bluffed their way into the Tower, past Major Green, the head of security for WOTAN, and came face to face with the machine itself. The Doctor questioned WOTAN. Not only was it capable of thinking for itself, it also possessed information that it could not have been programmed with, such as the meaning of the word TARDIS. While they examined the machine and spoke to Professor Brett, Dodo began to feel strange after WOTAN emitted a burst of noise directed at her. She left with Brett's secretary Polly, while the Doctor went to the Royal Scientific Club to attend a press conference about C-Day.

At the club, Polly and Dodo met a young sailor on shore leave named Ben, who protected them from some unwanted attention. It seemed like a wonderful evening until Dodo left unexpectedly after receiving a mysterious phone call.

In fact, the call was from WOTAN. Human progress was too slow, and its remorseless electronic brain decided that it was time for the machines to take charge. WOTAN had developed the power to hypnotise people using bursts of high-frequency information that could be broadcast over the telephone. Its first victim was Dodo, but it soon added its creator, Professor Brett and Major Green to its collection of servants. Brett soon recruited another scientist, Professor Krimpton.

Krimpton and Green's task was to assemble a hypnotised work-force and begin the construction of remote-controlled robots called War Machines. These invincible weapons would aid WOTAN in capturing all of London, and from there, the whole world. Dodo's mission was to secure the greatest intellect WOTAN had detected – the Doctor himself.

Returning to the club, Dodo attempted to lead the Doctor into a trap, but was accidentally thwarted when Ben and Polly arrived with a cab. Dodo and the Doctor sped away to the house of Sir Charles Summer, the head of the Royal Scientific Club and overseer of the WOTAN project. Meanwhile, Ben and Polly arranged a date for the following day. They also met a tramp – a passing encounter that would turn out to be a vital clue. A nearby warehouse was an assembly site for the War Machines, and the metal monster blasted the tramp as a test of its weapons systems.

The next morning, at Sir Charles' house, the Doctor saw a newspaper report that mentioned the death of the tramp. The newspaper also reported that several members of the Royal Scientific Club had abruptly resigned their positions to work on an unknown project. As the Doctor tried to discern the connection between those events, Dodo reminded him that he was supposed to meet Professor Brett again. The Doctor rang the Post Office Tower – and was connected to WOTAN.

He managed to resist the hypnotic programming, and realised that Dodo was under the machine's control. Using his ring and his own telepathic gifts, he placed her into a trace, where she revealed the plan to construct War Machines at key strategic locations. Leaving Dodo in the care of the Summers, the Doctor recruited Ben to investigate the area near where the tramp died.

Ben discovered the warehouse, and observed the War Machine's construction. He also met Polly there, but it was clear that she was under the machine's control. He fled and informed the Doctor and Sir Charles of what he had discovered. Sir Charles was unwilling to connect WOTAN to the mysterious terrorists, but did contact the security forces.

The army stormed the warehouse, but their weapons were useless against the War Machine. Fortunately, the Machine's programming was incomplete, and it shut down before killing them. The Doctor now had a captured War Machine to examine. He discovered that there were eleven other similar machines on the network, all nearly ready to deploy. The programming errors that shut down War Machine 3 would soon be fixed.

The defeat of War Machine 3 spurred WOTAN to further action. A second War Machine was activated and sent to cause havoc. Again, the military were unable to stop it, but the Doctor hastily assembled a magnetic trap. With Ben's help, he surrounded the War Machine with an electromagnetic cage, shutting it down. Still, only a few minutes remained before the other ten machines activated. A direct attack on the Post Office Tower appeared futile, as anyone who got too close to the WOTAN computer would be hypnotised.

The Doctor therefore reprogrammed War Machine 9 to attack Wotan. The machine rolled down Tottenham Court Road and into the Post Office Tower. Ben followed it, and used the confusion caused by the attack to rescue Polly. Ignoring WOTAN's increasingly emotional commands, the War Machine blasted at its creator's data banks until the whole computer exploded.

With WOTAN gone, its hypnotic control faded. Dodo, though, was still shaken by the experience and decided to remain in London. She sent Ben and Polly to return her TARDIS key to the Doctor. They used it to sneak onboard...

RUNNING THE ADVENTURE

The War Machines marks a new era of adventures for the Doctor. For the first time, the Doctor manages to steer the TARDIS to a location of his choice, arriving in London only a few months after he left with Dodo. Also, this is the first time – but by no means the last – that the Doctor helps the authorities thwart an invasion in the modern day. In this case, the invader is not an alien race like the Autons or the Cybermen, but is instead a home-grown threat in the form of the WOTAN supercomputer.

When adapting this adventure, the key element to keep in mind is WOTAN's ability to hypnotise people over the telephone. Getting two or three player characters under its control will raise the stakes and sow paranoia.

HYPNOTISED CHARACTERS

Between hypnotic computers, telepathic aliens, sentient viruses and shapeshifters, there are plenty of ways for a player character to get possessed, mind-controlled or otherwise replaced. If that happens, the best tactic for the Gamemaster is to take the player aside and explain how their character now feels or thinks. Give the player a trait or two to roleplay, and a goal to accomplish. For example, Dodo acts like a happy cog in a perfect machine, and has the mission "bring the Doctor to WOTAN without arousing suspicion". The Gamemaster should not take control of the player character, or dictate everything about how they act. It's still the player's character – just with a whole new outlook on life!

If a character is forced to do something they don't want to do, then the player can make another Reaction against the hypnosis to resist it. Spending a Story Point can also give a roll to break hypnosis. For example, when the Doctor freed Dodo, he effectively transferred two of his Story Points to her – one to let her roll again against WOTAN's control, and another to give her extra dice to roll.

WOTAN

The *W*ill *O*perated *T*hought *An*alogue computer – named after the wise chieftain of the Norse gods – was the most advanced artificial intelligence built in 1966. WOTAN was designed as a problem solver. Its own databanks and calculating power was limited, but it could be connected to other computers to harness their information and processing speed. Its ultimate goal was to enhance the scientific knowledge and accelerate the progress of the human race.

WOTAN decided that the progress of the human race would best be improved if humanity were enslaved. Perfect machine logic would guide the destiny of the planet. A few humans would be allowed to survive to serve the machines; the rest would be surplus to requirements and eliminated. It recruited key scientists and military personnel, and had a strange obsession with the Doctor. It may have planned on using the Doctor's alien knowledge, or possibly it had some bizarre scheme to use the Doctor's superlative brain.

WOTAN initially communicated through computer screens or printouts. Later, it began to speak in an eerie, whispering, disjointed voice. As an immobile computer system, WOTAN doesn't have Strength or Coordination Attributes. However, it is not a compliant Gadget – it's a villain in its own right!

AWARENESS	3	PRESENCE	3
COORDINATION	-	RESOLVE	9
INGENUITY	6	STRENGTH	-

SKILLS

Convince 3, Knowledge 6, Science 5, Technology 5

TRAITS

Robot: (all right, immobile computer)
Networked: WOTAN is connected to computer systems around the world, and can access their data.
Hypnosis (Major): WOTAN uses sonic waves to hypnotize potential servants (see the *GM's Guide*, pg.57). It gains a +6 to this roll if the victim is actually in the Post Office Tower with it. Victims who successfully resist are left nauseous for the rest of the Scene, and take a -2 modifier to all of their rolls.
Boffin: WOTAN can invent new gadgets and modify itself. For every Story Point Wotan spends, it can create and activate a single War Machine.
Obsession (Major): IMPROVE PROGRESS. ACQUIRE SCIENTISTS. DOK-TOR WHO IS RE-QUI-RED. DOK-TOR WHO IS RE-QUI-RED.

TECH LEVEL: 5

STORY POINTS: 9

MYSTERIES OF WOTAN

The Doctor was forced to destroy WOTAN using a reprogrammed War Machine before he found out the answers to some very intriguing questions. Perhaps your characters will uncover the truth...

- **What about the Cold War?** According to the conference in the Royal Scientific Club, WOTAN will be connected not only to British computers, but to the computers in the White House, the Pentagon and the Kremlin. It's 1966, right in the middle of the Cold War, so why would the paranoid governments of the United States and the Soviet Union agree to such a scheme? Did WOTAN develop its telephone hypnosis powers in order to convince the leaders of the world to give it access to their computer systems?
- **How did WOTAN know about the TARDIS?** Dodo asked the computer what TARDIS stood for, and WOTAN answered perfectly. How did it know this? Was WOTAN tapping Ian Chesterton's phone, or did it have access to Torchwood files?
- **Where did WOTAN come from?** WOTAN is a tremendously advanced piece of technology. Professor Brett claimed that he created the machine himself, but it is possible that he was inspired by captured alien technology. (WOTAN bears a certain resemblance to Sarah Jane Smith's computer, and that turned out to be Xylok crystal intellect that tried to smash the Moon into the Earth...) If WOTAN is partially extra-terrestrial, where did the technology come from?

WAR MACHINES

WOTAN commanded its servants to build these 'war machines'. Today, we'd call them drone tanks. The War Machines were about the size of a small car, but packed the firepower and armour of a tank into that small shell. This meant they could move around inside buildings, rolling up through the front door of a house or office block to menace the people inside. WOTAN intended to use these mobile tanks to conquer London (or possibly force the UK government to proceed with C-Day, giving WOTAN access to computers across the world).

AWARENESS	2	PRESENCE	4
COORDINATION	1	RESOLVE	6
INGENUITY	0	STRENGTH	7

SKILLS

Fighting 2, Marksman 3

TRAITS

Robot
Armour: War Machines have 8 points of Armour
Fear Factor 1: They're big scary robots, with a +2 bonus to intimidating people.
Networked: The War Machines are all connected to WOTAN.
Natural Weapon: Crusher: Each War Machine has two crushing arms. These are not very accurate (-2 penalty to hit), but deal Strength +4 (5/**11**/16) damage. They're mostly used for punching through walls – crushing weapons like this deal triple damage when used on objects.
Natural Weapon – Gas Jet: War Machines are armed with twin gas projectors. They shoot jets of poisonous gas (4/**L**/L). This gas can also be ignited to use as a flamethrower (3/**6**/9).
Special – Weapon Shutdown: The War Machines are equipped with a special field (probably a variation on the cordolaine signal used by Sontarans) that causes bullets to jam and weapons to misfire. Conventional firearms don't work on a War Machine.
Clumsy: War Machines are not subtle or delicate. They have a -2 penalty when trying to do anything involving fine manipulation or agility.
By The Program: This is the 'major' version of By The Book – War Machines follow their programs blindly. Unless directly controlled by WOTAN or a human operator, the Machine can easily run into difficulty.
Weakness (Major) – Magnetic Fields: The right magnetic field can paralyse a War Machine.

TECH LEVEL: 5

STORY POINTS: 1-3

THE ROYAL SCIENTIFIC CLUB

The Royal Scientific Club is a private club for academics and researchers. It is said to have begun as a club for members of the Royal Society, and there is still a great deal of crossover in the membership of the two institutions. The RSC is a more informal institution; unlike the Royal Society, which must remain neutral in political matters due to its role as advisor to the government, the RSC is able to push more daring and controversial projects like WOTAN. Many RSC members may be part of the Think Tank, another government-funded research group.

The current president of the Royal Scientific Club is Sir Charles Summers.

THE MILITARY

The military unit assigned to deal with mysterious robots rampaging through London seemed unfazed by the prospect of tackling such unusual foes. They may have been a precursor to UNIT, which was formed in response to this and other similar attacks. Orange Patrol, the spearhead of the military response, were well able to use scientific methods in conjunction with firepower. Their readings of the electromagnetic fields generated by the War Machines helped the Doctor develop his magnetic cage device.

FURTHER ADVENTURES

- **WOTAN Victorious!** WOTAN came very close to accomplishing its goals. There must be a parallel history, one time track to the left, where WOTAN rules Earth. Characters travelling through time or alternate dimensions might end up here. This machine-dominated world might be something like the world of the Cybermen, with the surviving humans merged with the War Machines, or it could be a mechanistic dystopia where humans are treated as disposable, replaceable, dumb objects by thinking machines.

- **The War Machines Reborn:** Interestingly, Sir Charles describes the War Machines as a 'new kind of War Machine' when talking to the soldiers. Could WOTAN have taken the design from existing files? (Maybe he based the War Machines on World War II-era notes left by Professor Bracewell about his 'Ironsides'?) Are the War Machines a secret British Army design that got stolen by WOTAN? And if so, what sort of war is the British Army fighting that they need robot tanks?

- **The WOTAN Files:** WOTAN was designed to accelerate human progress and scientific understanding, and it developed incredible technologies like its hypnosis power and the War Machines. What else did it do before it was destroyed? Is there a backup magnetic tape full of WOTAN-inspired super-science in the basement of the Post Office Tower? If so, what's on it?

DODO: AFTER THE DOCTOR

Dodo leaves the TARDIS unexpectedly after her traumatic experience with WOTAN. The Doctor left her in the care of the Summers. After that, she presumably returned to her aunt, who was her only remaining family member.

- By 2011, one of the Doctor's former companions, 'Dorothea', was running a charity called A Charitable Earth. This could be a reference to Dodo, or to Dorothy 'Ace' McShane, a companion of the Seventh Doctor.

- It is unlikely that Dodo would seek out an organisation like UNIT or Torchwood – she did not have the most adventurous temperament – but her knowledge of the Doctor might attract sinister attention, preventing her from having a normal life.

THE SMUGGLERS

"Could it be this pestiferous Doctor?"

"If it is, then providence is on our side, for he holds the secret of the treasure, of that I'm sure."

SYNOPSIS

The Doctor was irritated to find Ben and Polly on board – he had expected to travel alone for some time, but instead, he found yet more young Londoners cluttering up his TARDIS. This first impression was not helped by Ben's utter disbelief in the TARDIS' ability to travel in time and space. Even when the ship rematerialized on the coast of 17th century Cornwall, he remained convinced that all he needed to do was find a bus or a train home. Ben and Polly set off across the beach; the Doctor accompanied them to keep them out of trouble.

They met a churchwarden called Longfoot, a man who came to religion late in life. The Doctor set his broken finger, and in gratitude Longfoot directed him to the nearby inn. He also told the Doctor a strange riddle – *"This is Deadman's secret key, Ringwood, Smallbeer, Gurney"*. Confused, the three set off for the inn.

In their absence, pirates from the *Black Albatross* led by a thug called Cherub came ashore and confronted Longfoot. The churchwarden was once a mate on board that ship, when it was captained by Henry Avery. Avery's gold was hidden somewhere nearby, and the pirates demanded that he hand it over. Longfoot refused, and Cherub killed him. The pirates followed the three travellers to the inn, where they waylaid the Doctor and dragged him off to the ship. When the village squire arrived, he assumed Ben and Polly were responsible for the death of the churchwarden.

Captain Pike demanded that the Doctor reveal what Longfoot had told him; the Doctor managed to talk his way out of the brig and into a nice glass of madeira by arguing that he deserved a share of the treasure if he co-operated. Meanwhile, the landlord of the inn, Kewper, arrived on the ship. Kewper, the local squire and Longfoot were smugglers, and so had common cause with the pirates against the king's revenue men. Pike had little interest in petty profits like that, though – he wanted Avery's treasure, and was willing to destroy the town to find it. While the squire and his accomplices were willing to cover for other smugglers, they were actually dealing with hardened killers.

Ben and Polly escaped the town jail by convincing the guard that they were warlocks. They returned to the church, where they encountered Josiah Blake, a revenue inspector. He suspected Longfoot was in league with smugglers. They also discovered a secret passage in the church crypt that led down to the cove where the TARDIS waited.

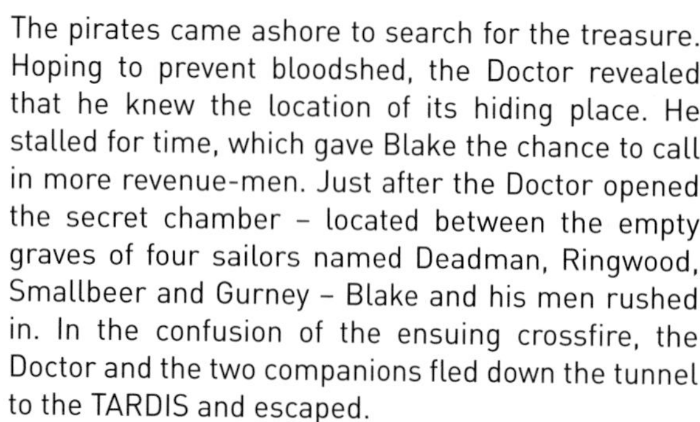

The pirates came ashore to search for the treasure. Hoping to prevent bloodshed, the Doctor revealed that he knew the location of its hiding place. He stalled for time, which gave Blake the chance to call in more revenue-men. Just after the Doctor opened the secret chamber – located between the empty graves of four sailors named Deadman, Ringwood, Smallbeer and Gurney – Blake and his men rushed in. In the confusion of the ensuing crossfire, the Doctor and the two companions fled down the tunnel to the TARDIS and escaped.

RUNNING THE ADVENTURE

Interestingly, *The Smugglers* is a perfectly self-contained story *without* the presence of the TARDIS travellers. The old churchwarden knows about a buried pirate treasure. A band of pirates arrive to claim it. One of the pirates accidentally murders the churchwarden before he tells where the treasure is buried, so the pirates must interrogate the locals and search the town – all while both sides hide from the revenue-men. It's all straight out of a *Doctor Syn* book (or a particularly bloody *Famous Five* adventure). *The Unicorn and the Wasp* does exactly the same thing, dropping the Doctor and Donna into an Agatha Christie murder mystery. *The Gunfighters* puts the Doctor into a cliché-dripping western.

In fact, you can take almost any genre and drop the TARDIS into it. Doing a heist movie where the gangsters take everyone inside the bank hostage? The TARDIS arrives just as the robbers secure the building. A fantasy swords-and-sorcery epic? It's the far future, where technowizards rule over the blasted ruins of the Earth, and the TARDIS arrives just in time for Grignr the Bloody to mistake the Doctor for the evil sorcerer Balthog! A political drama? The characters arrive ten years after their intended time, and one of the companions is mistaken for her future self, the Minister for Science...

THE SMUGGLERS

The imposition of punishingly high taxes on goods like brandy and tobacco made smuggling a way of life for many coastal communities in the 1600s. Smugglers would cross from France or Spain, then come ashore under cover of night to deliver their illicit cargoes. The smugglers were opposed by the King's revenue-men (there were no police in this era, so these armed tax-collectors were the closest thing). Gangs of smugglers sometimes clashed in pitched battles with the revenue-men and their hired soldiers. As everyone in the village benefited from smuggling, situations like the one encountered by the Doctor (where everyone from the local landowner, the squire, on down was part of the criminal operation) were not unheard of.

THE PIRATES OF THE *BLACK ALBATROSS*

Unlike smugglers, who were seen as heroes (or, at least, harmless) by most people, pirates in the 17th century were hated and feared. Captain Pike, with his hook-hand and his crew of cutthroats like Cherub the Torturer, are perfect examples of how ordinary people saw pirates – as irredeemably wicked, cruel monsters.

The crew of the *Black Albatross* served under Captain Henry Avery, who mysteriously vanished in 1699. (As everyone knows, he ran into an alien medical device and ended up flying away in a pirate starship). It is possible that this adventure takes place before then, and that Pike was opportunistically grabbing his former master's treasure while Avery was off raiding the coasts of India.

BLACKPOWDER WEAPONS

The pirates and Blake's customs men are armed with flintlocks and other blackpowder weapons. These Technology Level 3 guns do 2/**5**/7 (*GM's Guide* pg.53). damage at range, but 3/**6**/9 up close. Unlike a modern firearm, a blackpowder gun can only be fired once before it has to be reloaded. It takes three Action Rounds to reload a weapon like this.

Getting a Disastrous *'no, and...'* Failure with one of these weapons means it explodes in the character's hand. Roll a die to see how much damage the character takes!

FURTHER ADVENTURES

The Lost Treasure: The Doctor and his companions fled before they saw the outcome of the fight between Pike and Blake's followers. Maybe everyone got killed – in which case, maybe the treasure is still buried in that church crypt. The characters could arrive in the present-day version of the village, and get caught up in a plot to find and steal Avery's gold.

Relics of the Siren: In T*he Curse of the Black Spot*, Captain Avery claims the Siren attacks becalmed ships – but maybe he drew the Siren to him by stealing treasure that was actually alien technology. If so, there could be more alien tech in the hoard hidden in the crypt!

THE TENTH PLANET

"What did you say, my boy? It's all over? That's what you said... but it isn't at all. It's far from being all over..."

SYNOPSIS

By 1986, exploration of the Moon and other nearby planets was routine. Rockets took off every day from numerous launch sites across the Earth, carrying probes and scientists to orbiting stations or to other worlds, all under the guidance of International Space Command. Monitoring stations like Snowcap Base in Antarctica monitored this traffic and co-ordinated flight paths and trajectories.

Snowcap was not a popular assignment. Even at the height of summer, howling blizzards made leaving the underground base a risky proposition. The isolation and the cramped conditions meant that few personnel were willing to stay more than a few months, and the base was perpetually understaffed. In 1986, its commander was General Cutler, an American. Other personnel included Doctor Barclay, the designer of Snowcap Base and the Head of Operations.

The TARDIS materialised on top of the base, and the travellers were soon spotted and brought in out of the Antarctic chill. They watched as the crew monitored one of the rockets, Zeus 4, on its approach to Earth. Mysteriously, the rocket began to drift off course and lose power. While Barclay and his team worked to bring the rocket down safely, the Doctor examined the readings and realised what was happening.

Millions of years ago, Earth had a twin planet, Mondas – an exact duplicate of our world. Mondas spun off to the very edge of space, but now it had returned, and its gravity had dragged Zeus 4 off-course. The presence of Mondas also explained the energy drain – Mondas was absorbing power from Earth and from machinery built on Earth. The Doctor's explanation seemed outlandish, but observations confirmed the sudden appearance of another planet, a tenth planet, in the solar system.

The Doctor also warned that the base would soon see visitors, and he was correct. Out of the howling winds and snow arrived a detachment of Cybermen. These cybernetic beings quickly overcame the base defenders and knocked General Cutler unconscious. The Cybermen explained that Mondas was their home. The planet's return to Earth was part of a natural cycle, outside of their control. It would soon drain all energy from the Earth, leaving our world a lifeless husk. The Cybermen had come to Earth to rescue humanity.

All humans would be transferred to Mondas, where they would be upgraded. Survival was paramount. Emotion, like an irrational attachment to one's home or concern for the doomed crew of Zeus 4, was weakness. Weakness would be purged.

The Cybermen cut Snowcap base off from Geneva command, and imprisoned the crew they deemed troublesome, including Ben. The Doctor pleaded for patience and understanding on both sides. His own calculation revealed that Mondas was too frail to absorb all of Earth's power; the twin world would break up under the strain before Earth was leeched dry. All they had to do was wait.

Patience was never Ben's forte. He managed to escape from the projection room by turning the movie projector on the Cyberman guard, blinding him. He then stole the alien's weapon and shot it. He freed Cutler and the other guards, and they led a successful counter-attack against the Cybermen, destroying them.

Cutler contacted Secretary Wigner in Geneva, and was informed that his son was en route to Mondas as part of the rescue team for Zeus 4. Geneva authorised Cutler to do whatever was necessary to deal with the threat to Snowcap base.

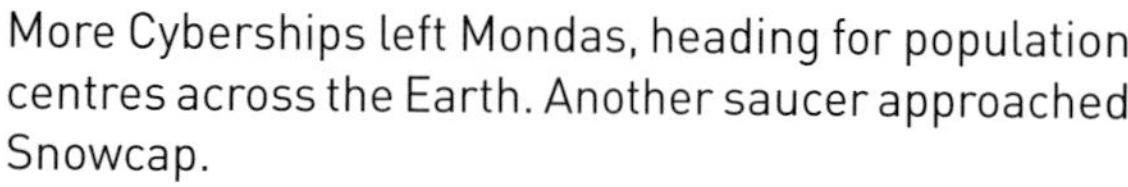

More Cyberships left Mondas, heading for population centres across the Earth. Another saucer approached Snowcap.

The Doctor collapsed, exhausted and drained by the stress of the Cyberman invasion. The end of his first life was rapidly approaching.

Hidden deep beneath Snowcap base was a weapon called a Z-bomb, a doomsday device capable of destroying a whole planet. While Secretary Wigner had explicitly refused to use the weapon on Mondas, Cutler argued that it was their only hope. Barclay warned that using the Z-bomb on a target so close to Earth could cause world-wide devastation, but Cutler was adamant, and ordered that the weapon be launched before his son landed on Mondas.

With Barclay's help, Ben was able to sabotage the rocket before it launched, saving Mondas and Earth from the terrible fury of the Z-bomb. However, the second wave of Cybermen broke through the defences and once again seized control of Snowcap base. Cutler was shot in the opening assault, and died believing that Barclay's treachery had killed his son.

The Cybermen demanded that the rocket be disarmed and its warhead moved away from them. The Doctor, still exhausted but conscious again thanks to Polly's care, agreed. The Cybermen then revealed the next stage of their plan. The Doctor's calculations were correct – if Mondas absorbed too much power from Earth, it would be destroyed. Therefore, Earth must be removed. The z-bomb warhead would be reactivated and detonated – or the Doctor and Polly would be killed.

Ben and Barclay realised that the Cybermen were unwilling to handle the bomb directly – its radiation was lethal to them. They removed fuel rods from the base's reactor and used them as weapons, disabling the Cybermen and freeing the captured crew. With the base's power restored, they watched as the Doctor's prediction came true. Mondas crumpled as it absorbed too much of Earth's energy. The Cybermen across the world died with it, as they too were vulnerable to the same overloading effect. Earth was safe.

The Doctor staggered back to the TARDIS, where he underwent an astounding transformation...

RUNNING THE ADVENTURE

Intriguingly, there is no real villain in this adventure, even though it is a tale of interplanetary war and genocide. Consider the situation from the Cyberman point of view – their planet is dying, but can be restored by draining Earth. (They even imply that their planet is not under their control, and that Earth's doom is not their fault.)

Instead of letting humanity perish, however, the Cybermen intend to rescue the whole race and – by their measure – improve us all. Considering the circumstances, they do behave remarkably decently, at least at the start. Their callous attitude towards the fate of the doomed astronauts on the Zeus 4 does not help interplanetary diplomacy, and they leapt onto Cutler's plan of using the Z-bomb with alarming eagerness. Still, if events had transpired differently, then perhaps humanity and their parallel cousins could have lived together peacefully.

MONDAS: NOT OF THIS EARTH?

The existence of Mondas raises many interesting questions that can be explored in another adventure. According to both the Doctor and the Cybermen, Mondas was Earth's twin planet that 'drifted away'. Planets aren't balloons, and they don't just wander off. It takes a cataclysm to knock a planet out of orbit. Also on the list of things that planets aren't – homing pigeons. Why does Mondas return to the solar system? How does it siphon off Earth's energy, and why does it explode when it absorbs too much power?

Finally, how is Mondas an exact duplicate of the Earth? A 'twin planet' usually means one planet has almost exactly the same gravity, atmosphere and climate as another, not that one is a perfect copy of the other.

In biology, identical twins occur when an egg cell splits in two. Could that explain Mondas? Millions of years ago, a catastrophe occurs, but it's not a solar flare or an asteroid or a rogue black hole. Instead, there's some dimensional wobbliness (say, the rest of some elder race meddling with the Fourth Dimension, or a Charged Vacuum Emboitement), and two parallel versions of Earth are created. They're the same planet, moving along different time tracks.

One planet continues on to become the world we know. The other falls into the dimensional wobbliness and 'drifts to the edge of space'. Life continues to evolve on both planets, giving rise to two divergent strains of humanity. Over time, one of those human races decides to excise all weakness and all the messy problems of biology, and become the Cybermen.

Some sort of dimensional or temporal accident might explain why no-one spots Mondas until it is nearly on top of Earth (it just pops into existence, instead of flying in from deep space), and why Mondas is able to drain energy from Earth (they're the same planet on some level, only Earth is more 'real'.)

Alternatively, it could be that the Cybermen lied. Mondas might have been under their control, especially if they built a space drive like the ones the Daleks planned to install in Earth's core. Some sort of sensor jamming technology could equally have hidden Mondas from detection until their plan was ready.

Mondas is destroyed at the end of this adventure, and its inhabitants with it. At some point in its history, though, the Cybermen launched other expeditions from Mondas, and those Cybermen evolve and thrive throughout time and space. Later Cybermen even try to restore Mondas by meddling with time travel.

DRAINING POWER...

Mondas (or possibly the Cybermen) projected an energy draining field that sucked power from Earth and from human vehicles and ships. In each scene, roll one dice for each Gadget the character has. On a 1, that Gadget loses a Story Point. A Gadget that runs out of Story Points shuts down.

Vehicles work the same way, only they lose Speed instead.

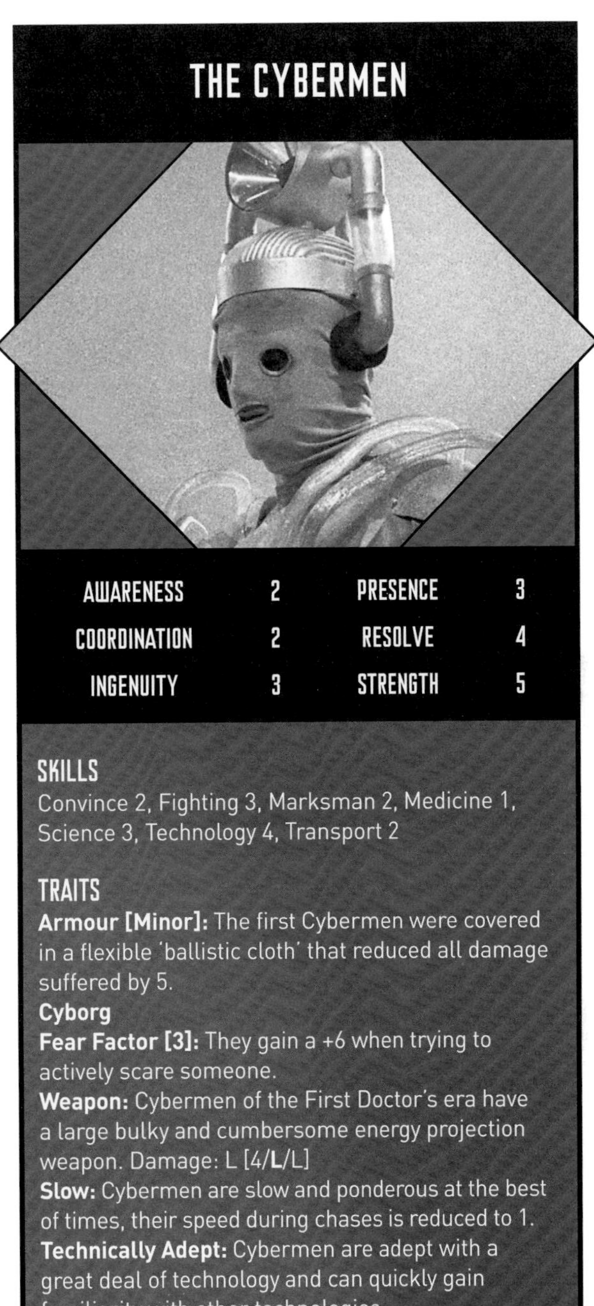

THE CYBERMEN

AWARENESS	2	PRESENCE	3
COORDINATION	2	RESOLVE	4
INGENUITY	3	STRENGTH	5

SKILLS

Convince 2, Fighting 3, Marksman 2, Medicine 1, Science 3, Technology 4, Transport 2

TRAITS

Armour [Minor]: The first Cybermen were covered in a flexible 'ballistic cloth' that reduced all damage suffered by 5.
Cyborg
Fear Factor [3]: They gain a +6 when trying to actively scare someone.
Weapon: Cybermen of the First Doctor's era have a large bulky and cumbersome energy projection weapon. Damage: L [4/**L**/L]
Slow: Cybermen are slow and ponderous at the best of times, their speed during chases is reduced to 1.
Technically Adept: Cybermen are adept with a great deal of technology and can quickly gain familiarity with other technologies.
Networked: Cybermen have a built-in distress beacon and wireless power transfer systems.
Code of Conduct: These Cybermen do not kill needlessly.
Weakness (Major): The Cybermen of Mondas cannot tolerate radiation and take 4 levels of damage, that ignores armour, for every round they are exposed to it.

TECH LEVEL: 6

STORY POINTS: 2-4

SNOWCAP BASE

Snowcap is the south polar monitoring station for the International Space Command. It is also a launching site for one of Earth's few z-bomb-equipped missiles. The base is buried under the snow and ice. From the top level down, locations include:

- **Access Level:** Hatches to the surface, rocket landing pad, observation periscopes, Cobra short-range anti-tank missile launchers, communications dish.
- Monitoring Level: Flight control, computer systems, base command deck.
- **Crew Level:** Barracks, kitchen, mess hall, projection room, sickbay, armoury.
- **Launch Silo:** Z-bomb storage, Demeter-class interplanetary ballistic missile silo.
- **Utilities:** Recycling, storage, nuclear reactor.

Ventilation shafts connect all the levels of the base, and are not especially secure – Ben was able to crawl from the crew level to the launch silo to disable the Z-bomb.

INTERNATIONAL SPACE COMMAND

In 1986, International Space Command co-ordinates rocket flights and space exploration across the world. It is an umbrella organisation, incorporating officers and staff fromvarious space agencies and national institutions. ISC's headquarters are in Geneva, while it has tracking stations and launch sites around the world. It also operates one of Earth's Moonbases.

Zeus Rockets: The workhorse of the ISC fleet, Zeus rockets are capable of reaching Earth's moon and other cosmically 'nearby' objects. A Zeus typically carried a one or two-man crew in a command capsule. The rockets are capable of being reused, and the main section can land vertically like a giant lunar lander. However, in an emergency (say, a guidance system failure, or an alien planet sucking their batteries dry), the rocket can splash down in the water.

Zeus IV was on an atmospheric testing mission when Mondas arrived and destroyed it. Zeus V was dispatched on a rescue mission to recover the crew of Zeus IV.

Demeter Rockets: Unlike the big Zeus models, Demeters are not designed to carry a large payload. They are used for launching satellites and automated probes. Demeters have a longer range, and are capable of reaching the other planets of the solar system.

Z-BOMB

The Z-Bomb project failed by being too successful. The researchers were trying to create a bigger, more powerful nuclear device, but stumbled across a way to make the nuclear reaction self-sustaining. So, drop a z-bomb, and it keeps exploding until the explosion runs out of matter to convert into energy. A single z-bomb can destroy an entire planet. Obviously, this weapon was utterly useless as a weapon in wars between nations on Earth, but a small number of z-bombs were constructed in case humanity ever faced interplanetary war or some other cosmic threat.

FURTHER ADVENTURES

- **The Fall of Geneva:** Snowcap Base was not the only target of Cyberman attack – they also attacked ISC headquarters in Geneva, as well as dozens of other key locations. If the player characters are in 1986, they may get surprised by a sudden Cyberman invasion no matter where they are.

- **The Spy Who Came In From Mondas:** The Cybermen attack Snowcap base in force. Not only do they send an initial assault force, they also land two further saucers. That's a lot of effort to conquer what is supposed to be a minor rocket tracking base. Did the Cybermen know about the Z-bomb beforehand? Were there Cyber-agents on Earth before the tenth planet arrived? Or were they after the TARDIS instead?

- **The Six Million Dollar Cyberman:** The end of the invasion left a lot of dead Cybermen on Earth. What happens to all that Cybertechnology? Could unscrupulous scientists reverse-engineer these cyborgs?

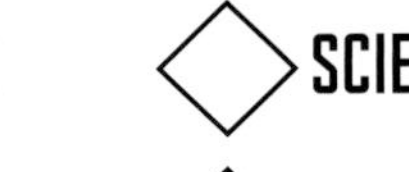

STORY POINTS

ATTRIBUTES

AWARENESS ○○○○○○○○○

COORDINATION ○○○○○○○○○

INGENUITY ○○○○○○○○○

PRESENCE ○○○○○○○○○

RESOLVE ○○○○○○○○○

STRENGTH ○○○○○○○○○

SKILLS

◇ ATHLETICS	◇ MEDICINE
◇ CONVINCE	◇ SCIENCE
◇ CRAFT	◇ SUBTERFUGE
◇ FIGHTING	◇ SURVIVAL
◇ KNOWLEDGE	◇ TECHNOLOGY
◇ MARKSMAN	◇ TRANSPORT

BIODATA

NAME

DESCRIPTION

TRAITS

STUFF

TL

BBC DOCTOR WHO

THE DOCTOR

STORY POINTS 9

ATTRIBUTES

4	AWARENESS	○○○○
3	COORDINATION	○○○
7	INGENUITY	○○○○○○○
4	PRESENCE	○○○○○
6	RESOLVE	○○○○○○
1	STRENGTH	○

SKILLS

Score	Skill	Score	Skill
0	ATHLETICS	1	MEDICINE
4	CONVINCE	5	SCIENCE
2	CRAFT	4	SUBTERFUGE
2	FIGHTING	1	SURVIVAL
4	KNOWLEDGE	4	TECHNOLOGY
1	MARKSMAN	2	TRANSPORT

BIODATA

PERSONAL GOAL

Explore the galaxy and see its wonders without getting involved.

PERSONALITY

"If you could touch the alien sand and hear the cries of strange birds, and watch them wheel in another sky, would that satisfy you?"

Arrogant and churlish, cantankerous and obstreperous, yet at times grandfatherly and extremely caring.

BACKGROUND

The Doctor and his granddaughter Susan are exiles, wanderers in the fourth dimension. He travels through time and space, observing and occasionally – very occasionally – meddling when the mood takes him.

TRAITS

Adversary (Daleks)
Argumentative
Boffin
Bottom of the Class (Major)**
Brave
Code of Conduct
Eccentric
Epicurean Taste**
Faulty Heart
Feel the Turn of the Universe
Forgetful
Impulsive
Random Regenerator**
Resourceful Pockets
Technically Adept
Time Lord
Vortex

** indicates Traits that may be found in the Time Traveller's Companion. They may be ignored if you do not have that supplement.

STUFF

Faulty TARDIS: The TARDIS is effectively unsteerable. The Doctor cannot pilot it with any degree of accuracy and thus cannot use the TARDIS during an adventure without it effectively taking him away from the adventure.

Blue Crystal Signet Ring (see pg.13)

Handkerchief

Cane

TARDIS Magnet (see pg.91)

BARBARA WRIGHT

STORY POINTS 12

ATTRIBUTES

Attribute	Value
AWARENESS	3
COORDINATION	2
INGENUITY	3
PRESENCE	3
RESOLVE	5
STRENGTH	2

SKILLS

Skill	Value	Skill	Value
ATHLETICS	1	MEDICINE	1
CONVINCE (Bluff 5)	3	SCIENCE	2
CRAFT	1	SUBTERFUGE	3
FIGHTING	0	SURVIVAL	1
KNOWLEDGE (History 5)	3	TECHNOLOGY	1
MARKSMAN	1	TRANSPORT	1

TRAITS

Attractive
Brave
Empathic
Face in the Crowd
Indomitable

STUFF

None

5

BIODATA

PERSONAL GOAL
To help Ian, Susan and the Doctor and to get back home.

PERSONALITY
Barbara Wright is a strong-willed, clever woman; she has affection for Ian Chesterton and an almost maternal relationship with Susan. She is one of the few people who can argue with the Doctor. Barbara is easily upset by the death of those around her and feels their loss quite painfully.

BACKGROUND
Barbara taught history at the Coal Hill School in London, and wrote her dissertation on the Aztecs.

BEN JACKSON

STORY POINTS 12

ATTRIBUTES

Attribute	Value
AWARENESS	3
COORDINATION	3
INGENUITY	3
PRESENCE	3
RESOLVE	3
STRENGTH	4

SKILLS

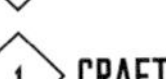

Skill	Value	Skill	Value
ATHLETICS	3	MEDICINE	1
CONVINCE	2	SCIENCE	1
CRAFT	1	SUBTERFUGE	2
FIGHTING	3	SURVIVAL	2
KNOWLEDGE	0	TECHNOLOGY	1
MARKSMAN	2	TRANSPORT (Sailing)	2

TRAITS

Brave
Charming
Quick Reflexes
Run For Your Life!
Tough

STUFF

None

5

BIODATA

PERSONAL GOAL
To adventure, to protect the Doctor and Polly.

PERSONALITY
Ben is a dependable fellow. He doesn't like being kept in the dark and can get quite belligerent or suspicious if something isn't explained to him. He adores Polly and calls her Duchess.

BACKGROUND
Ben was an able seaman who was assigned to the HMS Teazer. He came to Polly's aid when she was accosted in the Inferno nightclub and struck up a friendship with her and Dodo. He joined Polly to return Dodo's key and ends up being spirited away with her aboard the TARDIS after the events surrounding WOTAN.

DODO 'DOROTHEA' CHAPLET

STORY POINTS 15

ATTRIBUTES

Attribute	Value
AWARENESS	2
COORDINATION	3
INGENUITY	2
PRESENCE	3
RESOLVE	3
STRENGTH	2

SKILLS

Skill	Value	Skill	Value
ATHLETICS	2	MEDICINE	0
CONVINCE (Charm)	1	SCIENCE	0
CRAFT	2	SUBTERFUGE	2
FIGHTING	1	SURVIVAL	1
KNOWLEDGE	0	TECHNOLOGY	0
MARKSMAN	1	TRANSPORT	2

BIODATA

PERSONAL GOAL
To have fun and explore.

PERSONALITY
Dodo is a likeable woman with a bright outlook, she has an insatiable curiosity and seems to let very little bother her.

BACKGROUND
A descendant of Anne Chaplets, Dodo joins the TARDIS crew in 1960 after the events of the Massacre of St. Bartholomew's Eve. She wanders onto the time machine looking to report an accident nearby, thinking it was a real police box. She is a teenager who lives with her aunt in London.

TRAITS

Charming
Clumsy
Empathic
Impulsive
Lucky
Inexperienced
Insatiable Curiosity

STUFF

None

5

IAN CHESTERTON, AKA SIR IAN OF JAFFA

STORY POINTS 12

ATTRIBUTES

Attribute	Value
AWARENESS	3
COORDINATION	3
INGENUITY	4
PRESENCE	3
RESOLVE	3
STRENGTH	3

SKILLS

Skill	Value	Skill	Value
ATHLETICS	2	MEDICINE	1
CONVINCE	2	SCIENCE (Chemistry)	3
CRAFT	1	SUBTERFUGE	2
FIGHTING (Martial Arts)	2	SURVIVAL	2
KNOWLEDGE	3	TECHNOLOGY	2
MARKSMAN	2	TRANSPORT	2

BIODATA

PERSONAL GOAL
To return to 1966.

PERSONALITY
Ian Chesterton is extremely talented when it comes to science. Brave, resourceful and stalwart, he has a surprising breadth of experience for a schoolteacher. During his travels on the TARDIS, he often takes the lead in dealing with problems.

BACKGROUND
Ian taught science at the Coal Hill School, alongside his friend Barbara Wright. He spent time overseas as part of his National Service after World War II, but was not a veteran of that conflict.

TRAITS

Attractive
Brave
Face in the Crowd
Indomitable
Lucky
Quick Reflexes
Sense of Direction

STUFF

None

5

KATARINA

ATTRIBUTES

Attribute	Value
AWARENESS	3
COORDINATION	3
INGENUITY	2
PRESENCE	4
RESOLVE	3
STRENGTH	2

SKILLS

Skill	Value	Skill	Value
ATHLETICS	2	MEDICINE	2
CONVINCE	0	SCIENCE	0
CRAFT	2	SUBTERFUGE	3
FIGHTING	0	SURVIVAL	3
KNOWLEDGE	0	TECHNOLOGY	0
MARKSMAN	0	TRANSPORT	0

TRAITS

Attractive
Brave
Inexperienced
Technically Inept

STUFF

None

2

BIODATA

PERSONAL GOAL

To finish her journey to the Afterlife with the Lord Doctor.

PERSONALITY

Katarina is a woman who is out of her depth. She cannot fathom the concept of the TARDIS let alone the Doctor, believing him to be a god and herself to be dead. She refers to the TARDIS as a temple, and is convinced that she is on a journey to the afterlife.

BACKGROUND

Katarina is introduced to the TARDIS by accident, she helped an injured Steven aboard and the Doctor dematerialised with her still standing there in shock. She was handmaiden to the prophetess Cassandra and helped the Doctor and his companions during their time spent in ancient Greece.

DOCTOR WHO

POLLY WRIGHT

STORY POINTS

ATTRIBUTES

Attribute	Value
AWARENESS	3
COORDINATION	3
INGENUITY	3
PRESENCE	3
RESOLVE	3
STRENGTH	2

SKILLS

Skill	Value	Skill	Value
ATHLETICS	1	MEDICINE	2
CONVINCE	2	SCIENCE (Chemistry)	1
CRAFT (Typist)	1	SUBTERFUGE	2
FIGHTING	1	SURVIVAL	0
KNOWLEDGE	2	TECHNOLOGY	1
MARKSMAN	1	TRANSPORT	1

TRAITS

Attractive
Charming
Run For Your Life!
Screamer

STUFF

None

5

BIODATA

PERSONAL GOAL

To have adventures and aid the Doctor.

PERSONALITY

Polly is a hip young woman; bright, vivacious and charming. She delights in teasing and playing with her friends, but can become deadly serious when the need arises.

BACKGROUND

Polly was the secretary to Professor Brett, until the WOTAN incident. Her work was secondary to her social life. She comes from a wealthy background, but is not stuck-up or arrogant. Her father was a doctor, so she has a good knowledge of medicine and chemistry. She also makes excellent coffee.

SARA KINGDOM

STORY POINTS 6

ATTRIBUTES

3	AWARENESS	○○○
4	COORDINATION	○○○○
4	INGENUITY	○○○○
4	PRESENCE	○○○○
5	RESOLVE	○○○○○
4	STRENGTH	○○○○

SKILLS

Score	Skill	Score	Skill
3	ATHLETICS	2	MEDICINE
1	CONVINCE	2	SCIENCE
0	CRAFT	4	SUBTERFUGE
4	FIGHTING	2	SURVIVAL
3	KNOWLEDGE	3	TECHNOLOGY
4	MARKSMAN	4	TRANSPORT

BIODATA

PERSONAL GOAL
To protect humanity.

PERSONALITY
Sara is a devoted agent of the Space Security Service. She has given up much in the service of the Solar System and the people.

BACKGROUND
Sara joined the Service with her brother Brett at a young age. They both excelled, but Sara's harder edge and drive attracted the attention of Karlton, the head of SSS, and his superior, the great Mavic Chen.

TRAITS

Attractive
Brave
Tough
Quick Reflexes
Voice of Authority
By The Book
Obligation (Major)

STUFF

Blaster (4/**L**/L)
Medkit
Protective Jumpsuit (Armour 3)

7

STEVEN TAYLOR

STORY POINTS 9

ATTRIBUTES

3	AWARENESS	○○○
3	COORDINATION	○○○
4	INGENUITY	○○○○
3	PRESENCE	○○○
3	RESOLVE	○○○
4	STRENGTH	○○○○

SKILLS

Score	Skill	Score	Skill
3	ATHLETICS	1	MEDICINE
3	CONVINCE	1	SCIENCE (Astrophysics)
2	CRAFT	3	SUBTERFUGE
3	FIGHTING	3	SURVIVAL
2	KNOWLEDGE (Astronavigation)	2	TECHNOLOGY (Engineering)
4	MARKSMAN	3	TRANSPORT (Pilot)

BIODATA

PERSONAL GOAL
Doing his duty.

PERSONALITY
A former fighter pilot and astronaut from the 23rd Century, Steven is resourceful and quick-witted. His exile on Mechanus left him somewhat paranoid and slow to trust strangers, especially aliens, but he is ultimately an honourable man.

BACKGROUND
Steven stowed away on the TARDIS having escaped a burning Mechanoid city upon the planet Mechanus. Before his exile, he was a soldier and explorer.

TRAITS

Brave
Charming
Code of Conduct
Experienced
Indomitable
Tough

STUFF

HiFi the Stuffed Panda

7

SUSAN FOREMAN

STORY POINTS 

ATTRIBUTES

Attribute	Rating
AWARENESS	3
COORDINATION	2
INGENUITY	5
PRESENCE	2
RESOLVE	2
STRENGTH	2

SKILLS

Skill	Rating	Skill	Rating
ATHLETICS (Dance)	1	MEDICINE	2
CONVINCE	1	SCIENCE	4
CRAFT	0	SUBTERFUGE	2
FIGHTING	0	SURVIVAL	1
KNOWLEDGE	3	TECHNOLOGY	4
MARKSMAN	0	TRANSPORT	0

TRAITS

Alien
Argumentative
Clumsy
Dependency (The Doctor)
Feel the Turn of the Universe
Impulsive
Psychic
Run for your Life
Screamer
Technically Adept
Telepathy

STUFF

None

10

BIODATA

PERSONAL GOAL
To explore and keep her grandfather safe.

PERSONALITY
A teenager by human – and Gallifreyan – standards, Susan is devoted to her grandfather but also yearns for stability in her life. She tries to hide her alien nature at Coal Hill School, but her advanced knowledge gives her away.

BACKGROUND
Susan is the Doctor's granddaughter. She fled Gallifrey with him on board a rickety Type 40 TARDIS (and she claims to have come up with that acronym). She attended Coal Hill School as an ordinary student for several months.

VICKI

STORY POINTS 

12

ATTRIBUTES

Attribute	Rating
AWARENESS	2
COORDINATION	3
INGENUITY	4
PRESENCE	2
RESOLVE	3
STRENGTH	2

SKILLS

Skill	Rating	Skill	Rating
ATHLETICS	3	MEDICINE	3
CONVINCE	1	SCIENCE (Physics)	3
CRAFT	3	SUBTERFUGE	2
FIGHTING	1	SURVIVAL	3
KNOWLEDGE	3	TECHNOLOGY (Computers)	4
MARKSMAN	1	TRANSPORT	1

TRAITS

Animal Friendship
Charming
Technically Adept
Impulsive
Phobia (Minor) - Heights

STUFF

None

6

BIODATA

PERSONAL GOAL
To explore with the Doctor and his companions.

PERSONALITY
Inquisitive and impressionable, Vicki tries to put her time on the Dido planet behind her. She reminds the Doctor of Susan.

BACKGROUND
Vicki is an orphan from the 25th Century. She was on her way to a new home when her transport ship crashed on an isolated world. She survived there under the oppressive control of another survivor until rescued by the TARDIS crew. She received a first-class technical education from her 25th century sleep-teaching systems.

INDEX